An Outline History of the Great War

THE DESOLATION OF THE SALIENT

(The remains of Zonnebeke village, 1917)

An Outline History of the
Great War

for use in Schools

compiled by

G. V. CAREY
late Major, The Rifle Brigade;
sometime Fellow of Clare College, Cambridge;
Headmaster of Eastbourne College

&

H. S. SCOTT
late Captain, R.F.A.;
Assistant Master at Wellington College

CAMBRIDGE
At the University Press
1929

CAMBRIDGE UNIVERSITY PRESS
Cambridge, New York, Melbourne, Madrid, Cape Town,
Singapore, São Paulo, Delhi, Tokyo, Mexico City

Cambridge University Press
The Edinburgh Building, Cambridge CB2 8RU, UK

Published in the United States of America by
Cambridge University Press, New York

www.cambridge.org
Information on this title: www.cambridge.org/9781107648029

First published 1928
Second edition 1929
First paperback edition 2011

A catalogue record for this publication is available from the British Library

ISBN 978-1-107-64802-9 Paperback

PREFACE

To those on whom the events of the years 1914 to 1918 are branded as a living experience it is sometimes a shock to find that the youth of to-day is often ignorant of the very names of the chief battles of the War; so difficult is it to realise that even those whose school days are now closing were still in the nursery when the storm broke. It is in the belief that some knowledge of the War is of importance to the men and women of to-morrow, and of special interest to a generation whose parents helped to make the history of those critical years, that we have compiled this book.

To realise what the War *felt like* is even more important than to know its events in outline, and the false glamour which is apt to be shed on war, when viewed from a distance, finds no place in this narrative. In particular, an attempt has been made in the concluding chapter to summarise very briefly the attitude and experience of those who walked through the valley of the shadow of death. But to do full justice to the War's reactions, physical, mental, and moral, on the individual would have been impossible within the limits which we have deemed essential. Moreover, this "atmosphere" can be supplied, if not by the spoken word, by many excellent books, and suggestions in this direction will be found at the end of each chapter. We have essayed the more prosaic, but less common, task of setting down a narrative of the War in outline, short enough to be read in a single school term. To this end the severest compression has been necessary throughout; events outside the sphere of the main British campaigns have found little space, and political issues have been almost entirely excluded.

Amongst a number of works consulted we would mention in particular *Sir Douglas Haig's Despatches*, edited by Lt.-Col. J. H. Boraston (Dent), and the volumes of the *Official History of the War* by Brig.-Gen. Sir J. E. Edmonds (Macmillan) and Sir Julian Corbett (Longmans). Acknowledgements are also due to Lt.-Col. H. R. Sandilands (author of *The 23rd Division, 1914–1919*) for first-hand information on the British campaign in Italy, and to Mr F. A. Potts for helpful criticism. But to one anonymous friend, to whose name we would gladly have seen ours subordinated on the title-page, we owe a debt not to be measured in words; without him this book could not have been written.

G.V.C.
H.S.S.

September, 1928

NOTE ON THE SECOND EDITION

The authors are grateful to those who have pointed out one or two errors and have made suggestions for the improvement of certain passages in the book. Opportunity has been taken in this edition to benefit by these criticisms wherever possible.

It is, happily, no longer necessary that the friend referred to in our original Preface should remain anonymous; he is Lieut.-Colonel N. C. Rutherford, D.S.O., late R.A.M.C.

G. V. C.
H. S. S.

August, 1929

CONTENTS

ILLUSTRATIONS

MAPS

Chapter I: THE OUTBREAK OF WAR

Owing to the summary rejection by the German Government of the request made by His Majesty's Government for assurances that the neutrality of Belgium will be respected, His Majesty's Ambassador at Berlin has received his passports and His Majesty's Government have declared to the German Government that a state of war exists between Great Britain and Germany as from 11 p.m. on the 4th August.

At 12.15 a.m. on the 5th of August, 1914, the Foreign Office issued the foregoing statement. It ended a period of peace with her European neighbours which the United Kingdom had enjoyed since the Crimean War.

At the moment, Britain, France, and Russia were at war with Germany, and Austria was at war with Serbia. Belgium and Luxembourg had been forcibly entered by the German Armies, by way of attacking France from the north-east. Italy remained neutral, though long allied, offensively and defensively, to Austria and Germany. Turkey had ordered mobilisation on July 31st, the day following Austria's declaration of war on Serbia.

For more than a decade much care had been needed to keep peace in Western Europe. Smouldering fires lay along the frontiers of Germany, remains of the conflagrations of the nineteenth century. These, whilst uniting the German States under Prussian dominance, had injured Denmark, Poland, and France, not only territorially but in prestige. On the other hand, Germany lacked the wide political interests to which, she considered, her commercial and industrial growth should have led. Her colonies were few, scattered, and not rich enough to be attractive.

Germans, both scholars and statesmen, mourned bitterly the wars which had spoiled her in the eighteenth century and the migration of her swarming population to foreign states in modern times. In an era marked by great scientific progress she had played a prominent part, for she had shown surpassing ability in adapting new discoveries to industrial uses. Withal, she had a tradition alike in art, religion, learning, war, and politics. Such indeed was the charm and brilliance of twentieth-century Germany that the whole civilised world seemed to conspire to praise her and to forget the injuries she had done her neighbours. Doubtless this only added to her sense of frustration, whilst it intensified her fear of encirclement and her longing for a larger share of world dominion. Her rulers reiterated a demand for "a place in the sun".

Yet another spite in her lot tried her sorely. Prussia and her highly industrialised Silesian state had in Russia an unsettled and unsettling neighbour.

On the 28th of June, 1914, the Archduke Ferdinand, heir-apparent to the Austrian throne, whilst visiting Serajevo, was murdered by a Serbian student. For this Austria demanded as reparation from Serbia more than a sovereign nation could concede; and Germany stood firmly by Austria. In spite of Serbia's submission to almost all that was demanded, Austria, on July 30th, declared war. Russia, traditional champion of the Slavs, then ordered the mobilisation of her four southern armies as a threat to Austria. Germany had previously asked England, in vain, for an assurance of her neutrality if Russia should attack Austria; now she threatened to mobilise on both frontiers unless Russia ceased mobilising. Officially Germany took her first step in mobilisation on July 31st, at the same time presenting a twelve-hour ultimatum to Russia. At noon on the 1st of August this ultimatum expired, whereupon Germany ordered general mobilisation; and France followed suit, in support of her ally Russia.

Germany's military plan had long been known; it was, principally, to turn the fortified Franco-German frontier by way of Belgium. So, on July 31st, Great Britain demanded of Germany and France to know whether they would respect Belgian neutrality. France replied promptly that she would; Germany made an evasive answer. Two days later, at Brussels, a request was presented for the march of the German army through Belgium, twelve hours being allowed for a reply. Straightway Belgium appealed for diplomatic intervention by Great Britain. The British Minister for Foreign Affairs, Sir Edward Grey, announced in a speech to the

House of Commons on August 3rd that this country would not be committed to war on Serbia's account, but that England would honour her treaty engagement to uphold the integrity of Belgium.

At 6.45 p.m. on this day Germany declared war upon France, alleging frontier infringements since admitted to be imaginary. This step finally rendered useless Sir Edward Grey's desperate efforts to preserve peace in Western Europe. Summarising these, a year later, to a distinguished American, he writes: "Austria had presented a tremendous ultimatum to Serbia. Serbia had accepted nine-tenths of that ultimatum; Russia was prepared to leave the outstanding points to a conference of Germany, Italy, France, and ourselves. France, Italy, and ourselves were ready; Germany refused".

On the following day Germany declared war upon Belgium. The British Ambassador to Berlin was then instructed to ask for his passports if no satisfactory answer about Belgian neutrality were forthcoming by midnight. The interview at which our Ambassador imparted these instructions to von Bethmann-Hollweg, the German Chancellor, is a memorable one, for at it the Chancellor spoke of the Treaty to respect Belgian neutrality as a "scrap of paper".

Germany returned no answer, and Great Britain was at war.

THE INVASION OF FRANCE

Before the declaration of war, the British Grand Fleet had been ordered to its war station in the North; steps preliminary to the mobilising of the Army had also been taken. With the outbreak of war, decisions had to be made for its conduct, and among the first of these was the appointment of Earl Kitchener of Khartoum to be Secretary of State for War. It fell to him to administer a military system which had been devised, under Lord Haldane, by the recently formed General Staff. A war footing had been "established" for all troops, Regular and Territorial, the basis of which was the "infantry division". This was made up of all arms and services, in set proportion, with commanders and staff. Stores of war equipment had been provided for a force not exceeding six infantry divisions and a cavalry division; in addition, trains and ships to carry it, reinforcements, remounts, and Ordnance stores for its replenishment had all been prepared and tabulated. This was the Expeditionary Force. The General Staff had meanwhile concerned itself with the possibilities of the employment of our military forces in war and had studied the landing of an expeditionary force on the continent. A scheme of troop movements had been arranged, with the assistance of the Admiralty and the French General Staff; complete in every detail, down to a proper sequence of written telegrams, it lay at the War Office ready for use. Much of the credit for this detailed preparation is due to an officer who was to play a still more prominent part during the war itself, General Sir Henry Wilson.

The Cabinet now decided to send to France four infantry divisions and a cavalry division, under Sir John French. The transportation of this force occupied five days and was completed by August 13th; 1800 special trains were employed, and ships to an average tonnage of 52,000 a day carried troops and stores from various ports in the British Isles to Havre, Rouen, and Boulogne. Meanwhile two regular divisions and some mounted troops were retained in this country temporarily; these served to cover the mobilisation and concentration of the fourteen infantry divisions and fourteen mounted brigades of the Territorial Force against a possible enemy landing.

In the meantime the Belgian Army of six divisions and a cavalry division and the garrisons of the frontier fortress at Liège had been making an unexpectedly successful resistance to the German advance. Despite the use by the Germans of enormous howitzers, the last of the Liège forts did not fall until August 16th. Thus four or five days were gained for the Allies in which to complete the concentration of their troops. But even more valuable to them was the experience obtained of the limitations of fortress defence; and this was supplemented when the Belgians withdrew their Field Army successfully from the river Gette to Antwerp. There it remained menacing the German flank.

The French concentration would be finished by the 18th, and was covered by a cavalry corps under General Sordet, who reconnoitred to within nine miles of Liège during the first week of August, but withdrew in conformity with the Belgians. Thus the fortress was left to its fate; its gallant commander, General Leman, was taken unconscious from under a mass of masonry after its fall.

The French could oppose but five Armies to the Germans' seven; but the addition of the British and Belgian Armies made shift to equalise the number of Armies, if not their strengths. The German scheme was to overwhelm France with a huge concentration of 1,500,000 men, leaving only 250,000 to act with the Austrian Armies on the eastern frontier. No less than 600,000 were allotted to the two Armies of the right wing; these were to move through Belgium, outflank and envelop the enemy, pass west of Paris, and finally drive him against the Swiss frontier. Only one failure marred the early workings of this strategy: the Belgian Army remained unaccounted for.

In the third week of August the French First Army advanced south-eastward into Alsace. Simultaneously the French Fourth Army moved north-eastward against the inner flank and communications of the two German Armies entering Belgium. Both attacks were serious failures; they were tactically unsound in conception and the dispositions which resulted were all to the advantage of the invader. The four southern French Armies were thereafter held by four German Armies, leaving three on the shortest and easiest route to Paris opposed only by the French Fifth Army, under General Lanrezac, the small British force, and the six Belgian divisions—34 divisions against 20.

SUGGESTIONS FOR READING:

Twenty-five Years by Viscount Grey of Fallodon, vol. I, pp. 15, 77, 224, 304; vol. II, p. 39. *The War in the Air* by Sir W. Raleigh, vol. I, pp. 295–7. *The World Crisis, 1916–18* by W. S. Churchill, pt. I, pp. 37–8.

Chapter II: RETREAT AND RECOVERY

(See map on p. 16)

Sᴉʀ Jᴏʜɴ Fʀᴇɴᴄʜ's force, formed into two Army Corps commanded respectively by Sir Douglas Haig and Sir Horace Smith-Dorrien, had concentrated in the neighbourhood of Le Cateau by August 20th. On the 21st, by order of General Joffre, the French Commander-in-Chief, it moved forward on the left of the French Fifth Army towards the line of the Sambre and the Mons–Condé Canal. The changed conditions of war and its unchanging principles were well illustrated on this day, for at Maubeuge aerodrome, new to war, was the Royal Flying Corps, whilst in the evening the outposts of the 9th Infantry Brigade overlooked the battlefield of Malplaquet. They were found by the Lincolnshire Regiment, which, with the Royal Scots Fusiliers, had fought there under Marlborough.

THE BATTLE OF MONS

On the 22nd the French Fifth Army was heavily engaged on the Sambre and its centre was compelled to retire. This stopped the offensive movement of the British also, just as they were in the act of wheeling north-eastwards from the Mons-Condé canal; yet at the request of General Lanrezac they remained in position to assist the retirement of the French. And so it was that hereabouts the first clash of British and German arms took place, early in the morning of the 23rd of August. Actually, the German First Army broke like an oblique wave along the line held by the Second Corps round Mons and to the west of it, suffering great loss. The position was by no means strong, for it had been taken up by chance rather than choice the evening before. Its weakest point was a "salient" near the junction of our First and Second Corps. The First Corps (1st and 2nd Divisions) faced north-east, on a front of ten miles, whilst the Second Corps (3rd and 5th Divisions) lay along the canal to the west for seventeen miles.

The weakest section of the defence was the first attacked. Beginning at 6 a.m., the attack spread gradually westwards. Though German artillery hammered their salient defences, our men continued ceaselessly firing at the infantry advancing south-westwards across their front. The enemy's opening attacks at Jemappes, two miles west of Mons, and against the bridge at Mariette were similarly dealt with. At St Ghislain, still further to the west, an advanced company of the West Kents, north of the canal, clung to its position although the enemy launched a whole regiment (three battalions and a machine-gun company) against it. Under this pressure the company was withdrawn to the canal by successive platoons, though the enemy was within a hundred yards of its rear platoon; it lost about half its strength.

The situation of our men in the salient became very precarious in the afternoon, and reinforcements failed to improve it. But the troops were withdrawn in good order, though with heavy losses, through the devotion of the machine-gunners of the 2nd Royal Irish and 4th Middlesex Regiments. The latter, with the water boiling furiously in the jackets of their guns, fired their last rounds of ammunition into the masses of the enemy before being overpowered. The former had both their guns disabled by shell-fire, but set to work during a short retirement and made one serviceable gun out of the remains of the two. Elsewhere the retirement of our troops took place with little interference, the worst difficulty often being to persuade unshaken defenders to withdraw.

The night passed quietly on the main position a mile or two south of the canal. From the canal bank the German bugles could be heard at sunset sounding the "Cease Fire" all along their line. When it got dark the illuminating flares which their outposts used were seen by the British soldier for the first time—of countless times.

THE RETREAT FROM MONS

On the following day the British Army began the third and most splendid of the great retreats in its history; for General Joffre's offensive had failed. At a cost of 1600 casualties and two guns abandoned, two British divisions had held up six German divisions, delayed their advance a whole day, and demonstrated how high training and skill with the rifle can vie with faultless organisation and the fullest equipment. The Field Companies of the Royal Engineers added to the enemy's difficulties and to the great tradition of their Corps by the timely destruction of nearly all the canal bridges between Mons and Condé.

Next day the First Corps reached their destinations about Bavai without mishap, though greatly fatigued. Some battalions had marched 59 miles in the last 64 hours, so the men were hardly able to put one leg before the other; yet they sang as they marched in. The Second Corps was less fortunate, for von Kluck was straining every nerve to pin it to its ground and outflank it. He wished, in the words of his order for the day, to "force the enemy into Maubeuge". But German attacks were repulsed at Frameries, Wasmes, and Dour; at Wasmes the Germans reached the British position only to find it empty, and were blown out of it again promptly by their own artillery. Less fortunate but more glorious was a flank-guard action fought at Élouges by the 1st Norfolks, 1st Cheshires, and 119th Battery, R.F.A., assisted by the 2nd Cavalry Brigade and "L" Battery, R.H.A. Retirement could be resumed only with difficulty and guns had to be man-handled out of action under heavy fire. No orders to retire reached three companies of the Cheshires and a platoon of the Norfolks, and they defended themselves desperately until 7 p.m., when only forty of them remained unwounded. The Cheshires, 1000 strong that morning, mustered barely 200 at nightfall; but von Kluck's aim had been frustrated, and by the end of that day the main force had safely passed Maubeuge. Still the strain and the fatigue never ceased. Far into the night our men were slogging along past the Bavai cross-roads, the murmurous cadence of their going dimly mingling with the sound of many wheels. The anxieties of the Staff and its labours only grew, even though the 4th Division had that day begun detraining its fighting troops at Le Cateau.

THE BATTLE OF LE CATEAU

During the 25th von Kluck's Army followed hard upon the British as they retreated, the First Corps to the east and the Second Corps to the west of the Forest of Mormal. Though seriously checked at Solesmes, Landrecies, and Maroilles in the evening, the Germans were so close to our exhausted troops that the Second Corps Commander was forced to consider a change of plans. General Allenby, commanding the Cavalry Division, advised him that unless it were found feasible to continue the retreat again before daybreak, he must stand and fight. As troops were still coming in dead-beat at 4 a.m., and meanwhile the conditional assent of Sir John French had been obtained, Smith-Dorrien determined to give battle. For this purpose the 4th Division, Cavalry Division, and 19th Infantry Brigade were also placed under his orders.

Unhappily some battalions could not be warned of the change of plan in time. Thus a spur to the east of Le Cateau was evacuated early, the troops there moving off to resume the retreat, as originally ordered. This left the British right flank open.

The British line was manned by the 5th, 3rd, and 4th Divisions, with the Cavalry Division and 19th Infantry Brigade in reserve. It ran for about 12 miles roughly parallel to the Le Cateau–Cambrai road, but with its left flank bent back; in front of it the ground fell gently away, making a natural glacis. Von Kluck attempted to outflank it on the east, up the valley of the river Selle, which flows north-eastwards through Le Cateau, and on the west by way of Wambaix and Cattenières. He used great concentrations of artillery on both flanks, in the hope that, if he could not destroy the British, he might drive them southwards off what he believed to be their chosen line of retreat—westwards towards their bases on the Channel.

As at Mons, battle was first joined on the right of the line. The infantry and guns of the 5th Division took heavy toll of the enemy masses advancing from the east. But German infantry was not lightly baulked. Supported by enfilade artillery and machine-gun fire from the abandoned spur, which the enemy had lost no time in occupying, his infantry steadily closed round this flank. Yet it held out for the greater part of the day under the inspiration of sheer valour, although our infantry and guns were disposed merely in the temporary positions they had taken up, tired out, in the black dark and pouring rain of the previous evening. Gun after gun was put out of action; reinforcements and ammunition-carrying parties were swept away; the Suffolks and Argylls on the flank dwindled to a remnant. At 2.45 p.m. with a rush the enemy overwhelmed them. Notwithstanding this, the flank held until the Divisional order to retire reached those covering it. Meanwhile gallant deeds were done in the saving of most of the guns of four batteries. Of four other batteries, only one could be reached; two of its guns were got away, the four teams for the other guns being destroyed. An eye-witness records the "short, wild scene of galloping and falling horses, and then four guns standing derelict, a few limbers lying about, one on the sky-line with its pole vertical, and dead men and dead horses everywhere".

Along the westward reach of the position, heavy enemy attacks were repulsed so completely that no further effort was made until late in the day; but at dire cost, for the German artillery stood wheel to wheel and targets were assiduously sought for it by air. By then the thunder of the French "75's", away to the west, had assured General Smith-Dorrien that Sordet's Cavalry Corps would prevent von Kluck enveloping the British left. Ever since the 22nd, Sordet's tired mounted regiments had been labouring to cross the rear of the retreating British, to the mutual discomfort of both, on roads crowded with wretched refugees. So, after the first moments of doubt as to their identity had passed, the sound of Sordet's guns must have been a vast satisfaction to the British Corps Commander.

With nice judgement orders were issued at 1.40 p.m. for the resumption of the retreat. Dispositions had already been made to hold covering positions on the higher ground to the south and east whilst the front line troops withdrew in succession from the right. Inevitably, in certain cases, these

orders to infantry in action miscarry; and so it came about
that, scattered along the position, there remained odd companies, sometimes even the bulk of a battalion, doggedly
fighting on. Their presence caused the enemy to bombard
the otherwise empty positions with great fury until dark.
Some of these gallant bands even then followed up the retreat and rejoined; others, attempting this, were trapped in
the darkness and surrounded; others, wandering and fighting
their way through the German lines, eventually brought
their thinned ranks through to Antwerp or Boulogne. Yet
others, notably five platoons of the 2nd King's Own York-
shire Light Infantry, held on until overwhelmed, after in-
flicting tremendous punishment on the enemy.

The enemy tried to follow up the retirement of our left,
but was repulsed in the neighbourhood of Ligny. Any disposition he showed to mass and move forward on the right
was promptly checked by horse batteries and "heavies" in
position on the higher ground about Escaufort and Honnechy.
Of the 5th Division only the 15th Infantry Brigade retired as
a formed body; the remainder left the field—so says an eye-
witness—"like a crowd leaving a race meeting and making
its way earnestly to a railway station". Once on the Roman
Road, which had possibly borne the march of the legions
with which Julius Caesar overcame the Nervii, they formed
up and resumed the retreat towards St Quentin. Contact
with the enemy was practically lost when darkness fell.

So, in weather not unlike that of historic Crécy, the men
who fought on this its anniversary proved again the military
virtues shown by their race in 1346. Turning upon an enemy
twice as strong as they and with both their flanks open, they
had driven him to cover and caused him heavy casualties.
Finally they had withdrawn, having shaken off pursuit and
foiled the plan of the enemy commander. Yet more widely
considered, their doings had "*puissamment contribué à assurer la
sécurité du flanc gauche de l'Armée française*"—words used by
General Joffre in a congratulatory telegram which he sent
to Sir John French.

But it was a critical time. The news, confused and dis-
torted, as always, by rumour, stirred the country deeply, for

von Kluck claimed to have defeated the whole British Army, capturing several thousand prisoners and many guns. Actually the losses were 7812 men and 38 guns, the prisoners, including wounded, numbering 2600.

THE RETREAT RESUMED

During the night of August 26th, in order to restore the organisation, the troops of the Second Corps were sorted on the line of march. The difficulty of this was the greater because everyone dropped and slept wherever he halted and had to be kicked up to go on, stiff with cold and weak with hunger. The 3rd Division was worst off, being without rations from the 25th to the afternoon of the 27th. About St Quentin, the men of the 5th Division resumed their march cheerfully whistling and singing, after a rest of an hour or two. The rear-guards were unmolested, for von Kluck bore away in haste south-westwards on the 27th, under the impression that he had settled with the British and could now devote himself to the French assembled between the Somme and the Avre. By dawn on the 28th, Sir Horace Smith-Dorrien had brought the whole of his force across the Somme, 35 miles from the battlefield of Le Cateau. One of the crossings—that at Voyennes—had been passed by Henry V in his retreat northwards to Agincourt, four centuries earlier.

During this time the First Corps, accompanied by the 5th Cavalry Brigade, had been making its way southwards precariously, for a gap of a dozen miles, and widening, separated it from the Second Corps. The weather was extremely hot, and traffic difficulties hindered progress; indeed, at Le Grand Fayt, on the 26th, they directly caused a severe engagement whereby a rear-guard battalion (2nd Connaught Rangers) lost 300 officers and men. In an affair at Étreux on the following day the 2nd Munster Fusiliers and a section of a field battery were practically wiped out. Orders to retire failed to reach them, and they resisted an attack by twelve battalions of von Bülow's Army, supported by artillery, for twelve hours before they were overpowered. Meanwhile the First Corps passed through Guise—a critical operation.

The Second Corps reached the neighbourhood of Noyon on the 28th, a day of oppressive heat, whilst the First Corps halted at night south of La Fère. The fifteen-mile gap between was kept by two cavalry brigades, one of which fought a brilliant action near Cerisy.

When the 3rd Division halted at 6 p.m. on the 28th, just short of Noyon, it was worn out physically, having marched 68 miles in 50 hours; yet its spirit was unbroken. By this time Sir John French had convinced himself of the need to rest his army, so the British remained inactive on the 29th. General Joffre, however, had hoped to resume the offensive along the Oise and Somme on this day. But, as the British Commander-in-Chief could not support him, the French Fifth Army turned alone and heavily countered von Bülow at the crossings of the Oise.

On the 30th the retreat was continued; and an additional Army Corps, the Third, was formed of the 4th Division and the 19th Infantry Brigade. Both this and the following days were stiflingly hot, and the march of the Army was further hampered by crowds of unhappy refugees. On the 1st of September von Kluck returned hot-foot from the Avre, after, as he thought, disposing of the French Sixth Army, which was really only in process of assembling. Von Bülow had called upon him to complete the rout of the French Fifth Army, believing that he had defeated it two days before.

Marching south-eastwards early on the 1st, von Kluck brushed against the British rear-guards, with stirring effects. At Néry the 1st Cavalry Brigade and "L" Battery, R.H.A., were surrounded at 5.30 a.m. by a German cavalry division. The battery was in mass with the horses hooked in and the poles down, yet despite the fire of twelve enemy guns, two guns were man-handled round and one of them remained in action until it had exhausted its ammunition. Captain Bradbury was mortally wounded at this gun. His concern then was to conceal his dreadful injuries from the sight of those still serving it, B.S.M. Dorrell and Sgt. Nelson. All three were awarded the Victoria Cross. Ultimately, with the help of the 4th Cavalry Brigade and some infantry, the enemy was driven south into the woods, dispersed, and all his guns captured. Further to the east at Crépy-en-Valois and at Villers Cotterets other actions were fought. In the former the enemy lost heavily without getting to close quarters; in the latter the Guards Brigade only shook off the enemy about 6 p.m. after confused fighting in the forest. At Rond de la Reine, a forest glade, two platoons of Grenadiers fought to the last man.

The last stages of the retreat, down the west bank of the lower Ourcq and across the Marne, saw no serious fighting; but extreme measures were necessary to bring along the exhausted troops. On the 2nd of September, General Haig railed back half the ammunition carried by the Divisional Ammunition Columns and carried kits and exhausted men in the fifty waggons thus made available. Cases of heat-stroke occurred in the intense and suffocating heat of these last days, for though night marching was resorted to, the crowded state of the roads and the disorganisation of the civilian masses fleeing before the invasion made the marches long in time as well as distance.

There was now no gap in the British front. But it was necessary to make a critical manoeuvre in order to clear the defences of Paris and to get touch with the French Fifth Army eastwards. During this operation von Kluck made one last effort to grapple with the British, but this was anticipated and eluded by their, to him, uncanny mobility. Thus he was drawn on to the crossings of the Grand Morin. His advance-guards were aligned south of the river from Esternay to Crécy, but his right flank was insecure. Five German Armies had now penetrated into a vast armoured pocket, bulging round Chalons and flanked by the fortresses of Verdun and Paris. Sarrail's Third Army and Gallieni's Army of Paris (150,000 men), which included Maunoury's Sixth Army, faced inwards against their flanks, the western one being already overlapped from the north.

At this time the seat of French Government was transferred to Bordeaux, whilst its military chief aimed the blow which almost ended the war in 1914. On the 5th of September, General Maunoury began his attack eastwards at

Meaux and St Soupplets. The next day, the whole Allied line from Paris to Verdun and beyond along the Moselle turned on the enemy. The battle of the Marne had begun.

THE BATTLE OF THE MARNE

It is already claimed that the battle of the Marne ranks among the decisive battles of the world. It turned the tide of invasion and caused the German Armies to retreat in confusion; for eight days, indeed, the Armies of von Kluck and von Bülow remained in actual jeopardy. They fought again only when their commanders dared no longer risk the demoralisation of further withdrawal. Then they stood on the ridge between the valleys of the Aisne and Ailette, along which runs the Chemin des Dames. There on the 15th of September the crisis was overpassed, but only by dint of desperate efforts and in the nick of time.

When on the 6th of September the British force turned upon the enemy, it had got its "First Reinforcements"—10 per cent. of the original strength of its "units"; but there had been rather more than 15,000 casualties, and in addition, just as in all great retreats, there were absent some 20,000 men, most of whom, however, rejoined later. But during the next few days the work of the British Army, though tactically of decisive importance, did not entail any heavy fighting.

The retirement of the British on September 5th prevented them engaging the enemy profitably on the 6th, so as to hold him on the line of the Grand Morin. Von Kluck could therefore withdraw his troops as required to strengthen his right flank on the lower Ourcq against the Army of Paris. In their place he left a strong cavalry screen which, proving insufficient to hold up the British, he reinforced later with a division and a half.

On the 6th the Second Corps was able to secure and maintain a bridge-head north of the Grand Morin; but the First Corps was compelled to advance with extreme caution, for in the early morning strong columns of the enemy were everywhere, and their disappearance (towards the Ourcq flank) must have been difficult to understand or even to

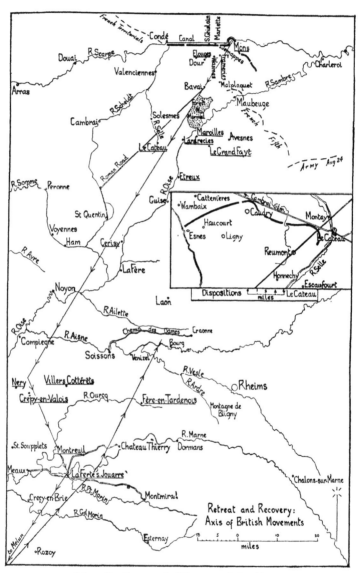

Mons, Le Cateau, the Marne, and the Aisne

credit. The Grand Morin was crossed on the 7th without serious incident. On the 8th the line of the Petit Morin was strongly held by two enemy cavalry corps, whilst the neighbourhood of the bridges over the Petit Morin and the Marne at La Ferté-sous-Jouarre was crowded with enemy troops on the way to the Ourcq. Crossings were forced soon after midday, and the enemy was defeated, after some furious fighting, in scattered actions along the Montmirail–La Ferté road. Though only part of La Ferté-sous-Jouarre could be occupied that evening, the British had opened up a gap of some twenty miles between the First German Army on the Ourcq and the Second German Army on the head-waters of the Petit Morin.

On the next day the Marne was crossed without opposition up-river towards Château Thierry, where the bridges remained undamaged. Lower down the enemy clung to La Ferté-sous-Jouarre and destroyed the bridges, so that only six battalions of the Third Corps had crossed by evening. This brought the right of the British advance to a standstill at the Château Thierry–Montreuil road, which runs along the ridges north of the river; opposition was very strong south of Montreuil, for here von Kluck had been compelled to throw in the division and a half already mentioned. The ease of the early advance of the British right had seemed to hold out the hope of cutting off the retreat of those of von Kluck's troops which remained in the Marne–Ourcq angle, but, much to the disappointment of the British, it was not fulfilled.

On the left of the British, Maunoury, using up the last of his reserves from Paris, fought hard all day, but was only able to report in the evening that von Kluck was retiring north-eastwards, covering his retreat with his heavy artillery. On the right the French Fifth Army had defeated von Bülow and enveloped his right.

During these four days, 6th–9th September, the British advanced 37 miles, across three rivers, in the face of a numerically superior enemy. This reflects the dogged spirit of men who had just endured the labours of a 200-mile retreat. The pressure they put on von Kluck kept him so intent upon his own peril that he refused to assist the despairing von Bülow. Von Bülow thereupon retired, and caused von Kluck to follow suit. By means of a converging retirement they hoped to reduce gradually the 25-mile gap between their two armies. If successful, this would squeeze out the British wedge, which seemed likely otherwise to bring about the isolation of the German First Army and the successive envelopment of the others from west to east. Ultimately the whole German line from the Ourcq to Verdun was withdrawn, and the fruitless attacks of their Sixth and Seventh Armies towards the Moselle came to an end.

The anxieties of the German Supreme Command at this time seem to have been too much for it. Though the Russians under Samsonow had been annihilated at Tannenberg by von Hindenburg on the 29th of August, the battle of the Masurian Lakes had but begun on September 8th, and the terrors of the invasion of East Prussia had raised a great popular outcry, which belittled the Supreme Command and idolised von Hindenburg. South-eastward the Austrians had been routed at Lemberg and driven headlong across the San. A Belgian sortie from Antwerp on September 9th had temporarily disorganised the German arrangements to reinforce the Armies of the western wing at a critical time. Von Moltke, the German Chief of Staff, now decided to place von Kluck, as at first, under von Bülow's command, and this was done as soon as the Supreme Command became aware of von Bülow's decision to retreat.

In cold rainy weather the British pursued the retreating enemy. Some 2000 prisoners were taken as a result of rearguard actions, south of the upper Ourcq on the 10th, and at the crossings of the Vesle on the 12th. First across the Aisne was General Hunter-Weston's 11th Infantry Brigade. At the end of a thirty-mile march, it crossed the damaged bridge at Venizel in single file during the night of the 12th-13th; it then seized the heights to the north of the river at the point of the bayonet just before dawn. Early on the 13th the First Corps began crossing further east at Bourg.

Difficulties at the Aisne crossings on this day delayed the advance, and no serious attempt to seize the Chemin des

Dames could be made until the 14th. It was then too late. The gap between the First and Second German Armies had been filled with two additional Army Corps. So, when the British divisions dribbled on to the battlefield over the Aisne crossings on the 14th, they found the enemy well posted, entrenched, and supported by 8-inch howitzers. Thinking no longer of retreat, he was even prepared to counter-attack and drive the Allies back across the river. So firm was the purpose of the enemy command, now directed by von Falkenhayn, who had superseded von Moltke, that on the 14th, when some much-tried troops showed a disposition to surrender, they were on two occasions shot down by their own guns. A day of fierce fighting ended without decisive result. It is now customary to regard this as the beginning of trench warfare.

The fortunes of the French Armies on the British flanks were similar to our own. The Fifth Army had hustled the hard-pressed von Bülow and penetrated even round to his rear, through the gap between him and von Kluck; but this advantage had to be given up on the arrival of reinforcements. The Sixth Army, delayed like the British at the Aisne, had failed to press von Kluck enough to prevent him reorganising his army and digging in. It attempted in vain to envelop his right by way of the western bank of the Oise, and this step began the prolongation of the northern flanks of the combatants, until finally they rested on the North Sea, without either succeeding in gaining a decisive advantage over the other.

Imperturbably cheery, the British force, augmented on the 16th of September by the 6th Division, established itself immovably in an impossible position just north of the river. To this it clung, in places without artillery support and in spite of violent bombardments with heavy shell. Its precarious communications lay across a wide valley and a swift stream; but they were improved and repaired so that reliefs, rations, and ammunition could always be got forward and casualties brought back. The tenacity and military aptitude of an unwarlike race could hardly be more strikingly revealed. The experience which followed, including even the

making of grenades from jam-tins emptied of their "plum
and apple", was to be of great value during October and
November. It was indeed the germ of the limited military
training of the years immediately following.

SUGGESTIONS FOR READING:

Military Operations, 1914, France and Belgium by Brig.-Gen. Sir J. E.
    Edmonds, vol. I, Appendix 8 and p. 244. *1914* by Viscount French
    of Ypres, pp. 95–103.

Chapter III: FLANDERS, 1914

(See maps on pp. 21, 49 *and* 29)

Tʜᴇ strategic situation at the beginning of October was
that neither side could pierce the line entrenched by the
other, between the Swiss frontier and the Oise at Noyon.
This was due to the straits both sides already were in for gun
ammunition; the expenditure of shells during the fortnight's
fighting on the Aisne had outrun the home production.
Moreover the holding of an entrenched line is a great saving
of strength, so both sides were automatically provided with
large mobile reserves. Armies in Alsace and Lorraine were
replaced by reserve troops, whilst those holding the remainder of the trench line were thinned out. The product
was used to attempt the envelopment of the adversary's
exposed north-western flank.

The succession of movements resulting has come to be
known as "the Race to the Sea" and was punctuated by
epic fighting: first on the line of the Somme; then for the
Vimy Ridge and the Aubers–Pérenchies Ridge; and finally
for the heights south-west to east of Ypres. The Allies aimed
at aligning with the Belgian Army about Antwerp and forming a continuous front which would secure Lille and cover
the coal-fields of Béthune and Lens. To prevent this the
Germans moved on Arras, gained the Vimy Ridge and even

a footing on the Lorette Ridge, and launched a cavalry
sweep through Flanders towards the Channel ports and the
lower Seine. At the same time they accelerated the operations against Antwerp.

Thus an opportunity presented itself for the withdrawal
of the British from the Aisne; so the whole force, now
amounting to six divisions, an infantry brigade, and two

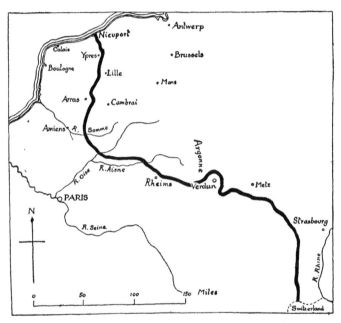

General trench-line on the Western Front, 1914–18

cavalry divisions, began moving in the first fortnight of
October to Flanders. The transfer greatly shortened its lines
of communication; fittingly, in the interests of England, imposed on it the duty of keeping the enemy from the Channel
ports; and once again made it recognisably the instrument
of our pledged word in Belgium. Attempts had been made

to devise further means for this purpose as soon as it was plain that the Aisne battle would reach a deadlock. The concentration near Dunkirk of an Allied force for the relief of Antwerp had been arranged; but time did not suffice.

The Germans, under von Falkenhayn, showed that they had thrown off the lethargy of defeat. The siege of Antwerp was pressed; 17-inch howitzers began the reduction of its outer forts on the night 27th–28th September, but the city was not surrendered until October 10th. The only assistance the British were able to give the doomed place was of a moral rather than of a material kind; it comprised the presence of Mr Winston Churchill and three Naval Brigades, mostly untrained and ill-equipped, whose bearing was nevertheless incredibly fine. Fortunately the Belgian Field Army was able again to withdraw in time and in order from German clutches; it evacuated Antwerp on October 8th. Its retreat was partly covered by a British force, the Fourth Corps (comprising the 7th Division and the 3rd Cavalry Division) under General Rawlinson, which had landed at Zeebrugge and Ostend on the 6th and 7th of October and operated towards Ghent.

During the second week in October, whilst the Fourth Corps was retiring westwards on the right of the Belgian Army, the main British force began to advance eastwards; the Second Corps first, towards La Bassée, then the Third Corps towards Armentières, and at the end of the third week the First Corps through and north of Ypres. They pivoted on the famous St Omer–Aire–La Bassée Canal defence line, one of Vauban's last conceptions, only carried out after his death.

The Second Corps encountered the enemy west of La Bassée on the 10th of October. After a fierce struggle it secured the Aubers end of the ridge which runs north-eastwards to Pérenchies and covers Lille, at a cost of 2000 casualties. Its attack gave out on the 20th a mile from La Bassée.

The Third Corps, after a costly success at Meteren on October 13th, drove back the enemy through Bailleul and Armentières. Fighting determinedly, it tried to establish its centre on the northern end of the Pérenchies Ridge about Ennetières, whence it could look down on Lille. It was hoped thus to command the crossings of the river Lys towards Menin, so that the Cavalry Corps, bearing down on them from the Messines–Wytschaete Ridge, might advance across the river against the flank of the German line. Secure behind these crossings, however, the German right was awaiting the advance through Belgium of a newly formed Army consisting mainly of young volunteers, with a stiffening of reservists. It was their task to "win the war...by successfully closing with the enemy".

FIRST BATTLE OF YPRES: FIRST PHASE

The British gave the enemy their wish. When the latter advanced against the northern spurs of the ridges running from south-west to north-east of Ypres, they found the Fourth Corps reconnoitring in force the passages of the Lys towards Menin, its cavalry about Passchendaele. Further north, French cavalry and Territorials were holding Houthulst Forest and the line of the canal from Ypres to Boesinghe. Behind the line of the Yser, north of Boesinghe and extending to the sea, lay the greatly enduring Belgian Army, supported by a French Naval Brigade.

A general attack by the two German Armies between La Bassée and the sea began on October 20th. The Belgians along the Yser had been strongly attacked two days previously in an attempt to break their line. This was the first sign of the coming storm north of the Lys. On the following day the vicinity of Audenarde was reported by our airmen to be crowded with troops and transport; more were noticed at Courtrai, and four long columns, heading south-westwards from the direction of Brussels, foreshadowed the approach of what one man in those ranks has called the *stahlgewitter* ("tempest of steel").

The portents were misunderstood by the Allies, and to this extent they were unprepared. So on the 20th, though the enemy was foiled at the first onset, his attempt to break through to Estaires pressed back the British line on the Aubers–Pérenchies Ridge and cost our 6th Division alone

2000 casualties. Meanwhile his enveloping movement in the north had caused us the loss, with hardly a fight, of the commanding Becelaere spur.

On this day the First Corps was just arriving at Ypres from the Aisne. On the following day it attacked north-eastwards towards Passchendaele and Poelcapelle and reached the crest of the Gravenstafel Ridge; but it was twenty-four hours too late to endanger the German right. Thenceforward the whole Allied line between Nieuport and La Bassée was thrown on the defensive and was lashed and battered with assault after assault by fresh troops and more and more heavy artillery. To the splendid bravery of the Germans the British soldier opposed the patient and stubborn resistance of perfect fitness and great skill. Day and night the struggle was waged without ceasing, so that the British troops got no rest and no time to prepare food, till by the 25th one German Army had fought itself to a standstill and, for lack of company officers, had little offensive value henceforth. Its young men, singing their battle-songs, had been mown down by guns gallantly run up to short range. They were the first-fruits of the great sacrifice to Moloch which the youth of the warring nations was to furnish during four ghastly years; the victims died the more nobly, having never had the opportunity to become trained soldiers.

The enemy's greatest success, though a temporary one, was obtained on the 24th. Early in the morning German troops penetrated into Polygon Wood, after annihilating the 2nd Wiltshires on Reutel spur. An effort by the 2nd Warwicks and Northumberland Hussars to counter-attack through the wood no more than checked the enemy's progress; but it is notable as the first serious engagement of a British Territorial unit in the war. When, about 11 a.m., troops of the 2nd Division arrived, the Germans had failed to press forward, though they were quite close to the headquarters of the 7th Division, which was prepared for a last stand. Immediately the 2nd Highland Light Infantry and 2nd Worcestershires counter-attacked north-eastwards, every seventh man carrying a 7 lb. tin of "bully beef", newly drawn. It was difficult to keep direction through the thick undergrowth, but suddenly they came on the Germans, just east of the race-course in Polygon Wood, and fell on them with the bayonet. After a short but stubborn resistance the enemy broke and was forced out of the wood. But the Reutel spur was left in the enemy's hands.

A smaller German success at the Kortekeer Cabaret, north of Pilckem, on the 22nd, was equally speedily neutralised by the 1st Division, whose counter-stroke caused the enemy to fear that his front was being rolled up north-eastwards to the sea. After this counter-attack such a feeling of hilarity possessed the Queen's and Loyals engaged that they could hardly be prevailed upon to cease collecting "souvenirs" and prepare their position against attack.

The 25th of October saw, therefore, the beginning of a lull in the enemy's operations about Ypres. But, to cover the exhaustion of the German Fourth Army, their Sixth Army, south of the Lys, made yet more frantic efforts to progress. Here was desperate fighting, which died down only on the utter exhaustion of both sides towards the end of the month. By then the Second and Third Corps and the 19th Infantry Brigade had been wrenched off the Aubers–Pérenchies Ridge on to the marshy flats west of it. In a last attack, on the 27th, Neuve Chapelle became the scene of a struggle for possession, into which the remnants of worn battalions were thrown by both sides during two terrible days. After the village had changed hands a number of times, neither side was able to claim possession of it; so it was wearily abandoned to the dead, who alone might inhabit it. During the October fighting south of the Lys our casualties had exceeded 20,000.

FIRST BATTLE OF YPRES: SECOND PHASE

At the end of this first phase of the battle, the Allied commanders regarded their situation optimistically. Considerable reserves were in hand, a French Corps having arrived on the previous day. This Corps now attacked north-eastwards and threw back the enemy from Zonnebeke and Langemarck. On its right the British 2nd Division gained a footing on the ridge towards Becelaere. Except for attacks at Messines and at Kruiseecke late in the day on the 25th, the German line from Nieuport to La Bassée made no offensive movement. It is indeed recorded that the principal action on the front of one Brigade of the 7th Division took place when burying-parties of the 2nd Royal Scots Fusiliers were fired on from a house; they attacked it, shovels in hand, and captured 20 Germans, including an officer. The action at Kruiseecke, a single street of houses on a knoll, gave some anxious moments, and was moreover a portent. The hamlet lay in a sharp salient of the front at the junction of its eastern and southern faces. On the next day a renewed attack, heralded by a three-hour bombardment from 8-inch howitzers, destroyed the 20th Brigade's trenches and buried numbers of the occupants. Nevertheless, an infantry attack by twelve German battalions did no more than occupy the angle.

The enemy was using up relentlessly such troops as were still capable of offence. But he was not using them aimlessly; he was preparing a tremendous effort against the south and east faces of the Ypres salient, assembling for the purpose a new Army Group, with more than 250 heavy guns, under von Fabeck. This force would give the Germans a twofold numerical superiority over the Allies.

On the 29th of October the cross-roads one mile east of Gheluvelt were attacked and taken by these fresh troops after a confused and bloody fight. But it was not until the 30th that the full storm broke round the whole perimeter and the fresh divisions were launched at the British line between Ploegsteert Wood and the Menin Road. The enemy concentrated on the effort north of the Lys, so the fighting about Neuve Chapelle forthwith died down; whereupon the Second Corps was relieved by the Indian Corps and its infantry moved north in reserve.

To judge the success of the troops who bore von Fabeck's attack, it must be accounted that the scale of material supplies provided for the Expeditionary Force was inadequate. Towards the end of October a limit had to be imposed in the use of gun ammunition, so a quarter of the Divisional Artillery was withdrawn, because it had nothing to fire. Eventually even the guns remaining in action could average not more than one shell every half-hour, though the enemy counter-batteries could "plaster" them constantly. Worse than this was the failure in quality of the rifle ammunition. Moreover rifle oil was unprocurable, and many a rifle, fouled by the sandy soil thrown about during bombardments, remained quite unserviceable for lack of it. To these two causes, in part, the loss of the Gheluvelt cross-roads and Kruiseecke have been attributed.

Diminishing in numbers day by day at an alarming rate, the British troops yet took toll for every yard of ground which the enemy's continually renewed strength and vastly increasing heavy artillery compelled them to cede. The battle of the 30th and 31st of October abounds in instances of dogged valour and self-sacrifice in the fighting line, and of the inspired and equally self-sacrificing leadership to which it offered opportunity. Individuals, regiments, and leaders can seldom before have risen to such splendour of military virtue, for never before had the conditions of war been so appallingly ghastly, the stakes so stupendous. What Agincourt owes to Shakespeare let those assess who may. The world will be the poorer if no Shakespeare or Homer arise to endue with immortality the lives of the ragged, haggard, weary men who fought at Ypres. As at Agincourt, even their very destitution helped the cause they fought for, by giving the enemy the idea that the British were completely exhausted.

When, therefore, on October 30th, the German attack carried Zandevoorde and Hollebeke against the scattered trenches of the 2nd and 3rd Cavalry Divisions, the enemy's hopes rose high, despite his heavy losses. The British line about Gheluvelt lay practically at his mercy, and he had got such a footing on the high ground towards Wytschaete and Messines that the "break-through" seemed imminent. The Kaiser himself appeared, to encourage his troops.

Not waiting for daylight on the 31st, German infantry furiously assaulted Messines and Gheluvelt. As the morning mists cleared, about 8 a.m., they were recoiling almost everywhere. Seeing this, their artillery blazed at the British defences and in places literally blew the occupants out of them with high explosive. After two hours of this bombardment, masses of infantry advanced to the assault, cheering and singing with enthusiasm at being under their Emperor's eye. At Messines they made a lodgement; north of Zandevoorde they pressed back the 7th Division and troops of the First Corps; at Gheluvelt they broke the line of the 1st Division. But the ground they had passed over was littered with their dead and dying in such numbers that the remnants became disorganised. Finally they were driven back, in spite of the undiscriminating fury of the German artillery.

To the north of the "break-in" at Gheluvelt, the remains of the 1st South Wales Borderers and a few Scots Guards steadily wheeled back their exposed right flank, the better to spring, it seemed; for, with all the dash of troops fresh to the fight, they charged, about noon, and drove the enemy from the grounds of the Château. An order to retire reached these two battalions shortly afterwards, but it was cancelled to the Scots Guards by their Brigadier, General Fitzclarence; whereupon the Borderers stayed with them. This fine conduct, and that of the gunners about Gheluvelt, who served their guns heedless of close-range rifle fire, made possible the subsequent defeat of the enemy there.

South of the gap at Gheluvelt, Gloucesters, Welch, Loyals, and King's Royal Rifle Corps went forward through a sustained fire of guns and rifles against an enemy who outnumbered them hopelessly. Their progress was too slow to save the 2nd Welch, 1st Queen's, and K.R.R.C., fighting to the last in the original front line; but they completed the disorganisation of the enemy's attack. Finally the line here was restored by the 2nd Worcesters early in the afternoon. No amount of shelling could stay their steady advance from Polygon Wood to engage the enemy infantry, which was inexorably thrust back east of Gheluvelt and made no further effort to advance until daylight the next day.

North of Zandevoorde, soon after noon, thick masses of Germans, supported by continuous heavy shelling, advanced against Shrewsbury Forest and Tower Hamlets. Our men kept shooting them down, but they could neither stay them nor remedy the peril threatening their flank from Gheluvelt.

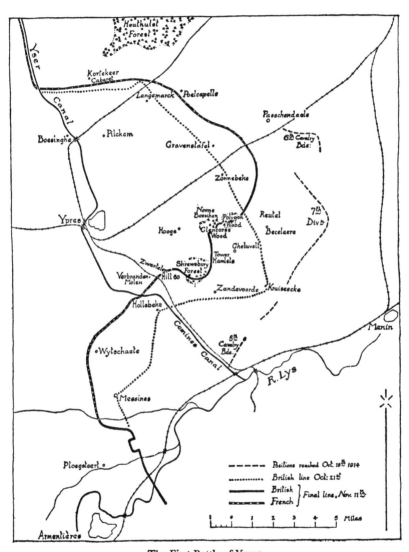

The First Battle of Ypres

On this flank the troops had been moved back as far as was advisable, and their situation was desperate. Suddenly, late in the afternoon, a battalion of Gordon Highlanders charged from behind the British line. The line north and south of them broke into flame, as if it were one huge machine-gun battery, for the space of a minute. Then Sussex, Northamptons, Oxfords, Royal Engineers, and Royal Dragoons joined in one wild rush with the bayonet and fought their way forward for half a mile before they could be brought to a halt. The charging "battalion" of Highlanders numbered originally just eighty all told!

At Messines the Inniskillings and two weak battalions just relieved elsewhere got back from the enemy all he had won, except his hold on the eastern half of the village.

Late in the day a platoon of the Hampshires did a great deed. Their trench was entered by the enemy after a bombardment which had lasted since morning. At once the 1st Somerset Light Infantry fell upon the assailants and brilliantly restored the line; but every man of the Hampshire platoon lay dead at his post.

The Belgian Army's hard lot was alleviated on this day. At high water on the 28th the lock gates at Nieuport had been opened, to let in the sea between the Yser and the embankment of the Dixmude–Nieuport railway. The inundation stopped the attacks on the Belgian Army on the 30th, and the Germans retired, abandoning wounded, arms, and ammunition.

Thus passed the most critical of all the critical days in the struggle for possession of the Channel ports. The British losses had been very heavy. The fighting Staffs of two divisions had been wiped out by one salvo which fell on the Château of Hooge, just at the time of greatest peril; subordinate commanders and company officers had fallen in numbers; rank and file had simply melted away. At the end of the day whole battalions were represented by a few score of lonely men; and yet, through all the excursions of the 31st of October, there appears neither failure of spirit nor disorganisation. The art of war had been used with credit. Primitive as it is, in practice it is the most difficult of all. It strives to avert imminent disorder and destruction under conditions which outrage every human sensibility. To have succeeded in doing this against heavy odds in men and heavier odds in weapons is the glory of the British Army this day.

The days that followed were relatively calm. New lines of resistance were prepared by the Allies in anticipation of coming trouble. French assistance arrived and shared the burden borne by the British troops. Yet it was necessary to shorten the front in order to organise reserves; so ground was ceded to the enemy, across which he hesitated to approach and close—and it was ground which neither side coveted, being dreadful with carnage. But the tide of battle still threw its earthy foam about Ploegsteert, Messines, and Wytschaete; the enemy was gradually gaining the crest from which he was so long to look down on the Ypres flats from the south and south-west. The German guns continued their bombardment and daily increased in number. A diarist remarks on the 5th of November "the Germans seemed to know it was Guy Fawkes Day". More British guns were withdrawn, starved of ammunition. The German infantry now approached by sapping and, when near enough, obeyed their orders to "attack somewhere every day" and give their adversary no rest. They lost heavily, particularly in prisoners, but the British losses were the more critical; in particular the casualties among officers had been excessive and remained irreparable.

FIRST BATTLE OF YPRES: THIRD AND LAST PHASE

There were some hopes that, with the coming of winter weather on November 7th, the enemy would cease his efforts for the Channel ports and occupy himself repairing his severe defeat before Warsaw, whence Hindenburg was withdrawing, having lost 40,000 men. But yet another great assault was intended. The enemy added yet more to the heavy artillery round the Salient and diverted to it ammunition allotted elsewhere. He drew divisions from his line as far off as Verdun in order to form one more Army Group, under von Linsingen, for this front. North of the Comines

Canal the British were to be "driven back and crushed" by corps containing Guards and Prussian troops of high repute, whilst elsewhere, from La Bassée to the sea, the German Sixth and Fourth Armies would make a general attack.

The God of Battles, in praise and worship of whom Queen Elizabeth struck a famous medal, decreed that on the morning of November 11th the burst-clouds of the German shells should be blown back into the faces of the assaulting infantry and swept clear of the British line, and that the defenders' trenches should be afforded the added shelter of trees felled by the German artillery. During the day there were three anxious moments, at Zwartelen, in Shrewsbury Forest, and at the Nonne Boschen ("Nun's Copse"). But there was no such crisis as on the last day of October, even at the last-named, where a crashing bombardment was followed by a massed infantry attack, which overran the front of Fitz-clarence's 1st Infantry Brigade north of the Menin Road. The jog-trot advance of the big Guard soldiers, the officers with drawn swords, the men with arms at the port, in the tradition of 1870, carried them forward among a number of scattered entrenched posts which the British dignified with the name of "strong-points"—for they were strong only in marksmanship. Turning against one and another of these, and against the trenches of the 1st King's along the southern edge of Polygon Wood, the German attack broke up and lost cohesion. Meanwhile the British guns effectively barred the advance of supports. Plodding on north-westwards, not firing much but mostly using the bayonet, men of the German Foot Guards passed through the Nonne Boschen to its western edge. Here they were driven back by point-blank gun fire and the rifle fire of cooks, messengers, headquarter details, stragglers, parties from heavy batteries, and the like. A wounded German officer captured here later, indicating the line of guns, asked "What is there behind?" Being told "Divisional Headquarters", he exclaimed with deep emotion "*Gott Allmächtig!*"

By this time the British reserves were on the move towards the copse from all directions. The Officer Commanding the 1st King's had in the meantime been ordered on no account to leave his trenches; he replied "No intention of quitting our trenches, but what about our rations?" At about 2 p.m. the Oxfordshires entered the north-western end of the wood, whilst the 5th Field Company R.E. charged down between it and Polygon Wood. They drove the Prussian Guardsmen on to the rifles of the Northamptons about Glencorse Wood, killing or taking all who stood their ground. The gap in the British line was then closed. Of the three Scots battalions of the 1st Brigade barely 300 survivors remained, and that night "the wondrous spirit that had inspired it...was stilled for ever". Whilst reconnoitring before leading the Irish Guards to retake his front line, General Fitzclarence— "O.C. Menin Road", as he was affectionately called—was killed by a rifle bullet.

The enemy's offensive did not entirely cease for some days; but wintry weather set in and both sides abandoned active operations in the third week of November. By this time another British division, the 8th, had arrived in Flanders and more than twenty Territorial battalions had crossed from England. The German Supreme Command, on the other hand, had ordered three Corps and all the cavalry from the Ypres front to Russia by the end of November.

The Allies then arranged that the British front should extend from the La Bassée Canal at Givenchy to opposite Wytschaete, the French holding the salient round Ypres and north to the Yser. Behind the Yser lay the Belgians. The French thus held 430 miles of the Western Front, the British 21, and the Belgians 15. The first illuminating pistols for sending up flares at night were issued to the British at this time. They were five in number and much less powerful than the hundreds in the enemy trenches, and they caused great hilarity among the Germans.

Officially the First Battle of Ypres ends on November 22nd, 1914. The cost of it to the British was almost military insolvency. Our losses between October 14th and November 30th alone amounted to more than 58,000, and our total casualties from the beginning of the war to the end of November were just under 90,000. The remains of the British battalions were, on the average, of the size of small platoons. Sufficient, however, remained slowly to leaven the New Armies and to make them invincible, a result due in no small part to the memory of the brilliant achievements of these splendid soldiers.

Two events of the early winter remain to be recorded. On the 14th of November the aged Field Marshal, Earl Roberts, died at St Omer, whilst on a visit to the troops; and two days later H.R.H. the Prince of Wales joined the Expeditionary Force, where his presence was destined to be an inspiration to troops in the line and an anxiety to those responsible for his safety.

SUGGESTIONS FOR READING:

Military Operations, 1914, France and Belgium by Brig.-Gen. Sir J. E. Edmonds, vol. II, pp. 264–6, 466. *The World Crisis, 1911–14* by W. S. Churchill, vol. I, pp. 332–3. *A Fatalist at War* by Rudolf Binding, pp. 13–31.

Chapter IV: NAVAL OPERATIONS, 1914–15

THE prosperity of the British Empire depends largely on its mastery of the oversea carrying-trade of the world. England owns more than a third of the world's tonnage and builds yearly more than two-thirds of the new construction. This industry enables our small islands to support the busy multitudes which throng them. So in war our world-girdling shipping must proceed, lest we starve. Moreover, to exert to the full the military power of the Empire the sea-routes of the world must be open.

On the outbreak of war the German Navy had squadrons and single fast ships abroad capable of preying upon commerce: a squadron, famous for its gunnery, on the China coast under Admiral von Spee; a fast light cruiser, *Nürnberg*, on the western sea-board of America; two fast light cruisers, *Emden* and *Königsberg*, in the Indian Ocean; two others, *Dresden* and *Karlsruhe*, and some armed merchantmen in the Atlantic. In the Mediterranean were the battle-cruiser *Goeben* and her consort the light cruiser *Breslau*.

On August 4th the *Goeben* and *Breslau* were found by

British battle-cruisers in the western Mediterranean and shadowed during the whole of that day. On the 6th they finally eluded the British squadrons and on the 10th sought refuge in the Dardanelles.

CORONEL AND THE FALKLAND ISLANDS

For long von Spee's ships were lost among the Pacific islands; during this time the *Dresden* and *Nürnberg* joined them. Meanwhile Allied squadrons keenly watched the horizons in the four corners of the Ocean. On the west coast of South America Admiral Cradock had an odd assortment of ships; too slow to bring the enemy to action, the squadron was yet too strong for von Spee to attack. This irked the spirited Cradock, so he cruised northwards without his supporting battleship, which was old and slow, and fell in with the Germans in rough weather off Coronel. The sun of the 1st of November went down on a southward-running fight. To landward the Germans, *Scharnhorst, Gneisenau,* and *Leipzig,* held off till sunset; afterwards they were obscured and suffered no damage. *Good Hope* and *Monmouth,* black against the after-glow, then bright in the fitful moonlight, were set on fire and sunk. Of their crews not one was saved; men of the pre-Dreadnought era, they strove only to close the enemy and never thought of surrender. The *Glasgow,* smothered in 8-inch salvoes, fought on alone till she lost her antagonists in the stormy darkness.

The German colony in Valparaiso feasted the victors and presented Admiral von Spee with a tribute of flowers. "They will do for my funeral", he said.

This disaster caused the Admiralty to send out the battle-cruisers *Inflexible* and *Invincible* to reinforce the squadron in the South Atlantic. They reached Port Stanley in the Falkland Islands on December 7th, accompanied by the armoured cruisers, *Kent, Cornwall,* and *Carnarvon,* the light cruisers *Glasgow* and *Bristol,* and the *Orama,* an armed merchantman. Admiral Sturdee was in command.

Whilst our ships were yet busy coaling on the following morning, von Spee's squadron appeared, to destroy the wireless station. It was *Gneisenau,* standing in close, which warned her consorts of their danger, and they steamed eastwards with the British ships in chase. Von Spee ordered his light cruisers to scatter and make for the mainland whilst the *Scharnhorst* and *Gneisenau* tried without avail to close their great antagonists. The *Scharnhorst*, with the Admiral and all hands, was sunk at four o'clock in the afternoon, but the *Gneisenau* fought on until nearly six; then, a helpless wreck, she opened her sea-cocks and went down. Meanwhile the *Dresden* was able to make good her escape; she was not accounted for until three months later in the roadstead of Mas-a-tierra (Juan Fernandez). The *Leipzig* was sunk by the *Cornwall* and *Glasgow*, the *Nürnberg* by the *Kent*; the *Leipzig* fought until she had fired her last round and was a flaming wreck; the *Nürnberg* surrendered at 7 p.m., having no longer a workable gun, and she sank half an hour later.

COMMERCE-RAIDERS

The *Emden* and *Königsberg* caused a considerable disturbance in the East. After a time the *Königsberg* sought the African coast and finally was destroyed in the Rufigi river. The *Emden* took many prizes, bombarded the coast of Madras, and was hospitably received at Diego Garcia, a British Colony unaware of the war; she even raided Penang with disastrous results to Allied shipping. Suddenly, on the 8th of November, 1914, the wireless at Cocos Island stuttered an abruptly ended message that a strange cruiser was approaching. It so happened that a large convoy of Australian and New Zealand troops was in the neighbourhood. One of the escort, the light cruiser *Sydney* of the Australian Navy, pursued, found the *Emden*, and within two hours left her stranded on North Keeling Island, a smoking wreck.

In the Atlantic Ocean the *Karlsruhe* narrowly escaped from the *Suffolk* and *Bristol* on the night of the 6–7th August. During the following three months she captured or sunk sixteen British vessels valued with their cargoes at over a million and a half sterling. But on the evening of November 4th, whilst on her way to the Bahamas bent on new mischief, she suddenly blew up. Of the German armed merchantmen only two kept the seas for any time; the damage they did was insignificant.

The loss which, it is computed, the German raiders inflicted on shipping was short of £7,000,000, whereas the total value of British sea commerce during the time of the German cruiser depredations was little short of £1,000,000,000. There is little pride in figures, but a loss of 0·7 per cent. represents solid achievement in naval effort. Against such a marvel of world-commerce protection the romantic deeds and nobly borne sufferings of the raiders must evoke admiration. Moreover, though for four months after the outbreak of war the further seas had held many menaces, the forces of the Empire were conveyed with safety and despatch towards the seat of the main conflict. By the end of the year five divisions of troops from India had been moved to Europe and Africa and their places taken by three divisions of Territorials. The overseas garrisons had been brought to England to form the 7th, 8th, 27th, 28th, and 29th Divisions. Twenty-five thousand Canadians and the Newfoundland Contingent had crossed the Atlantic to Plymouth, and two divisions of Australians and New Zealanders had been landed in Egypt.

THE GRAND FLEET IN BEING

Throughout this time the merchant shipping thronging to the ports of the United Kingdom was adequate for all purposes. Though the naval strength of Germany was almost wholly in home waters, it proved unable to limit our traffic by sea. This was the Grand Fleet's care; it drew a protecting cordon around what had once been called the German Ocean, and continually it swept into the obscurity of this North Sea, seeking an enemy who lurked behind minefields, submarine screens, and the defences of Heligoland.

Out of one of these sweeps arose the action in the Heligoland Bight. Towards the end of August a plan was laid to disturb the enemy's patrols of the waters about Heligoland. But the Germans gathered from the British wireless what was intended, so when the British light cruisers and destroyers steamed into the Bight at dawn on August 28th, the Germans were ready with a counter-offensive. From then until 4 p.m. fight after fight took place between the light

forces. The misty atmosphere blinded the island forts.
Finally the Battle-Cruiser Squadron under Admiral Beatty
held a course deep into the Bight and chanced on the
enemy's supporting light cruisers hurrying to reinforce. The
heavy armament of the *Lion* and *Princess Royal* blew the
Köln and the *Ariadne* out of the water; the fire of Beatty's
light cruisers silenced the *Mainz*; a German torpedo-boat
was sunk; the light cruisers *Stettin, Frauenlob,* and *Stralsund*
drew off much damaged, and a number of enemy destroyers were in like case. Over a thousand of the enemy
were killed, though 348 officers and men of the *Mainz* were
rescued by Commodore Keyes, who kept his destroyer
Lurcher alongside her till she sank. The damage sustained by
the British ships was comparatively slight.

The Germans, now aware of their beleaguered situation,
set themselves to make every use of the long winter nights
and the squally, misty days which favoured evasion by fast
or submersible craft. During the stormy weather towards
the end of September three old cruisers, *Hogue, Cressy,* and
Aboukir, patrolling off the Dutch coast, were torpedoed and
sunk by a submarine, *U 9.* Only about a third of their
aggregate complement of 2500 were saved. The danger
from submarines made the Grand Fleet shift its anchorage
often. While based on Lough Swilly, at the end of October,
one of the newest battleships, *Audacious,* was mined off Tory
Island and subsequently sank.

At dawn on the 16th of December units of the German
Fleet appeared off Scarborough and Hartlepool and shelled
the towns. The fort at Hartlepool put up a gallant fight; at
Scarborough there was no defence. Five hundred civilians
were killed and wounded in half an hour of violent ex-
plosions and falling masonry. Later two people were killed
and some wounded in Whitby.

Had fortune favoured as on August 28th, the German
raiders would have never returned. Intercepting their retreat off the southern edge of the Dogger Bank was the Battle-
Cruiser Squadron and a squadron of battleships, in overwhelming superiority. It had been possible to place them
there because the Admiralty had the German Naval cipher

and could read the enemy's wirelessed orders for forthcoming operations. A romantic story is told of the finding of the code and other books on the body of a German petty-officer after the wreck of the *Magdeburg* in the Baltic. In the morning twilight the British squadrons, unaware of what was beyond, engaged the screen of the High Seas Fleet, which turned at full speed for home. They then stood in shorewards to meet the raiders under Admiral Hipper, now unsupported. Twice a glimpse of the enemy was obtained amid squalls of rain and tumultuous seas, and once fire was opened; but Hipper's squadrons got clear away through the mist.

Having acted against our coast with impunity in December, the German squadrons sallied out again on the 23rd of January. Again the Admiralty was able to forecast the stroke. At 7 a.m. on Sunday the 24th, the battle-cruisers from the Forth and the light forces from Harwich sighted the enemy and gave chase. At 8.30 the *Lion* opened fire at 20,000 yards. Soon after 9.30 she could engage the leading German battle-cruiser, *Seydlitz*, at 17,000 yards. The *Blücher* had by then been crippled; her two after-turrets and over two hundred men were disabled. The *Moltke*, next ahead, was enduring heavy punishment from the *Princess Royal*. The stern of the *Seydlitz* and two turrets were ablaze; every man in the turrets from the gun-house above deck to the bilges eighty feet below perished. The *Lion* had been hit fourteen times, but the only damage was one gun out of action. At 10.52, however, she was hit again and her port engine disabled. Soon after this, what looked like the wash of a periscope was sighted to starboard and Admiral Beatty ordered a turn-away to the north-eastward. Subsequent signals were misunderstood, with the result that the destruction of the *Blücher* was completed whilst the rest of the German force made good their escape. The *Lion* was taken in tow and arrived in the Forth two days later at dawn.

The German Navy had again found that they were outwatched and outnumbered, and for long they eschewed aggressive action. The British Navy toiled and fretted meanwhile, getting never a gun-sight glimpse of an enemy ship.

An exemplary patience under the strain of duty and the restraint of public praise bespoke its endurance. The cheerless North Atlantic was continually patrolled and all traffic examined; contraband was prevented from reaching Germany, raiding vessels from reaching the high seas. The English Channel and the Irish Sea were as carefully and even more closely watched. The communications with France were vital. Out of their charmed safety grew the fame of the Dover Patrol.

THE FIRST SUBMARINE CAMPAIGN

The German Navy saw that its prestige was now at stake; it was impotent against the strangulation with which Germany was threatened from the sea. The German people, suffering the consequences, complained; the Army showed open contempt for the Navy. So the German naval leaders planned to retaliate from under the waters which they might not rule. Germany declared a blockade of the British Isles, threatening the summary destruction of all enemy vessels within the neighbouring waters.

The blockade began on February 18th, 1915, with the sinking unwarned of a British merchant ship. But the means to maintain it proved too slender. Only twenty-five "U boats" existed; only eight could be kept at sea at a time. In two and a half months they sank fifty-one ships, of which six were neutrals; and during this time over fifteen thousand vessels made and cleared port in the United Kingdom. It was obvious in May that the operations of the submarines had failed to bring about a blockade. In the autumn the campaign died down. The British merchant service had risen to the occasion nobly.

In the fight against enemy submarines much ingenuity was shown. Various nets with indicator floats or explosive pendants were laid and watched, or swept to entangle submerged marauders. Net barrages were constructed; one of these, closely guarded, stretched from coast to coast across the Straits of Dover. The first beginnings were made with decoy ships, apparently innocent merchantmen with masked batteries and specially trained crews of hardy sailormen.

By the laws and customs of the sea the U boat operations were sheer piracy. Many believed that the campaign had been launched without any hope of maintaining a blockade and for "frightfulness'" sake only. Colour was given to this view when the attempt to blockade had proved futile and yet the submarines waylaid great ships of famous passenger lines. Actually no such wantonness can be proved against the enemy. It was inevitable that war prepared for on the scale of that being waged could not be limited by the traditional safeguards of more limited times. War remains in all times a desperate issue. Moreover the German submarine campaign was part of a considered policy which aimed at provoking intervention in the cause of peace.

SUGGESTIONS FOR READING:

The Grand Fleet by Earl Jellicoe, pp. 140–1, 143–5. *The World Crisis, 1911–14* by W. S. Churchill, vol. 1, p. 462; *1915*, pp. 513–4. *Naval Operations* by Sir Julian Corbett, vol. 1, pp. 382–4.

Chapter V: THE WESTERN FRONT, 1915

(See maps on pp. 29 and 49)

THE Germans spent the winter ingeniously strengthening their new western "frontier" and preparing to deal decisively with the Russians in the spring. It was partly because the attention of the German Supreme Command had been distracted by events in Poland that it had eventually come to acknowledge the defeat of its attempts to reach the Channel ports and Paris. The Russian threat to Austria was serious. It menaced the fruitful plains of Hungary from the southern slopes of the Carpathians, and even German succour had failed before Warsaw to deal with the danger. Large forces were therefore moved from west to east to help guard against it. It was doubtless of a piece with this state of things that, when Christmas came, the German troops fraternised freely with their enemies wherever they could.

Both sides were very short of gun ammunition and used it sparingly in order to accumulate a reserve for future offence. The German reserve was needed for the projected advance against the Russians in Galicia. The British reserve would suffice for a short spring offensive; but meanwhile our batteries were rationed to three rounds per gun and one per howitzer per day.

The hardships of winter bore heavily on the British infantry. Standing in sodden boots and puttees in water-logged trenches caused them to suffer in thousands from a form of frost-bite known as "Trench Foot"; verminous shelters in the forward area brought about a low form of re-lapsing fever called "Trench Fever". To drain the trenches was impossible, as materials for the purpose were lacking; but body-lice were kept down by organising bathing and the disinfection of clothing. This service assumed a great im-portance as the war went on.

With the New Year, fresh divisions began to cross the Channel from England. The 27th, 28th, and 1st Canadian Divisions were followed by six divisions of Territorials—the 46th (North Midland), 47th (London), 48th (South Mid-land), 49th (West Riding), 50th (Northumbrian), and 51st (Highland). Later, in the spring, the Expeditionary Force was augmented by divisions of the New Army—9th, 12th, 14th, 15th, and 16th; though officially "New Army", they were generally spoken of as "Kitchener's Army". These troop-movements transported English youth in thousands through scenes famous in *Hereward the Wake* to ground familiar in *The Three Musketeers*, acquaintance with which was scraped anew with an entrenching tool. English troops found themselves billeted in some "Rue des Anglais" of an obscure village once the site of huts occupied by the troops of Malbrouck. A favourite ground for church parades was a circle of beeches on the edge of the Bois des Dames near Chocques, which had been planted by some of the Army of Occupation in 1815.

This increase in the numbers of the British Expeditionary Force did not add fighting power in proportion. To make an army fit for organised warfare takes years, even could the necessary guns, ammunition, stores, and equipment have been created by some miracle. Nevertheless offensive operations were undertaken which showed what the spirit of the troops and the ingenuity and dash of their leaders were capable of, lacking material means. First, however, the British line was extended northwards to Langemarck. Then the British Expeditionary Force was formed into two Armies, the First under Sir Douglas Haig and the Second under Sir Horace Smith-Dorrien.

NEUVE CHAPELLE AND HILL 60

During the winter the enemy had got a footing in Neuve Chapelle. On the 10th of March his trenches thereabout were first destroyed with a deluge of high explosive and then overrun by British and Indian infantry. The remains of the village and over 2000 prisoners were taken; at this stage the highest hopes were entertained that a great victory would be gained, but they were doomed to disappointment. Attempts to exploit the early success were foiled by the enemy's machine-gun defence at the Bois du Biez. Eventually indeed the enemy profited by this experience of the concentrated use of high explosive. He used the knowledge in his defence against the Allied attacks in the spring and adopted the method in his advance against the Russians in Galicia. More than one invaluable idea, in the course of the war, failed thus of its full effect through its premature use; but the needs of the moment were always pressing. Had this action served no other purpose, it provided an incentive to those at home who were concerned with the supply of munitions.

Hill 60, on which stand Zwartelen and Verbrandenmolen, less than two miles south-east of Ypres, was the scene of a mining operation early in April. Following the blowing of the mine, the British gained the crest and drove the enemy down the south-eastern slope. The advantage continued to be hotly contested for some days. More mines were blown and their craters fought for with great bitterness. Finally this fighting, which left neither side in full possession of Hill 60, merged into that of the first German gas attack.

At this time General Smith-Dorrien handed over the

command of the Second Army to General Sir Herbert Plumer and returned to England.

THE SECOND BATTLE OF YPRES

The time of the opening of the Spring Offensive was approaching, but it was not to arrive without a set-back. Having previously accused the Allies of using poisonous gases in the war, the German Supreme Command ordered cylinders to be installed in the front-line trenches so that gas-clouds could be discharged. The first experiment fell on some French Colonial troops near Langemarck on April 22nd. The resulting panic of Moroccan natives, which left a yawning gap in the line, was hardly expected by the enemy, who had made no other arrangements for the attack. This was fortunate for the Allied defence, but it did not save the British left flank, exposed by the retreat of the Moroccans. The Canadians holding it put up the first of many magnificent fights; the 50th (Northumbrian) Division, only just landed, was led straight into action to prolong the flank; the Cavalry Corps marched north all night, making the villages wonder sleepily at the endless clatter of hoofs on the *pavé*. They arrived to find the whole Salient aflame and the enemy busy with his new and surprisingly effective weapon wherever the wind favoured. Emergency res-pirators were devised from the knitted woollen cap-com-forters carried by the troops, wetted with any soda or ammonia procurable. In these, and in spite of them, men fought until they dropped and died suffocating miserably in their gas-filled trenches. In their sublime simplicity many even cast aside the poor protection of the hastily made respirator in order to fight with more freedom at close quarters. The result was the loss of a two-mile zone north and east of Ypres. The famous Salient was now narrowed to a radius of less than two miles from the city.

Thus yet another improvisation had been added to the war material of the improvident British. The jam-tin bombs they had used since the Aisne were barely superseded by the treacherous, wood-plugged, cast steel cylinders supplied by Ordnance; deft housewifely fingers were still busily stitching at badly needed sandbags by many an English fireside; and now factory girls were set to work day and night to provide an impregnated cotton-waste and gauze substitute for the "cap-comforter" respirator.

THE AUBERS RIDGE AND FESTUBERT

It was doubtless this emergency which postponed for a few days the projected Allied attacks on the Lorette and Aubers Ridges. The Germans actually displayed above their parapets chalked notices asking, "When are you coming, Tommy? We expected you last Sunday". The use of the microphone by the enemy was as yet unsuspected, and the information he garnered from the induced earth-currents set up by British field telephones was ignorantly attributed to espionage. The wireless age had hardly begun; such ignorance now would be pathetic.

Heavy gunfire throughout the night of 8–9th May left no doubt that the Germans' expectations were after all to be realised. The Lorette Ridge flamed and flickered, and spouted red and green signal rockets. The humid atmosphere of the close spring dawn throbbed and whined with field gun preparation. At sunrise the infantry advanced, and there began in Artois a struggle for the Lorette and Vimy Ridges which cost General Foch's Ninth Army some 200,000 casualties in three months. The vitally important Lorette heights passed finally from German hands and, unlike their counterpart in the north, Kemmel Hill, never served the enemy more. The crest of the Vimy Ridge remained for two more years unreclaimed, largely owing to the strength of a German redoubt, known as the Labyrinth, south of Vimy.

The British attack, which began on the Aubers Ridge and was continued at Festubert, was subsidiary and not meant to be pressed. When the 1st Black Watch reached the German front line opposite Festubert, they found it empty of the enemy and filled with water. A similar attack by the 7th Division, supplemented in its later stages by an assault of the Canadian Division on "the Orchard", near Givenchy, gained little permanent advantage. On May 24th an assault by a brigade of the 47th Division was shattered by enfilade artillery fire in the trenches it had captured. The brigade lost two-thirds of its strength in three days' fighting.

The German offensive against the Russians provided a very different spectacle. It opened in May with the crossing of the river Dunajec in Galicia after an unprecedently heavy bombardment by guns and trench-mortars. Pressing on, the Germans broke through the Russian line and caused them to withdraw from the Carpathians and finally to abandon Galicia and Poland.

After the unsuccessful attacks in the spring the British Army settled down to a routine of trench warfare. This lasted through the whole of a summer marked by fine weather, during which the new troops used themselves to the rough domesticity of campaigning. Withal a new Divisional *esprit de corps* arose which overlaid the old regimental tradition without altering it. It was a characteristic outcome of modern methods of fighting, which to be effective need the close co-operation of all arms and services.

One minor action of this summer introduced yet another new weapon, which, curiously enough, was never again used against the British on the same scale. On July 30th the Germans attacked the trenches at Hooge, then held by the 14th Division, with "flame-projectors", instruments which discharged jets of flame some 30 yards in length in the manner of a great blow-pipe. On this occasion all the conditions favoured their use, and the troops holding the sector were wiped out. A hastily conceived counter-attack a few hours later failed with heavy losses. In this literal baptism of fire the 14th Division fought grimly, and 2nd Lieutenant Sidney Woodroffe of the 8th Battalion, The Rifle Brigade, gave his life in earning for the New Army the proud distinction of their first Victoria Cross. Some days later, a carefully planned operation undertaken by the 6th Division recovered most of the lost ground.

THE BATTLE OF LOOS

As the summer drew to a close, preparations began to be made to attack the enemy lines before Lens. Saps were driven forward and joined, to make a new front line closer to the more important German strongholds. Fighting materials, including gas and scaling-ladders, were stowed in the new line. Dumps of all kinds were made and filled, a water-supply arranged, and battle headquarters built. The finishing touches were put to the training for battle by exercising over ground in rear marked out with flags and tapes to show the enemy's trenches and strong-points, as on a map.

It was intended that the attack should be opened by troops seasoned to trench warfare, whose duty would be to overrun the enemy defences. This done, three divisions of troops mostly straight from England, who had never seen an enemy trench, would carry on the advance and break through. A minor operation at Hooge would tie down the enemy's reserves. Cavalry would be at hand to push through and cover the infantry, if open warfare followed. For their use and that of the artillery, bridges were thrown across the forward trenches.

On the 21st of September the artillery opened the main bombardment; for some time previously wire-cutting had been going on. The infantry, engaged in making final reconnaissances of every detail of the enemy's defences, were heartened by the unusual strength and persistence of the shelling. Early in the morning of the 25th of September, poison-gas and smoke were discharged in clouds on the enemy for forty minutes. This was the first time the British had used gas, and it showed itself a treacherous weapon, for the wind changed. At 6.30 a.m. the infantry climbed out of their trenches and vanished into the smoke in the valley—one battalion, the London Irish Rifles, kicked a football in front of its line as it went.

The 47th Division was the right of the attack. Wheeling southwards it reached all its objectives and held them against counter-attacks. The 15th (Scottish) Division lost heavily in reaching Loos, but fought its way through the village, north of the famous pylons of the "Tower Bridge", a pit-head winding-gear which had withstood all the efforts of our 60-pounders. Further north the 1st Division captured Hulluch and entered Benifontaine. Meanwhile the 9th Division reached Cité St Elie and the 7th wheeled left against Fosse 8 and the Hohenzollern Redoubt.

A sad spectacle followed. With many a backward look a little straggling crowd of old men, women, and children toiled up the "Harrow Road" from Loos, the last remnant of its inhabitants. They had clung despairingly to their homes even when the enemy in defeat turned his guns on them. Last of them to leave was a young girl, who was later thanked and rewarded by the British Government for tending our wounded in Loos; her heroism gained her the Croix de Guerre also from her own people.

On the following day the enemy counter-attacks about Hulluch and Fosse 8 threw back the British line. South of this, gallant attempts to advance eastwards were shattered by machine-gun fire from the Bois Hugo and the reverse slopes of Hill 70. Little groups of heroic men filtered through, it is true, and some reached the western suburbs of Lens, where, cut off from all support, they perished. The remnants of the 15th Division were relieved that afternoon by the 3rd Cavalry Division, which had previously moved into Loos.

During the day the 21st and 24th Divisions arrived by forced marches from the coast, straight from England. Hungry and weary, they were thrown against Hill 70 and Fosse 8 respectively, suffering heavy casualties bootlessly.

A last great effort was made on the next day, September 27th, when the infantry of the newly formed Guards Division came on the field. Those who saw it will never forget the advance of the 3rd Guards Brigade to the attack of Hill 70. It moved in artillery formation across the open into the Loos valley, swept by heavy shrapnel bursts, and the perfect order maintained restored confidence in the many onlookers shaken by the confusion of the previous day. On the left of the 3rd, the 2nd Guards Brigade crossed the Lens–La Bassée road, but were unable to clear the Bois Hugo. This and Hill 70 remained insurmountable obstacles. Heavy fighting continued for many days, but the tactical battle was over by the 28th.

On October 8th a German counter-attack developed, but

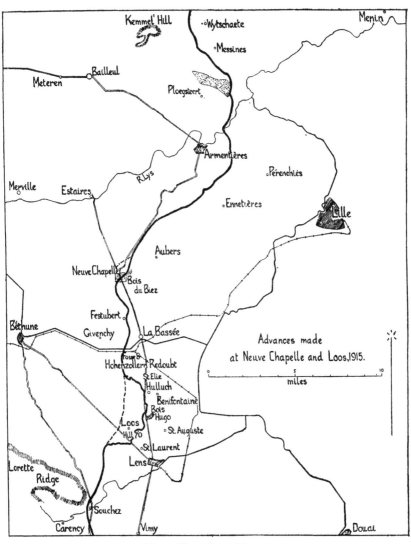

Advances made at Neuve Chapelle and Loos, 1915.

miles

Neuve Chapelle and Loos

it failed with great losses; in repulsing it one Corps alone used 9000 grenades in two and a half hours, evidence sufficient to show that guns and ammunition for them were lacking. Two years later a deluge of metal from hundreds of guns would have smothered any such movement of the enemy, just as the guns covering the subsidiary attack at Hooge, which met with scant success, would have had more than a meagre 500 rounds per battery.

On October the 13th the 1st Division attacked towards Hulluch, whilst the 46th assaulted the Hohenzollern Redoubt. Both had to abandon their gains and lost men in thousands.

Sixty thousand killed, wounded, and missing at the battle of Loos would not have been too heavy a price to pay for the "Great British Victory" vaunted by the posters in the streets of London. Actually it gained a little ground which, out of doggedness, had to be held at further cost. It may have helped the French to the possession of long-contested Souchez, just to the south. It may even have lightened the opposition to their great attack in Champagne. But the enemy remained unhampered on his eastern front, and even constrained the Allies to withdraw troops from France to oppose him in the Balkans.

SUGGESTIONS FOR READING:

The Irish Guards in the Great War by Rudyard Kipling, vol. 1, pp. 61–6. *The 47th (London) Division* by A. H. Maude, pp. 13–15. *Peter Jackson, Cigar Merchant* by Gilbert Frankau, pp. 158–203.

Chapter VI: THE SPREAD OF THE WAR

IT has been said that on August 4th, 1914, England was unprepared for war. The ease with which she preserved her land inviolate and kept the seas, "lest street-bred people die", shows exactly the extent of her preparedness. Yet it is true that she was unready to wage aggressive war, at a moment when only this could save not merely her own people, but Europe, from barbarism. Those who blame England err diversely. Some do so through pride in her power, others through over-confidence in her love of fairplay; both forget that in 1864 Denmark became Prussia's first victim only because England failed her. The Prussian appetite for subjugating her neighbours, thus aroused, grew with indulgence. Palmerston's betrayal of Denmark and Beaconsfield's infectious fear of Russia so whetted it that, within the space of six years, Austria and France were successively mangled by it. England, become conscious of her former error, had gone seriously to work to remedy it. King Edward VII himself set about forming a union of European hearts pure of aggressive intention. Lord Haldane tried repeatedly to get Germany to respect her neighbours' good faith. Sir Edward Grey steadily pursued a policy of conciliation, which he hoped would grow upon Europe, aided by the example of our dealings with the United States of America. Firmly and tactfully these statesmen strove with the dreadful political disease from which the Teutonic peoples were suffering; but to prepare to use force whilst professing peaceful aims was not to their mind. A proposal made by German notables to Lord Haldane in 1912, that England should stand aside whilst Russia and France were attacked, was even kept secret, lest it disturb the peaceful attitude of the English people. Yet German duplicity could appoint as ambassador to St James's the Prince Lichnowsky, a friend and admirer of England, whose tenure was honestly devoted to strenuous work for peace. Behind his back the finishing touches were being put to the other face of the German war-god.

Could England, warned by Lord Roberts, have raised and equipped an army on the continental scale, she might have subdued German aggressiveness without a shot fired. But it has abundantly been proved that this was not within the sphere of practical politics. As it was, her army was regarded by Germany as contemptibly little, and even Mr Walter Page, the American Ambassador in London, writes with critical sympathy: "England has just one big land gun—no more" (this was probably the 9·2-inch howitzer our men were to call "Mother"). At the same time he remarks in our people qualities, equally characteristic of the citizens of the United States, which he believes are directly to blame for the war, qualities perhaps as much the cause as the outcome of their industry, devotion to sport, and peculiar bent for domestic political wrangling.

So Colonel House, President Wilson's confidential friend, found England, in June 1914, utterly unable to grasp the realities of the international situation. He had made the journey to Berlin, Paris, and London at the instance of the President, who saw the trend of European politics and anticipated disaster. Having interviewed the Kaiser on June 1st, he retained a vivid memory of the words addressed to him at parting: "Every nation in Europe has its bayonets pointed at Germany. But we are ready!" He found Paris exercised to the limits of its emotional capacity by domestic intrigues. Official London seemed almost as confused by the Women's Suffrage disturbances and the imminence of civil war over the old Irish quarrel. For the moment Germany was forgotten. So when war came, the British conscience, like the French and Russian, could clear itself of the guilt of actively provoking it; but it was to be wrung during two mortal years by the consequences of military unreadiness. The youth of the land had to be sacrificed, its treasures poured out, its energies wasted in experiments, its imperial prestige mortgaged, and even its standing with neutral nations endangered; and all in championing the cause of freedom.

The appointment of Lord Kitchener to be Secretary of State for War was popularly approved. His name was a talisman of Cadmean power; recruiting offices were besieged at his summons to "join the Army to-day". His wisdom in predicting that the war would last five years did not convince everyone, but it furnished moral strength even after he was dead. On him and on Mr Winston Churchill the Cabinet, dismally failing to grasp the situation, gladly devolved the task of making war and preparing to make it on an ever increasing scale. As the burden of this "snow-balled" and politicians completed their apprenticeship to the new work, they gradually came to share it or help in the distributing of it. Thus Mr Lloyd George, who had greatly distinguished himself by his financial ability on the outbreak of war, succeeded, with the support of an able staff, in reorganising British industries for the making of munitions. Under his impulse the country became ultimately one vast arsenal and war-store.

Sir Edward Grey at the Foreign Office turned from his sorrow at the waste of his life's work for peace and took up the fatigue of endless dealings with neutral nations over cargoes shipped by them to Germany. It was not worth while actually to declare a blockade of the 200 miles of German coast. Ports in Holland, Denmark, and Sweden always shared largely in Germany's trade and, after the outbreak of war, could cope with it all. It would have been an act of war against Holland and Denmark to blockade Rotterdam and Copenhagen, so the Allied navies systematically stopped on the high seas ships suspected of carrying contraband of war, and took them into port to search them. If munitions of war (contraband), food or materials for the manufacture of munitions (conditional contraband) were found, they were seized and bought by the British Government, after which the ship was allowed to proceed. Under a declared blockade not only the cargo, but the ship too, is seized and becomes prize of war.

The plan adopted followed the precedent set up by President Lincoln during the American Civil War. The British Government, however, extended its scheme of "measures short of blockade" to include conditional contraband, the chief of which was, of course, foodstuffs. The result was that the Foreign Office was inundated with complaints from neutrals and became engaged in continuous controversy with the American Secretary of State. The controversy put a strain on British-American official relations, and the fact that the breaking-point was never reached was due mainly to Mr Walter Page's loyal friendship for Great Britain. Sir Edward Grey's dealings with the American Ambassador were always guided by their joint conviction that the friendship of the United States would determine the issue of the

war. Both believed, moreover, that any cause of estrange-
ment would be the blackest crime in history, for it would
mean the collapse of British-American co-operation and the
destruction of ideals.

On September 5th, 1914, Great Britain, France, and
Russia signed the Pact of London, binding themselves to
make war and peace as one. Having thus secured their own
political front, they proceeded by diplomacy to prevent the
enemy reaching out to conquests which he was known to
have coveted previously and, in his present extremity, to
need desperately.

In the Balkan Peninsula a number of unprogressive peoples
had been emerging gradually from Ottoman domination
and, having freed themselves in 1912, proceeded to dispute
the spoils in 1913. Turkey and Bulgaria had suffered; Serbia,
Greece, and Montenegro had profited politically; Roumania
had added to what she believed to be her prestige. Mutual
hatreds flourished, and German agents fished assiduously in
the troubled waters. Greece was, not unwontedly, divided
against herself, but through her Premier, Venizelos, she
offered, on the outbreak of war, to occupy the Gallipoli
Peninsula and keep open the Dardanelles. For two reasons
the Foreign Office refused this offer. To provoke war with
Turkey would be a poor return to Russia for the heroism
with which she had saved the Allies during September and
October 1914; and it might imperil the passage of the Indian
troops through the Suez Canal or disaffect the Mahometans
among them. Therefore, on the one hand, great indulgence
was shown to Turkish breaches of neutrality (particularly in
harbouring the *Goeben* and *Breslau*) and everything was done
diplomatically to pacify her and detach her from her German
allegiance. On the other hand, Russia pressed Greece to
give way to Turkish demands concerning the Aegean Islands,
lest Turkey and Bulgaria should combine against her. But
in October the Turkish Fleet in the Black Sea, acting with
the *Goeben* and *Breslau* under Admiral Souchon, made an
unheralded attack on Allied shipping and Russian ports.
War with Turkey followed inevitably.

Even then England could not accept the Greek offer to

land on the Gallipoli Peninsula, for Russia could not tolerate the slightest prospect of King Constantine of Greece making a triumphal entry into Constantinople, and Russia's last hope of a maritime outlet free of ice the year round would be destroyed. These complications had led to the conclusion of a secret treaty according Russia the ultimate possession of Constantinople, and so to the impulse to deal a mortal blow at Turkey through the Dardanelles. Naval attacks on the Straits in November 1914 and February and March 1915 merely served to put the enemy on his guard, and ultimately the Army was drawn in to undertake a major operation against Gallipoli. Its failure by the narrowest of margins, at an agonising cost, will be described in detail.

But the most trying of all the tasks set the Foreign Office was that of preventing Bulgaria from drifting into alliance with the Central Powers. No one expected she could remain neutral; her grievances against Serbia, Greece, and Roumania arising out of the Second Balkan War were too deep. To satisfy them proved more than the "Entente" Ministers could do, though they laboured without stint. Both Serbia and Greece halted exasperatingly on the idea of making timely restitution of territory to their former ally, though by the defeat of the Austrians and their backers, the Germans, they both stood to gain territory northwards and westwards far exceeding that demanded by Bulgaria in the south-east. Rather than resign a part, they would lose all—and did lose all. What was worse, they brought even the Entente into jeopardy when the day of reckoning came upon them. In the autumn of 1915 Bulgaria saw that her moment had come, and joined the Central Powers.

By then the Russian line had been forced back hundreds of miles; the Serbian people was being driven mercilessly from its homes; Greek unity—a not uncouth dream—dissolved in tumult. Germany, Austria, Bulgaria, and Turkey presented a victorious front from the Baltic nearly to the Persian Gulf. Behind it lurked, for a while, Roumania, waiting and watching, but only to discover disaster. The German vision of overlordship in two continents seemed realised.

One encouragement, only one, gladdened Allied statesmen during this time. Italy, peculiarly exposed to the sea and desiring to improve her land frontier with Austria, allied herself for this purpose with the Entente Powers and made war upon her former ally on the 24th of May, 1915. Our Mediterranean sea-route was thus improved and the French could cease their watch on the Franco-Italian border.

The navies of Germany and Austria dared not dispute the command of the seas, now in Allied keeping. But von Tirpitz, admiral-politician, conceived a clever project. Submarines could evade the surface patrols and prey unseen upon shipping; it was much simpler than the ordinary way of making prizes. Soon ships were torpedoed without warning, even neutral vessels unmistakeably ensigned. The scourge was made only the more vicious by the arming of merchantmen against it, and it irritated neutrals against the whole blockade system, to the advantage of the Central Powers. Thus it was soon apparent that a policy of submarine outrage was, indirectly, Germany's best peace-lever, apart from its military value.

On May 7th, 1915, whilst Colonel House was visiting London on a peace errand, news was received there of "the greatest infamy since St Bartholomew". The liner *Lusitania* had been sunk by a submarine off the Old Head of Kinsale, with the loss of more than a thousand lives, of whom 124 were American men, women, and children. At dinner that evening Colonel House declared "We shall be at war with Germany within a month". It was expected that President Wilson would hold Germany to that "strict accountability" which, he had previously warned all nations, he would exact for American lives lost by illegal submarine attack. Germany, however, was able to hold this off for the time and pursued her submarine campaign, unaffected by the President's "Notes". The exchange of these seemed indeed to turn the President's displeasure upon the British blockade of Germany, which was being pressed the more in reprisal for submarine outrages.

Meanwhile, when once the seas had been cleared of the German squadrons and commerce-raiders, no time was lost in assembling the military strength of the Empire towards the main conflict in the European theatre of war. First the German Imperial flag was hauled down in distant parts of the earth. The islands of the Pacific, China, South-West Africa, and Camerun knew it no more, though it was kept flying perilously for a time by the devotion and resource of a guerilla remnant in East Africa. These exploits were the work of troops from the nearest Dominions, and from India and Japan. In South-West Africa they were led by General Louis Botha and in East Africa by General Smuts, both of whom had first won renown in war against England.

England herself was trying heroically to rise to the greatness of the task set her. She began the practice of a rigid economy. This appears in the cutting, at the Christmas performances in 1915, of the most beautiful of the scenes in Barrie's "Peter Pan." Money might not be spent on the luxurious staging of the lagoon; and tenderness for the many who suffered could not abide the expense of feeling at Peter's words: "To die is such a very big adventure". Her wealth in manhood and material had to be gathered in and the means of doing this had to be devised on a great scale, which caused her to purchase largely in the United States. Hut camps, hangars, hospitals, mills, forges, furnaces, factories, slip-ways were improvised, extended, or built. All got to work, confusedly at first, but later in orderly productiveness. Strikes were at times a great hindrance, for there was much unrest in trades depleted by recruiting and made up again ("diluted") with unskilled men, among whom were some who sought to avoid the call to arms. Wages soared. Lord Derby's attestation scheme gave a last impetus to voluntary enlistment. Married men responded in great part, whilst single men in good work hung back; this did much to point the need for compulsory military service, in fairness to all.

Such was the preparation which England had to undergo before she could really fight again for the peace she had determined on. It was a phase which lasted unchanged until July 1st, 1916.

SUGGESTIONS FOR READING:

Twenty-five Years by Viscount Grey of Fallodon, vol. I, pp. 50–2; vol. II, pp. 55–7. *The Memoirs of W. H. Page*, vol. II, pp. 1–6, 56, 92.

Chapter VII: GALLIPOLI

(*See map on p.* 71)

"Soldiers of France and of the King. Before us lies an adventure unprecedented in modern war. Together with our comrades of the Fleet, we are about to force a landing upon an open beach in the face of positions which have been vaunted by our enemies as impregnable."

So ran the preamble to Sir Ian Hamilton's characteristic message to the Mediterranean Expeditionary Force at the setting out for the Gallipoli Peninsula. How the adventurers lived, laboured, and died in the spirit evoked by these words has been set out by John Masefield in his "Gallipoli." The immediate response was an outburst of cheering which deeply moved all who heard it. Ship after ship leaving Mudros harbour for Tenedos, on St George's Day, 1915, took up the wonderful sound. The warships answered—British, French, and Russian—and even the busy shore details joined in.

In the dawn of the day after next, boat-loads of these men uttered hardly a murmur, though many of them were agonising and dying in their places. Close ahead lay the shores of the peninsula, the shallows and beaches mined and wired. Around the boats the sea was thrashed with machine-gun, rifle, and shrapnel bullets. This desperate attempt to land was the outcome of what may be described as naval coquetry with the forts of the Dardanelles. In November 1914 these forts had been somewhat aimlessly bombarded; in February 1915 an operation had been begun to force a way to Constantinople with the Fleet. This had ended in drawing in the Army, not just to back the naval operations, but to point them in an endeavour to deal a mortal blow at Turkey through the Straits. That the many warnings of possible trouble had not been lost upon the Turks and their German instructors was evidenced by the opposition to the boat-loads of invaders struggling to land.

THE LANDINGS

Men of the Australian and New Zealand Army Corps landed before daylight just north of Gaba Tepe. By 5.35 a.m. four thousand had got ashore, scattered a Turkish battalion with the bayonet, and were scaling the cliffs towards Sari Bair as only perfect athletes can. As they climbed in groups and singly about the puzzling spurs and gulleys through waist-deep undergrowth, they fought whatever Turks appeared to oppose them and stalked the many who lay low and sniped. Nothing stopped them. Could the landing of supports, stores, and guns have kept pace with their vehemence, the day had been won in its very dawn.

At 5 a.m. the *River Clyde*, a collier, with the 1st Munsters, half the 2nd Hampshires, part of the 1st Dublin Fusiliers, and a West Riding Territorial Field Company on board, stranded at Sedd el Bahr ("V" Beach). Great sally-ports had been cut in the collier's sides, from which platforms projected; barges swept into position under her bows connected these to the shore as long as the lashings held against the storm of bullets. When they parted, sailors dropped into the water, ropes in their teeth, and secured them again.

Three companies of the Dublin Fusiliers in thirty boats passed ahead of the *River Clyde* when she grounded. The boats were shot to pieces on the beach; a few survivors lay the whole day under cover of the slope of a sand-bank, unable to stir; by midday the blood of the remainder and of those who tried to land from the collier had stained the waters of the bay. The Turkish trenches in the little amphitheatre above seemed proof against salvoes from the 6-inch guns of the *Queen Elizabeth*, the Navy's greatest battleship.

The fire from these trenches never ceased until dusk. Then the troops landed from the *River Clyde* almost scatheless. When in the moonlight the Turks sallied on to the beach, they were met with the bayonet and pressed back through the ruins of Sedd el Bahr. But it was not until the morning that they were finally driven from the place, after the guns of the Fleet had concentrated a terrific fire on the slopes above the bay.

Two thousand yards away, as far west of Cape Helles as the *River Clyde* lay east of it, the 1st Lancashire Fusiliers landed from ship's boats in a little bay ("W" Beach) near Tekke Burnu. Losing men by the score in the boats and on the beach, they struggled through the entanglements into shelter at the foot of the cliffs. Taking breath whilst the warships' guns pounded the slopes at close range, they then stormed the heights and took the Turkish trenches. Landing in support, the 4th Worcesters tried to pass eastwards to Sedd el Bahr. But the enemy's flanking belts of wire were too cunningly sited. The cool steadfastness of the Fusiliers and Worcesters, unceasingly cutting their way through by hand, will remain an undying glory.

Less than a thousand yards north of Tekke Burnu the 2nd Royal Fusiliers and the "Anson" Battalion of the Royal Naval Division landed under cover of the guns of H.M.S. *Implacable*. They took the enemy's defences and, moving inland, met a counter-attack in force, which they stopped dead. After this they prolonged their line southwards to link up with the Lancashire Fusiliers.

Two other landings were made. The 2nd South Wales Borderers got ashore within the Straits on the eastern reach of Morto Bay ("S" Beach) below De Tott's Battery; the 1st King's Own Scottish Borderers and the "Plymouth" Battalion, Royal Naval Division, scaled the sheer cliffs above the Aegean ("Y" Beach) which lie nearest the village of Krithia. Both these landings had been designed as feints, but both were so surprisingly successful that the Commander-in-Chief was tempted to alter his dispositions in order to improve the unexpected advantages resulting from them. His general reserve, the bulk of the Royal Naval Division, was under his hand; it had cruised in its transports towards Bulair during the night. However, he forebore to change his plan lest the minutely detailed disembarkation scheme be disorganised.

The cruise of the Naval Division towards Bulair was the occasion of a feat quite classical in its quality. Its distinction is the greater that it is in great part high comedy. Blind Homer would have laughed and made his Olympians do so

immoderately whilst he told how one naked man made a
noise like an army, the report of which filled the Constantinople newspapers next day. Lieut. Freyberg, R.N.D., swam
ashore from the transports, towing a little raft loaded with
flares. Some he burned as he swam, the rest he lit up and
down the country near Bulair. The large Turkish force there
got the impression that they were beating off a great attack,
and were thus kept from reinforcing the divisions at Helles.
On the return swim Freyberg missed his destroyer-tender in
the dark. He swam many miles, and when picked up at last
was nearly dead from exhaustion and exposure.

A more serious diversion than that by the Royal Naval
Division transports was made by the Corps Expéditionnaire
de l'Orient at Kum Kale, on the Asiatic shore of the Straits.
A French brigade landed and took the village at the point
of the bayonet, making 400 prisoners. This action diverted
the fire of the Turkish howitzers from the beaches of the
peninsula, besides keeping away reinforcements.

On the morning of the 26th of April Sir Ian Hamilton
cabled to Lord Kitchener that 29,000 men had been landed
upon six beaches. The cost of the operation was not unduly
high, seeing that it could be supported only by naval
artillery, the use of which differs radically from that of
artillery on land. The *Queen Elizabeth's* 6-inch battery had
had but little effect on the Turkish trenches at Sedd el Bahr;
yet on the following day, her balloon up, with her first shot
she put to flight the German battle-cruiser *Goeben* at the
Narrows and then sank a crowded transport with two more
rounds. The Dublin Fusiliers and the Lancashire Fusiliers
lost three-fifths of their strength, the Royal Fusiliers one half.
One Australian battalion lost 422 out of 900. Battalions
attacking in France about this time lost three-quarters of
their numbers without gaining anything so important as a
landing on enemy territory.

Nevertheless the landing would remain a "Balaklava"
epic unless the troops put ashore could go speedily on to the
capture of Krithia with its precious wells, and drive the
Turks from Achi Baba or Sari Bair. These were the first
steps to positions commanding the Narrows, whence the

Turkish communications with Asia could be interrupted and the Fleet's passage to the Sea of Marmora assisted.

THE ADVANCE FROM THE BEACHES

By noon on the 26th the first counter-attacks had been met and foiled. Save opposite Krithia, where the troops had re-embarked, and at Anzac, where the fighting was terrific, no ground had been yielded. During this day the French division, withdrawn after its success at Kum Kale, landed at Sedd el Bahr. The Royal Naval Division was put ashore at Anzac, where the Turkish attacks were most desperate.

The disembarkation of guns and stores never ceased, though the difficulties were very great. From the ship's side forward to the fighting line everything had to be man-handled. No draught animal and no derrick was available. The huge working-parties needed left only one-third of the 29th Division for fighting. So the advance northwards from Helles began only on the 27th, when the French on the right advanced two miles and the 29th Division nearly three. The resistance was spasmodic but desperate. The Turks began to evacuate Krithia, but, being reinforced from Asia, reoccupied it and turned upon the Allies. Exhausted by their great labours, the Allies gave ground.

The enemy's main blow came two days later. All his un-certainty concerning Sir Ian Hamilton's intentions was then over, so for four days and nights he strove in desperate fashion to drive the invaders back to the beaches.

The onslaught began on the night of the 1st of May. The fighting was as fierce as ever Saracen and Christian have waged in all the centuries of their conflict. At 10.30 p.m., after half-an-hour's bombardment, the Turks crept forward silently and then charged the Allies' trenches in close order. They got through to the support line and there followed such fighting in the darkness as no words can describe. The waning moon was unrisen; only the glare of shell-bursts, rifle flashes, and flares lit by the Turkish officers showed the dreadful work. At the first onset 9000 Turks were held, then routed; 12,000 more followed these. They died in thousands, with their battle-cry of "Allah Hu" and the name of Enver

Pasha on their lips. When the dawn broke, the remnant fled over the slopes of Achi Baba. But our wearied troops could not pursue. Sir Ian Hamilton records: "Our advance at dawn was half heroic, half lamentable. The men were so beat that if they tripped and fell they lay like dead things". Nightly the Turkish attacks were repeated until the 5th of May. By day hardly a sound of war could be heard; the dead were gathered and the wounded brought back through a paradise of rare spring flowers. Below lay the incredibly blue Aegean, above spread an azure sky. So prodigal of contrast is Nature.

On the 6th the Allies attempted the capture of Achi Baba. Delay might have increased their strength and added to their small stock of ammunition; but this would not match the enemy's increase of strength, by mere digging, in the interval. Attacking with the French went a brigade of the Naval Division, and on the left of the 29th Division was the Fusilier Brigade of the 42nd (East Lancashire Territorial) Division, newly landed. The advance made nowhere exceeded three hundred yards. On the left, along the Saghir water-course, the Territorial brigade could make no progress at all.

CONSOLIDATION AND NAVAL EXPLOITS

Operations were continued on the 7th and 8th, for though all hope of a victorious advance was gone, the dangers of the defence were a source of great anxiety. The fighting line was much too close to the beaches, and it was menaced by the Bluff Redoubt, on the Saghir water-course west of Krithia, and the Haricot Redoubt, south of the village. Krithia too, was not only an obstacle to the British but a "sally-port" for the Turk. Despite every effort, none of these key positions was taken. Five days later, however, the Bluff Redoubt fell to an attack by the Indian Brigade. Meanwhile the heights above Anzac Cove had been firmly held against the fury of the Turks.

On May 9th, Vice-Admiral de Robeck, whose Chief of Staff was the spirited Commodore Sir Roger Keyes, offered the Admiralty to attempt the passage of the Straits with his ships. It was hoped that mutually supporting major operations by sea and land might prove decisive. The offer was not approved. Still the Navy found itself able to do more than just fetch and carry and give artillery support. This careful nursing of the Gallipoli army was an evident source of cheer to the troops; but the nurse had yet a free arm with which to fend for her charge in other ways. In December 1914 Lieut.-Commander Norman Holbrook had passed the mine-fields with Submarine *B 11* and sunk the Turkish cruiser *Messudieh* in the Sea of Marmora. The British submarines gallantly followed this lead, with the result that the enemy's sea communications had to be abandoned. *E 11* (Commander Nasmith) and *E 14* (Lieut.-Commander Boyle) braved unheard-of dangers in passing to and fro. They sank scores of enemy vessels and destroyed thousands of Turkish troops, bombarded roads and railways along the shore, and even torpedoed a vessel in the harbour of Constantinople itself.

It was quite clear now that the Mediterranean Expeditionary Force could not do more than maintain its hold on Helles and Anzac, and the difficulty of doing this was increasing. On May 9th Admiral de Robeck was warned to expect enemy submarines. The first was sighted from Gaba Tepe on the 22nd, and shortly afterwards the battleship *Triumph* was torpedoed and sunk. The cheerful activity of the Fleet about the Peninsula then ceased. The sea communications from Lemnos and Tenedos had to be reorganised. Submarine-indicator nets gradually came into use. Artillery support was given by Monitors and various other craft provided with "bulges" below water.

To carry out the original programme, once the first onset had been stemmed, required " 50,000 more men, and shells, *shells*, SHELLS!" Unhappily shells were at their shortest, even in France. The Turks on the other hand were fairly well supplied and were never short of small-arm ammunition and hand-grenades.

The British force had already been strengthened by the addition of the 42nd Division and an Indian Infantry Brigade from Egypt, and Lord Kitchener now ordered out the 52nd (Lowland Territorial) Division. But formations already engaged were starved of reinforcements. The loss of

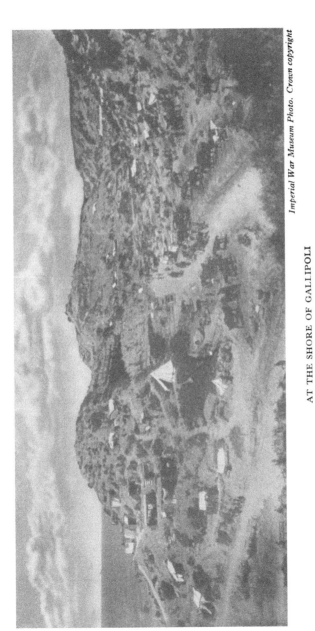

AT THE SHORE OF GALLIPOLI

Imperial War Museum Photo. Crown copyright

power so caused was fatal, so incalculably virile is the fighting kindred that forms between men already battle-worn and ardent new drafts. The tale of Gallipoli might have been vastly different had the 29th Division been provided with even the regular ten-per-cent reinforcement. Fortunately the Dominion troops at Anzac escaped this worst of starvations, but not without a struggle. Had they not escaped it, their precarious position could not have been maintained and the Turks could have turned their full strength against Helles.

The struggle to make the position at Helles merely tenable lasted until the end of June. In this period the British line was pushed forward the thousand yards needed to put the beaches beyond extreme field-gun range. The French had taken and lost the "Haricot" time after time from May 22nd. Could they have held it on the 4th of June, the Manchester Brigade (42nd Division) might have held Achi Baba; they had pierced the enemy's infantry defences and lay within reach of his naked gun positions on the slopes of the hill. At last, on June 22nd, the French, now comprising two divisions under General Gouraud ("the Lion of the Argonne"), attacked and took the "Haricot". On the 30th they improved this success by taking another strong redoubt. Abreast of this, on the left of the line, the Border Regiment with splendid dash took the "Boomerang", a redoubt on the Saghir water-course. Krithia, several times entered, could never be held.

Meanwhile heavy Turkish attacks by troops newly arrived from Adrianople and Syria were repulsed on the 8th and 19th of June. On the latter date the 5th Royal Scots, the only Territorial infantry in the 29th Division, greatly distinguished itself. The 52nd Division, to which this battalion originally belonged, arrived shortly afterwards, and was in time to take part in the last of the actions undertaken to improve the defensive security. All the formations now on the peninsula were supported by about one-third of their proportion of artillery. Moreover they had no heavy weapons to counter "Asiatic Annie", as the troops named any heavy gun shelling them from beyond the Straits.

SUVLA

The idea of a Russian Army Corps landing on the Bosphorus had now been abandoned owing to the German advance in Poland and Galicia. However, to General Hamilton's satisfaction, he was informed on the 8th of June that he would be sent three divisions of the New Army. Here were the 50,000 men he had prayed for. Whereupon he made plans to attack the enemy at the narrowest part of the peninsula. It was intended first to carry Sari Bair. Thence the Turkish communications down the peninsula, and from Chanak on the Asiatic side of the Narrows, could be commanded. Only two anxieties clouded the hopeful spirit of the Commander-in-Chief: would there be a sufficiency of artillery ammunition? would the higher leading of the new troops fit the novel conditions?

The arrangements for the new effort were extremely intricate. The military and naval staffs worked out the landings of the new troops and timed the strokes at Helles, Anzac, and Suvla Bay with minute care. New contrivances were available which would save labour in keeping up supplies of food, water, and ammunition at Suvla. Drinking-water brought from Egypt was to be stored ashore.

The labours of the troops already engaged in a trying defence were added to; but far from feeling overtasked, they showed a toughening of fibre and a raising of spirit. Secrecy was of the first importance. Every preparatory move had to be made in the dark hours, during the moonless nights of the first week in August. The most critical of these was the landing of the 13th Division, 29th Infantry Brigade (10th Division), and 29th Indian Infantry Brigade, 25,000 men in all, at Anzac on the nights of the 3rd, 4th, and 5th of August. To land fifteen hundred men per hour and conceal them underground with their supplies, including the eighty tons of water required daily and a number of animals, is a heavy task under any conditions. That it was carried out before daylight could reveal anything unusual to enemy airmen, within the narrow confines of Anzac, seems incredible. But it was done, and the enemy was no whit the wiser.

The action began just before 4 p.m. on the 6th of August, when the 29th Division attacked at Helles. The Turkish trenches were found fully manned for an attack on the British. During the next few days the struggle centred on the possession of a vineyard near Krithia. For days the Turks could not regain it, and when at last they stormed it at night, they were straightway bombed out of it. So the Turks used up thousands of men urgently needed elsewhere.

Just after the beginning of the action at Helles, about 5 p.m. on the 6th, the 1st Australian Brigade stormed Lone Pine, a little plateau overlooking Gaba Tepe, as if to force their way towards Maidos and the Narrows. The Turkish redoubt on this position was a tunnel trench with head-cover of heavy timber and earth. The attackers lost heavily from artillery and machine-gun fire in crossing the plateau. Some intrepid men dashed over the roof of the trench and entered by the open communications, but only when the third line of the attack, carrying picks and shovels, arrived was it possible to break in. Then followed a fight with bayonet, knife, and bomb in the half light of the tunnel such as has no equal in military history. It was waged across barricades for five days and nights with indescribable ferocity. At the end of it about one quarter of the men who had dashed to the attack lay dead in the trench.

By these two attacks the enemy's attention was turned from the decisive theatre. Operations in this theatre began about 10 p.m. on the 6th. In the words of the Commander-in-Chief's order, they aimed at "securing Suvla Bay as a base of operations, driving the enemy off the Sari Bair, and eventually securing a position astride the Gallipoli Peninsula from the neighbourhood of Gaba Tepe to the straits north of Maidos".

The approaches to the Sari Bair lay up the three water-courses, Sazli Beit, Chailak, and Aghyl. The four Turkish positions covering them were brilliantly captured by New Zealand infantry, whilst Welsh troops of the 13th Division, moving out to their left, established themselves on the spurs to the north of the Aghyl. Regarded only as a feat of mountaineering, in daylight, the progress of these troops would be remarkable. As a military operation in an unknown and ruggedly desolate country against a stubborn enemy entrenched and hidden in waist-high bush, it becomes a proud achievement.

The main attack in three columns followed. New Zealanders cleared the Sazli Beit ravine and English troops the Chailak. Meanwhile Australian and Indian troops fought their way up the Aghyl to Hill "Q". They paid a heavy price in lives and in physical endurance, but they never faltered.

For the final assault on Sari Bair yet a further force was landed just south of Suvla Bay. It was intended to prolong the left of the Australian line before Hill "Q" and Koja Chemen Tepe, and its impulse was to carry the whole to victory by enveloping the right flank of the Turks. Thirty thousand troops of the 10th and 11th Divisions embarked at Imbros, Lemnos, and Mitylene in destroyers and "beetles" (special armoured motor-lighters). They were landed mostly on the spit ("C" Beach) south of Suvla Bay between midnight and 10 a.m. on August 7th. One brigade was put ashore within the bay and later four battalions at a small cove on the northern shore ("A" Beach).

In the dark sharp fighting took place at the beaches, where some two thousand Turks opposed the landing; and when daylight came, the Suvla troops had driven these from Lala Baba and from Hill 10 on the shores of the bay. Unfortunately the resulting confusion caused delay and seriously hindered the continuation of the disembarkation. The brigades at Suvla should have moved early against the Anafarta position on outliers and foot-hills of the Sari Bair. Could they dislodge the enfilading artillery and settle with the enemy infantry, the way would be open to the assault of the summits from the north-west. Under threat of this advance the enemy's guns were actually withdrawn. But owing to the confusion at the beaches the troops suffered acutely from thirst and heat-exhaustion. Had they but gained the precious wells in the Anafarta villages, their privation was at an end, their fighting fitness refreshed, and the labours of their communications vastly eased. The salient truth of the Suvla failure lay at the bottom of those wells, repeating the early set-back at Krithia. So at nightfall only the Chocolate Hills were known to have been taken. Actually the important Scimitar Hill was held too.

Notwithstanding, the troops from Anzac had assaulted the summits of Sari Bair at noon, after fourteen hours of fighting and climbing. Though the assault was beaten back, no ground was lost, and it was manifest that the Turks, though reinforced, were hard pressed. Therefore New Zealand infantry made a second attempt on Chunuk Bair. This also was defeated; whereupon these troops dug in just below the crest, ready for a further effort. It was expected that this would be made when the troops from Suvla won through on the lower ground—which they never did. Mazed in the thick bush, much of which was on fire, gasping with thirst, and their brigade command disorganised, they ceased to have any value in the scheme of operations. They even failed to make safe their shore bases and became a source of anxiety to G.H.Q. Their evil fate resembles very much in its miseries that of the 21st and 24th Divisions of New Army troops at Loos six weeks later. It is in strong contrast with the glories which their companion division, the 13th, and the detached 29th Brigade of the 10th Division shared with the Anzac Corps and the 29th Indian Brigade on Sari Bair.

Night fell on the heights without any sign of aid coming from Suvla. So arrangements were made for the brigades from Anzac to storm the crests of the Sari Bair at dawn on August 8th. The New Zealanders and the 9th Gloucesters then took and held Chunuk Bair. At Hill "Q", English and Indian troops were held, as also were the Australians trying to reach Koja Chemen. Their failure was so narrow that it may be best described as almost victory. As it was, the taking of Chunuk Bair was the next thing to victory—could it but be held!

As the afternoon wore on, the Gloucesters were fighting under section leaders; not an officer or senior N.C.O. remained. The New Zealanders were reduced to three officers and fifty men. Reinforcements of the Duke of Wellington's were dribbled up to them and stoutly filled the gaps in the ranks of the stormers. Still the Turks fought on, until their counter-attack should assemble and advance.

That night three columns formed in the water-courses of the Sari Bair for a fresh assault at dawn on the 9th. At 4.30 a.m. a concentrated fire of artillery from every ship and gun that could be brought to bear scourged the crests. Then a flood of Warwicks and South Lancashires overran the Chunuk Bair, whilst the 6th Gurkhas cleared the col towards Hill "Q". The Turks fled down the forward slopes and our men beheld the Hellespont at last. But two disasters were to break the wave of victory even now. The one was due to the third column straying in taking up its assault position, so that it arrived too late to pass left of the troops on the col towards Hill "Q" and Koja Chemen. The other was caused by faulty timing of the covering bombardment. Salvoes of heavy shell fell among the troops as they began the pursuit of the fleeing Turks. The Turks, seeing this, returned and beat back the remnant from all but the south-western part of Chunuk.

That night the 6th Loyal North Lancashires relieved the garrison of Chunuk, and before dawn the 5th Wiltshires moved up in support. Shortly afterwards the 8th Turkish Division in mass, led by Mustapha Kemal (then a newly made Corps Commander) in person, attacked the ill-sited British trenches. Though suffering heavy losses, they overwhelmed the garrison, of which only a few of the Loyals survived; the Wiltshires were annihilated. Almost at the same moment two Turkish divisions from Bulair met the belated attack of the Suvla troops against the Anafarta Ridge, and stopped it, although it had been reinforced by troops of the 53rd (Welsh) Division.

A fine effort by the 6th East Yorks had even then almost changed the day, for it delayed the arrival of the divisions from Bulair which the German Commander-in-Chief, Liman von Sanders, was impatiently awaiting on the Anafarta Ridge. On the 8th this battalion was on Scimitar Hill with the 9th West Yorks. One of its patrols had driven the Turkish covering troops from Tekke Tepe northwards. At dawn on the 9th it had been withdrawn by order from

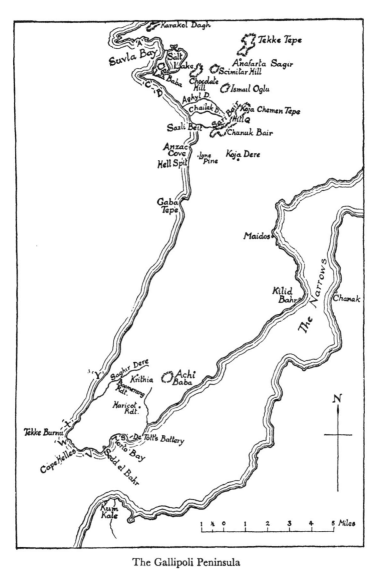

The Gallipoli Peninsula

Scimitar Hill. Then Sir Ian Hamilton's order to attack Tekke Tepe reached Colonel Moore, O.C. 6th East Yorks. This order was the outcome of a visit paid by the Commander-in-Chief to Suvla on the 8th, as soon as he became aware of the paralysis there; it seems never to have reached the other battalions of the 32nd Brigade. So only part of the 8th Duke of Wellington's, who were in the vicinity, supported Colonel Moore when, at the head of his leading company, he set out for Tekke Tepe. A force of Turks outnumbering them three to one opposed them, and "a free-for-all bayonet affair" ended in thirty of them reaching the summit. Only five of these trusty men survived to be taken prisoner. Had Brigades and Divisions been capable of leading such troops as these, no Turk from Bulair would ever have reached Anafarta and at this last moment the original scheme might have been carried through.

One further attempt to envelop the Turk by way of a ridge along the coast north of Suvla appears to have been critical, according to their German commander. It was made on the 15th of August by the 54th (East Anglian) Division and two brigades of the 10th Division, supported by ships off the coast. But it failed also. After one more attack a week later on Ismail Oglu by the 29th Division and the Yeomanry Division, dismounted, the two exhausted armies abandoned active operations.

In addition to the support the Fleet gave these attacks by bombardment, its submarine campaign in the Sea of Marmora was carried on with magnificent vigour. A net spread by the Turks at Nagara in the Straits was "charged" repeatedly and only once unsuccessfully; the mine-fields were passed boldly. The total "bag" was thus raised to 1 battleship (*Barbarossa*), 1 cruiser (*Messudieh*), 1 destroyer, 5 gunboats, 11 transports, 44 steamers, and 148 sailing vessels.

In the last week of November a blizzard raged for two days. Its effects seem to have decided the issue. Hundreds of men died of exposure and thousands became unfit for further service through their sufferings. The shores of the peninsula were strewn with the wreckage of supply-boats.

THE EVACUATION

Suvla and Anzac were evacuated on the night of the 19–20th December, Helles twenty days later. The miracle of the evacuation, which took place almost unmolested, can only be understood by those who know the workings of the Oriental mind and have some measure of the sufferings of the Turkish Army in this campaign. In the belief that it would be impossible to withdraw the troops from Gallipoli without a crowning disaster, both the Cabinet and the General Staff had been unable to face the idea of evacuation; and it was not until Lord Kitchener, after a personal visit, advocated this course, that the decision was taken. In the event, marvellous organisation made the withdrawal one of the greatest feats of the war.

In a little over eight months the British casualties were roughly 115,000. Those of the enemy will never be known, but there is no doubt that they were equally heavy. Health as well as life was levied upon in the struggle. In the warm weather a low form of dysentery affected almost all; in the winter frost-bite and lung diseases disabled many.

It is disputable whether success in the Gallipoli campaign would have exercised any great influence on the struggle in Europe. It certainly dissipated effort which might otherwise have been close-knit. The most valuable result would have been the opening of the Black Sea for the supply of the Russian Army with munitions; but at no time in 1915 were the munitions forthcoming, and all the summer the Russian Empire was agonising to dissolution under the terrific blows of the Prussian war machine. In 1906 the British General Staff had reported that the Dardanelles was an impregnable fortress. By 1915 the fortifications had been greatly strengthened. Yet since all the warfare in which the British Army was engaged was fortress warfare of the most terrifying description, a change of values in respect of the Dardanelles seems not unnatural.

Thus another chapter was added to the long military history of the Hellespont and its escarpment the Chersonese. The Hellespont seems to own allegiance to barbarism. It has floated the pontoons over which Xerxes carried slaughter and destruction into Greece. It has borne five hundred sail of the Goths, fresh from the sack of "ancient noble Cyzicus", to the plunder of the temple of Diana at Ephesus. Twelve hundred years later it harboured Barbarossa and his Ottoman corsairs and offered a refuge to the remnant of them which, after maiming Cervantes, escaped Don John of Austria at Lepanto. It has tried the faith of Crusaders and fretted the love of Leander. The politics of all the empires of Europe and the thoughts of all its peoples have betrayed unceasingly their fear of the sinister Hellespont. They are preoccupied with visions of yet another terror which may issue from it to spoil the rich peace of the Mediterranean.

This is the historical character of the Hellespont—for there is a character of places just as there is a character of men. Events reveal it periodically, and the history of the events is no bare chronicle; except as a study of character it is profitless. The Greeks subdued the Hellespont for the sake of a civilised ideal, the ideal of hospitality outraged by rude Paris. Ages afterwards the pick of British manhood from the ends of the earth fought there for ideals equally virtuous. Their physical perfection, so apparent to Hamilton and Masefield, perished; but their immortality is ours to cherish. Rupert Brooke died well in these men's company.

SUGGESTIONS FOR READING:

Gallipoli by John Masefield. *The Gallipoli Diary* by Gen. Sir Ian Hamilton, vol. I, pp. 58–9, 256–7, 311–13; vol. II, pp. 61–5, 100, 132. *The Secret Battle* by A. P. Herbert, pp. 8–110.

Chapter VIII: SALONICA, EGYPT, AND MESOPOTAMIA, TO MID-1916

(See maps on pp. 79 and 138)

THE Turks had foiled two attempts to force the Dardanelles to the relief of Russia; but there was still a chance that another attempt would succeed. The Allies' grip on the

Gallipoli Peninsula was almost a strangle-hold on Turkey, under which she might suddenly collapse. So long as it was maintained, Turkey was powerless against Egypt and the Suez Canal, harmless in the Balkans and Arabia, even too weak to defend herself in Armenia and Mesopotamia.

Germany, afraid that the Turks would fail, ceased in August 1915 to press her attack against Russia. Austria protested, desiring that Russia should be utterly crushed, but without avail. Warsaw had fallen on the 15th, Kovno on the 17th, Brest Litovsk on the 25th. The front ran straight southwards from the Gulf of Riga to the Roumanian frontier. It had been greatly shortened during the German advance; any further advance would lengthen it. Troops could therefore be spared to save Constantinople and then realise for Germany her dream of Eastern overlordship. Years before, the Kaiser, visiting the Middle East, had demonstratively entered Jerusalem through a gate specially opened for him in the western wall of the Holy City.

But first the Serbians must be swept from the path. Accordingly Austrian and German divisions assembled on the Danube late in August. This intimidated Roumania and Greece, whilst it emboldened Bulgaria. Disaster to Serbia was inevitable. Twice within a year she had heroically driven invading Austrians from her territory. Now Bulgaria was to fasten on her flank and help harry her wretched people from their homes.

Both the French and the British were disquieted by German ambitions in the Middle East, but they disagreed about how to thwart them. In the face of the new developments a small rift in Franco-British unity caused by the Gallipoli campaign almost became a gulf, and for a time the bonds of the Entente were strained nearly to breaking. The French wished to form an "Armée d'Orient" at Salonica, sending four divisions from France and withdrawing their two divisions from the Gallipoli Peninsula. But they could not muster the transport, so applied for it to the Admiralty. The British were unwilling to multiply the lines of sea communication; they wished to strike again at the Dardanelles with just the added weight represented by the four divisions from France. Hoping that this idea might prevail, the Admiralty made shift to comply with the French request for ships.

To complicate matters still further, on the eve of Loos the Greek and Serbian premiers jointly asked the Allies for the support of 150,000 troops. At the moment the Bulgarian Opposition was resisting a German alliance. Prompt compliance by the Allies seemed called for if Serbia, Bulgaria, and Roumania were to be enabled to unite in resistance to the German invaders. But prompt action was the last thing possible in the prevailing state of the Allies' counsels. Only when it was clear that the fighting at Loos and in Champagne would end without advantage gained did the Allied War Council decide to support the Serbians and Greeks. By this time the Bulgarians were mobilising, ominously.

On October 1st one British and one French division were withdrawn from Gallipoli to go to Salonica. Simultaneously, four French and two British divisions from the Western Front began embarking at Marseilles. At this juncture, however, the Greek Premier, Venizelos, resigned, King Constantine having informed him that he had exceeded his authority in inviting Allied assistance. The British troops from Gallipoli were therefore held back; not so the French. Enthusiastic for Serbia, the French persisted in their plan. They seemed blind to the strategic difficulties and failed to realise the extra strain on transport by sea which the new theatre of war would create. General Sarrail, the commander of the Armée d'Orient, hurriedly secured his base at Salonica and began to advance along the railway up the valley of the Vardar, in order to protect the Serbian right.

Meanwhile Russia quite independently had taken a fatal step. Though unable to give military support in the Balkans, she yet saw fit to send an ultimatum to Bulgaria, which was rejected on the 6th of October. On the 14th Bulgaria declared war on Serbia, and shortly afterwards cut the rail·way line north of Veles. England, her hand thus forced by France and Russia, regretfully declared war on Bulgaria on October 15th. France, Italy, and Russia in succession took this course also during the next few days.

Events at Salonica were most disturbing for some weeks. The situation of Greece was pitiable. The German Army, the British Fleet, and a fiercely vengeful Bulgaria all seemed to have her at a disadvantage. Serbia, her only ally, was being barbarously subjugated. Though offered Cyprus as the price of an alliance with the Entente Powers, King Constantine refused, stating that no inducement would make him take sides. A declaration of neutrality was made accordingly, friendly to the Allies, however, to the extent of allowing them to use Salonica as a base.

Salonica was a poor base, difficult to secure against submarines and, like the railway into Serbia, inadequate for a large army. Moreover the Greek Army was concentrating about Salonica as it moved to take up its watch on the Bulgarian frontier. Congestion, confusion, and ill-feeling resulted. The French were much hampered. The British hung back; new risks, which civil discord and the doubtful mood of the Greek Army made unfathomably grave, could not be accepted whilst prestige was still at stake on fateful Gallipoli. The Greeks for their part mistrusted the Allies' presence, and even Venizelos was momentarily alarmed lest their purpose was to compel the cession of the region to Bulgaria. Under these conditions little was done for Serbia. By the end of October the whole nation was fugitive before the army of von Mackensen and the Bulgarians.

It remained for Lord Kitchener to make an arrangement with the Greeks. He went to Athens after visiting the Gallipoli Peninsula. By his confident forecast of the outcome of the war he won King Constantine's trust as he had already won England's, another tribute to his almost prophetic insight. The safety of Salonica as a base for the Allies was assured and a promise made that their retreat would be unmolested. This overcame the most disturbing initial difficulty, though it did not remove its cause.

THE INVASION OF SERBIA

Three French divisions advanced up the valley of the Vardar and pressed on towards Veles. A huge advanced base was formed just inside the Serbian border at Ghevgeli.

Then, resting their right flank on Strumnitza, the French prolonged their left up the valley until it reached Gradsko. Farther they could not get to the succour of the Serbs, for the Bulgarians had driven in between. The Serbians were forced from Veles to their next hold, the Babouna Pass in the Moglena Mountains. To get help to them there the French had to operate across the difficult country within the loop of the river Cerna, north of Prilep. Though made with amazing skill and tenacity, efforts to do so failed, and the Serbs resumed their retreat into exile.

Meanwhile the first British division, the 10th, had begun to reach Dedeli, north-west of Lake Doiran. On October 28th it was in position to cover the right of the French. When on the 16th of November the Serbs fell back from the Babouna Pass to Prilep and Monastir, the French began to withdraw down the Vardar, and the 10th Division guarded the exposed flank of the French retreat. On December 6th it was attacked by the Germans and Bulgars east of Dedeli and, heavily outnumbered, was forced back to a line across the Dedeli Pass, where it held on until the depôt of stores at Ghevgeli was evacuated and the French rear-guards were clear of the place. By mid-December all the Allied troops had withdrawn across the Greek frontier; the enemy did not violate it.

The unfortunate Serbs made a retreat across the mountains of Albania in snow, and it is recorded that they perished in numbers at every ford and pass. The survivors, in three batches, reached the shores of the Adriatic, whence they were taken to the island of Corfu to rest and refit.

The political situation at Salonica continued to be an anxious one. In order to exercise a certain restraint upon the ill-disposed Greek Army, the Allies in December declared a blockade of the Greek coast. At the same time they busied themselves with what the troops called the "Bird-Cage", the entrenched camp of Salonica. The perimeter of this work, extending from the west shore of the Gulf of Orfano to the marshes of the Vardar delta, lay along the northern slope of the Derbend Ridge, at no point nearer than eight miles to the city. Good roads were carefully made within it.

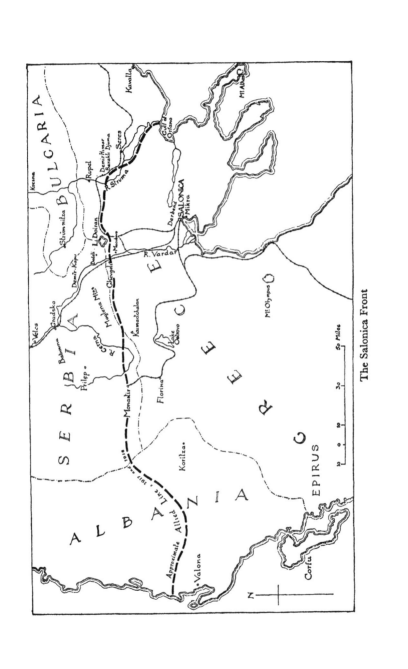

The Salonica Front

Although the Greek Armies were facing the Bulgars and Germans across their borders, it was half expected that the enemy might attempt to push the Allies into the sea, and no illusions were entertained that this would be distasteful to the Greek Army. So the Allied columns patrolled Macedonia, in spite of the veiled hostility of the Greek military authorities and the obstructiveness of their troops. To perform the same duty in Epirus, 30,000 Italians landed at Valona.

By the month of May 1916 the strength of the Allies at Salonica exceeded 300,000 men, to be increased during the summer by 80,000 Serbians from Corfu. These had been re-armed by the French, whilst the British and French shared responsibility for their maintenance. By that time it was clear that the Bulgars would not make a general advance, so the Allies moved out and fronted the enemy's entrenched positions along the Greek frontier. This line of battle altered little in the following two and a quarter years.

GERMANY, TURKEY, AND EGYPT

The Germans were fully alive to the importance of Egypt to the British Empire, so when war with the British Empire came upon Germany, their statesmen quickly prepared a shrewd blow at that country. For some years a German military mission had worked with the Turkish Army, and its members had gained the enthusiastic attachment of the younger and more adventurous spirits among the Turkish generals, such as Enver Pasha. After the outbreak of war in Europe the prestige of this faction in Turkey was so raised by the presence of the *Goeben* and *Breslau* at Constantinople as ultimately to bring Turkey into the war on the side of the Central Powers. She was the tool for Germany's blow at Egypt which was designed to re-establish Turkish sway at the sensitive nodal point of the British Empire's communications.

On December 18th, 1914, the title of "Khedive" lapsed and Prince Hussein Kamel Pasha became Sultan of Egypt, which was at the same time proclaimed a British Protectorate. Thus Britain assumed responsibility for the defence of Egypt.

During January 1915 an extremely courageous and enter-prising expedition was made by Turkish troops from Pales-tine across the Sinai Desert. Fifteen thousand men with some artillery succeeded in reaching the Suez Canal on February 2nd, after a march of 150 miles over barren and waterless country. They put up a stout fight and were successful in getting three pontoon-loads of men (all made prisoners) across the Canal. The Indian troops guarding the Canal were, however, able satisfactorily to deal with the situation, and the Turkish column retired with extremely heavy losses. A further attempt was made on the Canal near Suez on March 22nd, but was easily driven off.

Egypt was also invaded from the west. A number of Turkish officers was landed by a submarine in the Bay of Sollum, late in 1915. They raised the Senussi and before the end of the year had gained the Baharia Oasis, 200 miles south-west of Cairo. Steady pressure by British columns overcame the invaders during January 1916. The last re-mains of rebellion among the Senussi were stamped out soon after the middle of March, in spite of trying weather, scarcity of water, and the obligation of feeding the popula-tion of our enemies the while.

Early in 1916 preparations (which did not escape the British Intelligence authorities) were being made by the Turks in Syria, under German superintendence, for an attack on the Canal upon a more serious scale. This attack was delayed by the Hedjaz revolt, an Arab rebellion against the Turkish sway, headed by the Sherif of Mecca, in June 1916. The Arabs seized Mecca and the port of Jeddah, be-sieged Medina, and by destroying part of the Hedjaz rail-way prevented the arrival of Turkish reinforcements from Syria. This open hostility of the Arabs was destined to grow under the hand of Colonel T. E. Lawrence and be a thorn in the side of the Turks during the next two years, providing us with a useful ally. The Turkish invasion, thus postponed, materialised in August, when a Turkish force, 18,000 strong and under the command of a German General, von Kres-senstein, reached Romani. There they were opposed by British troops, including the Australian and New Zealand

Mounted Division, and after 36 hours' fighting the Turks were defeated and a pursuit of over 20 miles left us with 4000 prisoners and large quantities of material.

MESOPOTAMIA

The campaign in Mesopotamia grew from small beginnings. In the middle of October 1914 an infantry brigade had been sent from India to the Persian Gulf, with the purpose of protecting the oil export by occupying Abadan Island. Oil reached the coast through a pipe-line from Persian Arabistan, 150 miles away, and the source of supply was a valuable one to the Admiralty. After the declaration of war upon Turkey in November, the rest of the 6th (Poona) Division was sent to the Gulf. Two of its brigades made a landing below Basra, drove the Turks from their positions covering the port, and entered it on November 22nd. An advance was then made to Kurna, which lies in the angle at which the Tigris and Euphrates join to form the Shatt el Arab, and 1200 prisoners and 9 guns were captured.

The country along the rivers in lower Mesopotamia becomes inundated in the spring through the melting of the snows in Armenia and Kurdistan, and in order to carry on the campaign the troops had to be practised in the use of "balams", light native boats each capable of transporting ten fully equipped soldiers. During the period of training two further infantry brigades arrived from India and occupied Ahwaz on the oil-fields. This force was called the 12th Division.

The Turks, taking advantage of the delay, attacked an entrenched camp at Shaiba, south of Basra, on April 14th, and the issue was long in doubt. Ultimately the two Indian brigades and some cavalry holding Shaiba beat off their assailants, who retreated in disorder to Naziriya; pursued farther by the Euphrates river-flotilla, they lost heavily in men and material. Henceforward the Arabs (who had made up the bulk of the Turkish force against Shaiba) showed themselves as ready to turn against their Turkish rulers in defeat as they were to plunder the invaders at any favourable opportunity.

On May 4th the 12th Division advanced westwards from Ahwaz, but the enemy made a rapid and safe retreat. Persian Arabistan with its oil-fields and pipe-line was now secure. Still, the British hold on lower Mesopotamia remained hazardous; it had to be extended before it could be regarded as firm.

On May 31st, in the first fierce heat of Mesopotamian summer, a whole brigade embarked in "balams" at Kurna and started poling and paddling its way laboriously through the high reeds towards the Turkish position. A flotilla of sloops and launches on the Tigris supported the "balams" with the fire of their guns.

The Turkish position was on a group of sandy knolls rising out of inundations, which seemed to stretch from horizon to horizon. Only one redoubt could be reached by land along the left bank of the river; it was taken from its Arab defenders early in the action. The other forward redoubts were smothered with artillery fire from the flotilla and from Kurna whilst the "balams" were approaching them. Toiling by every means to get forward; pulling, pushing, punting; sweating at every pore in the intense moist heat and expecting every moment to be sunk by shrapnel, the amphibious battalions slowly approached and took the nearer knolls. The Turkish force then abandoned the main position and fled up the river to Amara. Informed of this early next day by the first aeroplane reconnaissance made in Mesopotamia, the General commanding the 6th Division, Major-General C. V. F. Townshend, set off in pursuit with the river flotilla. After some minor actions Townshend reached Amara, 90 miles from Kurna, early on the 3rd of June, and the town and its garrison surrendered.

Having thus boldly and successfully extended its hold on the Tigris, the British force turned to the Euphrates. A yet riskier amphibious operation was planned against Naziriya, 80 miles from Kurna along the old Euphrates channel. During the inundations no other approach was possible. The advance along the Tigris in "balams" from Kurna had been an out-of-the-way operation even for British enterprise. But the steaming of the little armada along the old Euphrates beggars amazement. Its escort was three stern-wheel sloops and an armed launch of the Royal Navy. Three river-steamers, each mounting two 18-pounder field guns, played the part of transports to a brigade of the 12th Division. In tow were strings of "mahailas" (river sailing-vessels) carrying supplies, also many "balams", some in pairs with mountain guns. Even heavy artillery was afloat, two 4·7-inch guns, each in a horse-boat.

The expedition sounded its way through Hammar Lake, about 40 miles from Kurna, on June 27th. Proceeding, it found that the channel leading from the lake to the main stream had been sufficiently dammed six miles short of the Euphrates. In overpowering heat a passage was blasted through the obstruction and the vessels man-handled past it. Mine-sweeping parties preceded the ships. The reed-grown banks were cleared by a battalion advancing along each, with parties in "balams" fanned out across the inundations to right and left. Serious enemy opposition was encountered at the entrance to the Euphrates, but it was overcome. The Turkish defenders were cut off by a "balam" flotilla and their Arab supporters dispersed through the marshes.

Entering the Euphrates, the expedition was checked six miles below Naziriya. A very critical time followed. The heat was unbearable and caused much sickness; the streams were fast subsiding. Nevertheless by heroic work in a furnace-like atmosphere, reinforcements were brought up, although Lake Hammar by then was more mud than water. On July 24th the Turkish position was carried and Naziriya surrendered on the following day. The enemy, 2000 strong, retreated by the Hai river to Kut on the Tigris.

Possessed of Amara on the Tigris and Naziriya on the Euphrates, the Mesopotamian Expeditionary Force was well posted to defend the province of Basra. Thus it had achieved the design of the Indian Government. But just beyond the limits of the province lay the town of Kut-el-Amara. To both British and Turks it was an ideal jumping-off ground for offensive operations. To deny it to the Turk would be to deprive him of alternative lines of operations against Amara along the Tigris or against Naziriya along the Hai.

The Turks entrenched themselves on both banks of the Tigris at Es Sinn, eight miles below Kut. They also boomed the river channel between. After long and careful preparation this position was attacked on September 27th. First a feint was made at the enemy's position south of the river by the main body of troops marching up that bank, and next morning a frontal attack was pressed against the enemy's trenches just north of the river.

During the night the main body had crossed the river by a pontoon bridge and marched northwards to turn the enemy's left, south of the Ataba Marsh. It made too wide a detour and had hard fighting in the heat of a day remarkable for its dust-storms. However, by 2 p.m. the turning force had captured the northern half of the enemy's position; but the troops were without water and short of ammunition. The water in the marshes proved to be undrinkable, although a cavalry reconnaissance had reported otherwise. Moreover the 6th Division had no water-carts nor any means of carrying water; it depended on river transport for almost everything. Notwithstanding, at 5 p.m. the turning force began to move south towards the river behind the Turkish position. Here it encountered the enemy's reserve of three battalions and routed it with the bayonet.

The troops were now utterly exhausted after their 18-mile march, the hardships endured, and the heavy fighting. Night was at hand to prevent the cavalry pursuing. With the river-flotilla lay the only chance of complete victory. Accordingly Commander Cookson in the *Comet* undertook to break the boom between the enemy trenches. Gun-fire and ramming having failed, he went himself in a dinghy and with an axe hacked at the cables securing the obstruction. He was killed at this work, and his name was fittingly added to the roll of those who died "For Valour". The Turks, who had suffered 1700 casualties, withdrew in the night and began to retreat to Baghdad. The British casualties were 1200.

It was at this juncture that the strategic importance of Mesopotamia was enhanced by the events in Russia and the Near East. The failure at Suvla and the infirmity of purpose of the Allies as to Salonica made of Baghdad an objective almost as desirable under the changed conditions as Constantinople had been up to this moment. The result was to precipitate an advance upon Baghdad. Such a resounding deed of arms as an entry into the city caliphate would, it was thought, impress the whole East. This would more than neutralise the loss of prestige apprehended from the successful defence of the Dardanelles by the Turks. There had always been a hope of dashing up to Baghdad with the river-flotilla after a success at Kut, much as Amara had been rushed after the victory at Kurna; but little idea of holding the city had been entertained. As it proved, the difficulty of navigating the river at its lowest not only prevented the pursuit of the Turks from Kut but hampered even the subsequent steady forward concentration.

Tempted, however, by the achievements of the "invincible" 6th Division and the gallant little flotilla on which it depended, political aspirations outran discretion, and the difficulties and dangers of the hazard were discounted. So it came about that another was added to the "forlorn hope" adventures abounding in British naval and military history.

The change in the plan of campaign could not be as readily arranged as it was suddenly made. In the operations to secure the Basra province, river communications had sufficed. More than this would be necessary to encompass the possession of Baghdad; to give the troops full power of manoeuvre land transport must be provided. Even at the battle of Es Sinn the lack of land transport had caused much hardship and limited the scope of the victory. Moreover it was clear that in the dry season the upper Tigris channel would be increasingly difficult for the supporting flotilla and unreliable for the daily supplies. Nearly two months elapsed before the 6th Division was completely fitted out.

Having completed his concentration at Aziziya on November 11th, General Townshend began the final stage of his advance. A night approach march brought the British, at dawn on the 22nd of November, within striking distance of the Turkish position at Ctesiphon. This was straightway turned, and masses of Turks were retreating by 8 a.m.; many more were fleeing towards the river before the attack of a widely extended half-battalion of the 2nd Dorsets. The remainder of the Dorsets, backed by the 30th Brigade, pierced the Turkish second line at about 11 a.m. and captured some guns. The flotilla, however, was prevented from advancing by the enemy's command of the north-eastward reach of the river below Ctesiphon. For this reason it could not support the attack on the second line; nor could it range on the enemy masses fleeing from the first line, owing to the height of the river banks.

At this juncture a fresh Corps of Turks, recently transferred from the Caucasus, began to reach the field from Baghdad. A tremendous fight for the Turkish second line followed. Great numbers were killed and wounded on both sides, including a large proportion of the British officers of the Indian regiments. Constrained by this and by a harassing cross-fire from the enemy's guns on the right bank, a withdrawal to the first line was ordered. Soon the plain became covered with troops walking slowly back.

The night was passed in the Turkish trenches, and in the morning no enemy was nigh. Air reconnaissance revealed the Turks occupying the west bank of the Diala, seven miles back, and their boat-bridge being towed up the river. At a cost of over 4000 casualties the British had ousted the Turks from a strong position and taken 1300 prisoners. But no hope remained that the little force would cover the last eighteen miles of the four hundred from Basra to Baghdad. The way which the finger of destiny pointed was the weary road to Kut and starvation—and not unmolested.

On the night of the 23rd, from nine o'clock until two in the morning, the Turks assailed the British position, but were driven off. The following day was passed by the British in reorganising and sending down the sick and wounded. The weak brigades were now each less than a thousand strong, their British battalions reduced to the strength of companies. So they slowly drew off southwards, harassed by large bodies of the treacherous Arabs, but taking their prisoners with them.

They were overtaken in the early morning of December 1st. They had heard the sound of wheels as the enemy too confidently closed on them in the night. At daybreak the waiting guns of the flotilla and field batteries opened on the massed Turks and severely handled them, so that it was possible to resume the retreat at 7.30 a.m. in perfect order. The flotilla was not so fortunate. The navigation of the shallow stream was slow work and the barge convoy of sick and wounded and stores was continually in difficulties. As a result of the devotion shown by the fighting ships in the work of salvage, only the *Sumana* survived. The little column marched all day and far into the night to shake off the pursuit, making 36 miles. Then they lay down and slept in column, foodless. At dawn the next day the retreat was continued and Kut was reached on December 3rd. There the 6th Division and the 30th Brigade were beleaguered for just on five months, during which the troops suffered great privation.

A force was meanwhile assembled down-river which before the fall of Kut attained a strength of 30,000 men with 133 guns. But it failed in its attempts at relief. This "Tigris Corps" pressed back the Turkish covering force from position after position to Sannaiyat; but there it was decisively checked. Enemy reinforcements for the investing and covering forces were arriving in strength, and they were able to multiply the entrenched positions before Kut and across the path of the Tigris Corps. Though the British casualties in the effort to reach Kut amounted to nearly 20,000, the effort was fruitless.

Adequate supplies could not be got to the starving garrison by air, so an attempt was made on April 24th to revictual the town by river. The steamer *Julnar* was loaded with 270 tons of supplies and steamed at the boom defences. But her propeller fouled the chains, both her officers were killed, and she fell into the hands of the enemy. Five days later, on the 29th of April, 1916, all guns, ammunition, and stores in Kut were destroyed, and the garrison, numbering 2970 British and 6000 Indians, surrendered. During the last few days of the siege twenty men a day had been dying of starvation and all were very weak. Their lot in captivity was such that many more died from disease and in despair.

Thus, in spite of a good beginning, the campaign in Mesopotamia came to grief. Rumours spread that the conduct of the affair was discreditable, and this was borne out at an official enquiry. In particular there was a grave scandal of the hardships suffered by the sick and wounded during their removal from the area of operations. The serious strategic situation was the sole origin of all the administrative troubles. A step had been resolved upon rashly after the crowning success of Es Sinn in September. This was recklessly gambled on at Ctesiphon, a victory for the British soldier but a complete strategic disaster. Hasty remedies and expedients thereafter brought about disorganisation; so in the instant of victory the tide of success turned against the magnificent 6th (Poona) Division.

SUGGESTIONS FOR READING:

Twenty-five Years by Viscount Grey of Fallodon, vol. ii, p. 215. *Naval Operations* by Sir Julian Corbett, vol. iii, pp. 165–72, 190–4.

Chapter IX: THE WESTERN FRONT, OCTOBER 1915–JUNE 1916

Despite the despatch of two divisions from the Western Front to Salonica, the stream of divisions from England had added the strength of another Army to the Expeditionary Force by October 1915 and the British Third Army came into being. General Allenby assumed command and took over the front from the Somme to Hebuterne. The command of the Expeditionary Force was relinquished by Sir John French in December 1915 and General Sir Douglas Haig was appointed in his place.

MEN, MATERIAL, AND TRAINING

At the battle of Loos the New Army had been generously blooded in the surgical sense. There followed a period unbroken by any considerable action until the Battle of the Somme in July 1916. The Germans worked hard everywhere to strengthen their well-sited line. They had plenty of materials, particularly timber and wire, and well-organised railways. Thus they were able to provide protection and even comfort for their troops holding the defences. This maintained their health and moral. Before Verdun preparations went steadily forward to strike hard at the French in the coming year.

In the British lines conditions were very different. The number of troops used to hold the crumbling trench system was excessive, as was the wastage from hardship and wounds. The autumn and winter rains of northern Europe are insistent. The digging of trenches even in the chalk of Artois is a bootless labour if materials for revetting, flooring, and draining them are not to hand. In the loam of Flanders the front-line trenches were in many places little more than ragged waterlogged ditches, and many of the communication trenches, in so far as they existed at all, were waist-deep in water. Thus the plight of our trench garrisons was pitiable, apart from persistent and accurate enemy shell-fire. The Germans on the other hand had already begun to realise that continuous trenches could not be maintained in Flanders soil and had started to evolve a defensive system consisting mainly of small concrete shelters called "pill-boxes"; within less than two years, indeed, there were to be practically no German front-line trenches in the Salient.

In the area immediately behind the line the roads were worn out; the streets of the towns swam inches deep in mud and water; the neighbouring fields were churned into sloughs by men and horses. The busiest traffic was that to and from the shale dumps of coal-mines. From these ballast for gun-pits, roads, horse-standings, camps, and dumps was drawn by the thousands of tons.

From this period the training of the Army in defence began to take shape in the minds of its leaders. Further, the offensive spirit had to be fostered by the Higher Command according to the policy adopted by the British in the "war of attrition". In estimating the difficulties which the enforcement of this policy encountered a few words must be given to some of the peculiarities of trench warfare. In the course of an infantry battalion's "tour of duty" lasting, say,

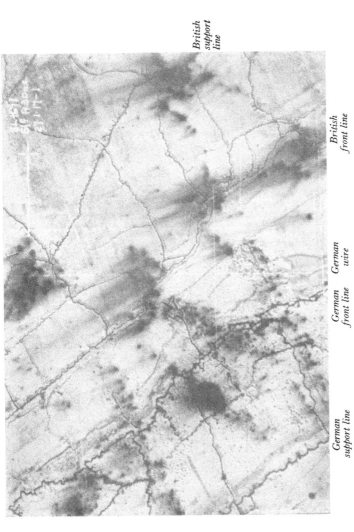

German
support line

German
front line

German
wire

British
front line

British
support
line

THE OPPOSING TRENCH-LINES AFTER A SNOW-FALL

(A rise in the ground makes the two front lines invisible to each other, and the Germans have
pushed out saps from which they can watch the British line. The black smudges show the action of
explosives on the snow; a bombardment of the German front line by the British artillery has brought
retaliation in the form of a trench-mortar bombardment, aimed chiefly at the British trench-
junctions. The pock-marks are old shell-holes under the snow.)

ten days, the maintenance of several miles of trenches—front line, support, and communication—was the first charge. Under the circumstances already described this in itself was a matter of great difficulty. Moreover, a great part of the energies of the infantry was taken up in mere carrying duties. Frequently an entire company was told off to meet the transport at a perilous rendez-vous soon after dusk, load up with sacks of rations, mails, and stores, and in the confusion of darkness and shelling deliver them to the other companies' headquarters, situated in various obscure corners of the maze of trenches. The rations often went astray, even though a quarter of the battalion strength was absorbed in this exhausting duty; at best, the task lasted most of the night and galling casualties were suffered in cold blood. Again, in the excitement of the moving battle the offensive spirit is natural to man; but in trench warfare the artilleries of both sides, not subject to the same frequent changes as the infantry and accurately registered upon the trench systems, instantly retaliated for any offensive step, however trifling. In a few minutes a hundred yards of trench might be battered to ruin and its garrison buried or blown to fragments without any possibility of resistance. The courage which can long endure this strain is of a rarer type than that which inspires the soldier to attack, and there is a point at which the endurance of the bravest man snaps.

At the battle of Loos the enemy defences were remarkable for the amount of uncut wire remaining after days of bombardment. "Dud" British ammunition lay about everywhere. During the ensuing twelve months the quality of the shell, and particularly of the fuses, used remained poor. Shells failed to explode, or exploded prematurely, damaging our own men. But by the time the battle of the Somme was well begun "prematures" and unexploded shell were much fewer. British factories had increased their output and improved their products, so that the poor supplies from the United States need no longer be contracted for.

Behind the front all formations which could be spared from the line went periodically into training in open and trench warfare. To facilitate this, cavalry volunteered and formed a composite dismounted division which served a tour in the line; at other times the cavalry abandoned saddle, lance, and sabre to wield shovels on reserve defence schemes. Schools of gunnery, telephony, bombing, bayonet-fighting, trench-mortar and anti-gas instruction got to work everywhere. Specialist training for cooks, water-duty men, sanitary men, chiropodists, farriers was provided. The work of preparation was intensively done. The leaven of new knowledge was forced continually into the lump, and the effect of it began to show gradually as its application in practice grew.

VERDUN

On the 21st of February, 1916, the Germans began an attack upon the French lines about Verdun. Being well informed of the enemy's intentions, the French were fully prepared. The arrangements for the defence had been planned with great care and ingenuity. Advanced works lightly held masked a strong battle zone. The two systems were so laid out as to break up an assault into parts which would be enfiladed as the attackers advanced or changed direction under compulsion of the defence. Field artillery and machine-gun barrages were mainly relied upon to crush the stormers. Communications had been provided for with particular care. Signal lines had been deeply buried and multiplied, and pigeons and war-dogs supplemented these means of transmission. The upkeep of roads and railways leading to the salient employed great gangs continually. Supplies were dumped in quantities in each sector and pipelines were laid to ensure the water-supply of the whole perimeter, so that the labour of carrying-parties was reduced to a minimum. Trench, road, and railway traffic were strictly controlled.

The struggle was prolonged and very fierce. Division by division the greater parts of the French and German Armies became involved in it, yet neither side succumbed to the terror it represented. "On ne passera pas" said the French; then, as the months went by, there flamed the characteristic "On les aura!" of Gallic exultation. The Germans had failed

early to get in a decisive blow; their subsequent efforts to turn
failure into victory were stemmed by the desperate heroism
of their opponents and came to an end soon after the battle
of the Somme began.

During the great struggle at Verdun rumour was continually busy in the British lines; divisions withdrawn for
training believed often that they were to be, not trained, but
entrained for Verdun. The assistance which the British
Army actually gave its ally took a less direct form; early in
March the First Army took over the defences on the Vimy
Ridge from the French, and a little later the Third Army
relieved the French troops holding the Arras front. Towards
the end of the month General Rawlinson's Fourth Army was
formed and it relieved the right of the Third Army. Thus
the British front stretched from Boesinghe to the Somme—
and still the divisions poured across the Channel, while their
French comrades turned eastwards to the fiery ordeal of
Verdun, the eyes of a whole breathless world upon them.

GERMAN ATTACKS AT YPRES AND VIMY

In the middle of February the enemy exploded mines at
"the Bluff", north of the Ypres-Comines Canal, and at
Hooge. At Hooge his infantry was driven off; at the Bluff
he maintained a lodgment for over a fortnight before he was
ejected by a brilliantly conceived counter-attack, which saw
the first use of "Stokes guns" and other novel features. In
this action a great part was played by one of the most
accomplished and gallant soldiers produced by the war,
Major W. la T. Congreve, who earned all the most coveted
decorations before his death on the Somme at the age of
twenty-five.

Late in March six large mines were exploded in an attempt
to thrust the Germans out of a commanding position at
St Eloi on the Wytschaete Ridge. After many days of confused fighting the ground became a quagmire, in which it
was practically impossible to say whether any progress had
been made or not. The new craters were dominated by the
enemy artillery, so the British line remained much as it was
before the action began.

94 The Western Front: October 1915–June 1916

The General Staff appreciation of the British position on the Vimy Ridge stated that, if attacked, it must be hung on to with "nails and knees". The enemy attempted to fraternise with the first British troops in occupation. After repeated warnings it was necessary to teach him a sharp lesson. The reason of his persistence shortly showed—a mine went up which buried forty of the British garrison. For two months thereafter both sides mined assiduously. Ultimately, using 20,000 lb. of ammonal, the British blew a huge crater, from the lip of which the eastern slope of the ridge could be observed.

With this the Germans were ill content, and in the evening of Sunday, May 21st, they attacked the northern end of the ridge. The assault was prefaced with a bombardment which British gunners described as highly scientific. The forward area was plastered with shrapnel and torn with high explosive; communications and battery positions were drenched with tear-gas shell which was so put down that the wind carried it in belts north-eastwards across gun positions and trench junctions. Roads and villages in rear were attacked with heavy metal. After some days and nights of ragged struggle, however, the position was stabilised with little loss of ground. Throughout the nights of terrific clamour the famous nightingales of the Carency valley sang full-throated. In each of the odd intervals to which the shelling of those times was subject, the throb of their song from the shattered woodlands had a beauty which was eerie.

All these minor actions emphasised that the enemy held the initiative; they were a proper use of his advantages in observation, held since the first year of the war, and it is remarkable that he should not have had any striking success against raw troops. But actually these troops were eager to "get on with the war"; a break, however bloody and futile, in the viewless routine of trench warfare was welcomed.

The time was at hand.

SUGGESTIONS FOR READING:
The Irish Guards in the Great War by Rudyard Kipling, vol. ii, pp. 73–4.
A Subaltern on the Somme by "Mark VII", pp. 94–7.

Chapter X: THE BATTLE OF JUTLAND

At dawn on the 10th of April, 1916, the German High Seas Fleet made the east coast of England aware that it had abandoned its quiescence. First Yarmouth and then Lowestoft were awakened to the terror of a bombardment from the sea. The damage done was considerable, and when the assailants got away unharmed public feeling was much disturbed. To protect the East Coast towns without prejudice to the unity of the Grand Fleet was the Admiralty's particular dilemma. To split the Grand Fleet and destroy its parts was the only hope the Germans had of victory at sea. The best face the Admiralty could put on this troublesome matter was that the enemy's raids on the coast were likely to give the Grand Fleet the hoped-for opportunity of engaging the High Seas Fleet decisively.

During May the enemy awaited favourable weather for the bombardment of Sunderland, intending to draw the British squadrons out over lurking submarines. At 2 a.m. on May 31st his scouting squadrons started northwards. This became known to the Admiralty at once, and a Grand Fleet rendez-vous was appointed for 2.30 p.m. off the coast of Jutland. The squadrons proceeded without loss from submarines.

A chance event brought the scouting forces into contact. The light cruisers *Galatea* and *Elbing*, twenty-two miles apart, sighted a steamer which each thought fit to examine. They opened fire on each other at 2.28 p.m. Admiral Hipper turned to support the *Elbing* with his five battle-cruisers. Admiral Beatty with six battle-cruisers and four fast battleships had already turned north towards the appointed rendez-vous, but he now turned again with the battle-cruisers only and steamed at full speed to cut off the enemy's retreat. Sixty-five miles to the north, Admiral Jellicoe read *Galatea's* report at 2.43 p.m.; he immediately increased the speed of his battle-fleet and steered for the fight.

An hour later a seaplane from the carrier *Engadine* reported that the German battle-cruisers had turned back, and at 3.48 the battle-cruiser action began at 13,000 yards range. Soon both the *Lion* and the *Tiger* were hulled twice. Admiral Hipper then turned his ships away south-eastwards, and immediately afterwards the British squadrons turned away also, taking a parallel course. On both sides the rate of fire was increased, and about this time, just before 4 p.m., the *Derfflinger*, her decks cascading tons of sea-water from shells bursting about her, received her first direct hit.

At this time one of the *Lion's* turrets was wrecked and the crews of both guns killed. The complete destruction of the ship was only prevented by the promptness of the turret-commander, Major F. J. W. Harvey, R.M.L.I., who, at the point of death from dreadful wounds, gave orders to flood the magazines. He gained the Victoria Cross for his action. The flagship blazed furiously for some time.

A minute or two later the *Indefatigable*, rear ship of the battle-cruiser line, was hit by three shells from the *von der Tann* which pierced her deck and caused a great explosion. She staggered from her course, was struck by a second salvo, and disappeared in a sheet of flame. Not one survived of her complement of over a thousand officers and men. The *von der Tann* was immediately attacked from another direction; Rear-Admiral Evan Thomas' colossal flagship *Barham* straddled her with 15-inch shell at 19,000 yards.

After an interval of some ten minutes the battle-cruisers resumed the action at extreme range. The *Lion* was still obscured in smoke and the *Queen Mary* was the mark of much of the enemy's fire. At last she was hit by a double salvo which fired her magazines. A great red flame rose from her, and only a lofty column of dark smoke remained where she had dived under with her propellers still revolving. Only two officers and five men, all wounded, out of her crew of 57 officers and 1209 men, were subsequently rescued by German destroyers. Meanwhile the fast battleships under Evan Thomas had so far overtaken the cruiser fight that the *Barham* and *Valiant* were engaging the *Moltke* and *von der Tann*, and at 4.15 p.m. both sides delivered destroyer attacks. The gallant little craft were whelmed in shell-bursts from each others' guns and from the secondary armaments of the bigger ships. Two German torpedo-boats were sunk and two British destroyers, *Nomad* and *Nestor*, lay wrecked between the careering squadrons. The big ships avoided the torpedoes.

At 4.30 p.m. a complete change came over the action. Two miles ahead of the *Lion*, Commodore Goodenough in the *Southampton*, leading the 2nd Light Cruiser Squadron, signalled "Battleships S.E.". Admiral Beatty thereupon signalled his squadrons to turn northwards, towards the Commander-in-Chief. Commodore Goodenough was not content until, at 12,000 yards, he had seen the whole long line of Admiral Scheer's twenty-two battleships deployed for battle. Under an avalanche of screaming shells the light cruisers steered hither and thither, gathered news as swallows gather gnats, and got away with it. Evan Thomas, too, held on southwards, his four great ships now firing in pairs on the luckless *Moltke* and *von der Tann*; at last he saw a chance of giving the stricken battle-cruiser force a respite. In eight minutes the two squadrons, the sum of their speeds almost a mile a minute, had met. So the battleships turned in the wake of the battle-cruisers with the enemy firing heavily on their turning-point. The rear ship, *Malaya*, turned in a hurricane of six salvoes a minute. Only the *Valiant*, by a miracle, was untouched.

Left to their fate, the helpless little *Nomad* and *Nestor* were destroyed by the guns of the approaching High Seas Fleet, but not before they had fired their last torpedoes at their mighty opponents. *Nicator* and *Petard*, destroyers, also attacked the advancing enemy, and one of their torpedoes hit the *Seydlitz*, damaging her seriously. The boldness of the destroyers' work was amazing; they beat off the attacking German torpedo craft and forced the German battle-cruisers away whilst the British squadrons were turning.

Meanwhile the British battle squadrons were reading Jellicoe's signal: "Enemy's battle-fleet coming north".

All the ships in action were now steaming northwards at full speed. The *Lion* was again set on fire and only saved from the fate of her two sisters by the prompt closing of a

magazine door. The *Malaya* was constantly straddled for
twenty minutes. At 5.10 p.m. the battle-cruisers had run out
of range of the enemy. Ten minutes later Evan Thomas
turned NNW in Beatty's wake, but kept Hipper's ships and
Scheer's van under fire for a time.

At 5.40 the fight was resumed. Less than twenty miles
away was the British battle-fleet, twenty-four Dreadnoughts
led by three battle-cruisers and screened by numerous
smaller vessels. Visual touch with it had been established
at 5.33.

Sir John Jellicoe had now to form line of battle from
cruising order in six parallel divisions of four battleships
each. The information he had of the enemy's course and
bearing and distance was of the meagrest. His responsi-
bilities defied reckoning. He questioned Admiral Beatty.
The answer read: "26–30 battleships probably bearing
SSE steering SE". Obviously the message had been
garbled. But no man is an admiral commanding-in-chief
for nothing. The critical evolution was ultimately performed
at 6.26 p.m. with great skill and perfect judgement.

With their engines exceeding the maximum revolutions
they were designed to give, Beatty's four remaining battle-
cruisers foamed into their assigned position and led the
battle line. Ship by ship it appeared out of the mist and
smoke, uncountable and menacing. Last of the long array
and last word in strength, speed, and gun-power, steamed
Rear-Admiral Evan Thomas' Fifth Battle Squadron—
Barham, *Valiant*, *Warspite*, and *Malaya*. These ships had
hitherto supported the diminished battle-cruisers against
their more numerous antagonists with a skill that matched
their devotion. Up to the moment of separation they gave
of their magnificent best and helped to force Hipper's
blazing, battered ships away eastwards without the invaluable knowledge of the reinforcement at hand. Then,
unable to follow Beatty's battle-cruisers without hampering
Jellicoe's manoeuvre, Evan Thomas had turned aside,
drawing past him the enemy's van battleships under his
fire.

Meanwhile the advanced ships of Jellicoe's fleet, cruisers,

light cruisers, and destroyers, with battle-cruisers in support, had found and set upon those of the enemy. Well ahead, south-eastwards, were the light cruisers *Chester* and *Canterbury*; they led on either hand of Admiral Hood's battle-cruisers, *Invincible*, *Inflexible*, and *Indomitable*. The *Chester* found and attacked three light cruisers. She was immediately swept by a storm of shell which wrecked her decks, disabled three of her guns forward, and killed their crews. A solitary figure remained erect, receivers on ears, amid the carnage around one of the useless guns. Though mortally wounded, he awaited orders from the distributing station. This was the boy Jack Cornwell, posthumously awarded the Victoria Cross.

Whilst the *Chester* zig-zagged out of action, the "Invincibles" engaged the German light cruisers. The *Wiesbaden* was completely disabled, her consorts *Frankfort* and *Pillau* severely damaged. Admiral Hood's escorting destroyers then repelled a torpedo attack, and the battle-cruisers turned westwards to join Admiral Beatty. But two destroyers were left crippled, the *Shark* hopelessly; the other, *Acasta*, offered a tow, which was firmly refused. The *Shark* was still bravely fighting her after-gun. Directing the gun stood Commander Loftus Jones until he lost a leg at the knee; then he lay on her deck and it began to trouble him that the *Shark*'s ensign gaff had been shot away. Able Seaman Hope ascertained that his Captain was "upset" because the ensign was drooping; so he climbed and unbent it, then rehoisted it at the yard-arm, and the *Shark* went down in the midmost fight with her flag flying. Only six wounded survivors of her company were eventually found on the life-saving raft to which they had carried their Captain. He had died, but had left a name behind him among the heroes of the Victoria Cross.

The fight thundered all about. The British line was bearing down from the north-west, whilst Hipper, his flagship *Lutzow* in flames, had gamely turned again and was approaching from the south-west with Scheer's battleships closely following. Seeing this, the dauntless *Acasta*, her merciful intent frustrated, had turned to torpedo; so had Evan Thomas' *Onslow*, far away on Hipper's other bow.

Acasta's torpedo appeared to hit, and she careered off out of the storm she had provoked, like a tattered mad thing, her engines and helm uncontrollable. The *Onslow* was at once riddled with shell and could only get off one torpedo, which missed. Helpless as she had become, she yet found a mark on the equally helpless *Wiesbaden*. Her last torpedo she fired at the German battle fleet only 8000 yards away. Yet she survived the day.

The stricken *Wiesbaden* fought on; her submerged torpedo-tubes were a standing menace, and Hipper was coming to her rescue. Admiral Arbuthnot with the 1st Cruiser Squadron, determined to forestall him. With a complete disregard of the odds against him, he raced *Defence* and *Warrior* to within 5500 yards of their target. They fought under a continuous rain of salvoes from battle-cruisers and battleships. At last two heavy salvoes struck the *Defence* and she was consumed in a great burst of flame. The *Warrior* remained hardly more than afloat.

There followed a miraculous happening. The *Warspite*, last but one of Evan Thomas' great ships, was turning into the line of battle when she hoisted the signal "Not under control". Her self-chosen course took her in circles right-handed round the mortally-wounded *Warrior*. She continued to fire with every gun, though she was the target of the whole German line proceeding north-eastwards.

About 6.30 p.m. the head of the German line came under a devastating fire. The *Lutzow*, still burning, had fallen out of line; she was nearing her end. The rest of Hipper's squadron, unable to face the hurricane of explosive being poured into them at 9000 yards by the "Invincibles", turned away. Suddenly the *Invincible* herself appeared to the Germans standing out on a light background. The change was characteristic of the patchy visibility in the North Sea; it was fatal to her, for she was promptly deluged with salvoes from the *Derfflinger* and the *König*. A great explosion completely destroyed her, only two officers and four men of the control-top being saved out of over a thousand aboard her.

In anything like clear weather the German Fleet must have been destroyed at this juncture. Its line lay radial to an arc occupied by the Grand Fleet south-east and north-east of its course. Even the chance obscurities which prevented the British from seeing more than a ship or two at a time and different ships at different times could not save it from unbearable punishment. At 6.35, therefore, Scheer ordered his ships to turn about individually. The evolution in itself is risky; with crippled units close to the enemy the risk was very great. But the German Fleet had practised it assiduously, and now boldly performed it. Aided by the low visibility and covered by the German destroyers, the evasion brought immediate relief.

At 7 p.m. the High Seas Fleet was still in a precarious position, with the British between it and its base. It therefore attempted to break back across its enemy's wake, firing at the vagrant *Warspite* as it passed. By this time, however, the *Southampton* had found it for the second time that day and reported its whereabouts. So again Admiral Scheer found the whole British battle-fleet enveloping him with flashes 9000 yards away, and again he ordered the individual turn-away. But a more serious diversion was necessary to cover the turn this time. The four remaining German battle-cruisers, all badly damaged, were ordered to sacrifice themselves—to steam on; also a succession of destroyer attacks laid a smoke screen and fired a large number of torpedoes. From these Jellicoe's ships had to turn away, to escape almost certain destruction.

By 7.20 p.m. the German battle-fleet, in serious disorder, had disappeared completely; even the shattered battle-cruisers, recalled, escaped the doom they had courted. In the failing light Jellicoe had difficulty in finding the enemy. Beatty could still just discern some of them, and he began heading them off from their line of retreat southwards. Meanwhile the Commander-in-Chief had hardly got contact again with the enemy and reformed line of battle when Scheer turned his ships away westwards. They were then lost in the gathering darkness. At 9 p.m. guns were still firing, but the fight soon died away.

In the hope that he might cut the enemy off and be favourably circumstanced to locate him at daylight, Admiral

Jellicoe ordered a course southwards at half speed, in close formation. Beatty's squadrons were sent ahead and the destroyer flotillas were echeloned astern. Further, the *Abdiel* was sent to lay mines in the German swept channel by the Horn Reefs and the Amrum Bank. Submarines of the Harwich Flotilla already lay in wait on the bottom there.

The night fell very dark. At 9.30 the German Admiral began to edge eastwards to the Horn Reefs, designing to pass astern of his enemy. Shortly afterwards occurred the first of a series of terrific encounters with the light forces astern of the Grand Fleet. The general character of all these was much the same. Shapes dimly seen loomed close in the darkness. Recognition lights twinkled. Perhaps no answer came, perhaps even the correct response—in either case breathless and dreadful and sometimes paralysing uncertainty, which not even a blaze of searchlights and a storm of shell quite removed. A few moments of hellish uproar and destruction; feverish work with breech mechanisms and torpedo tubes; searchlights smashed and extinguished; ships ablaze like beacons by which to continue the dreadful work; ships sinking torpedoed; ships rammed, their plating stripped or their structure shorn through. And then darkness again and the scend of the sea.

The *Black Prince* of the 1st Cruiser Squadron was destroyed in such circumstances. She had been far to the west on the wing of the Grand Fleet's advance. Ignorant of the fate of her flagship, *Defence*, she steamed through the night in search of her consorts. What she found no one of her company lived to tell.

Another of these clashes furnished the destroyer *Spitfire* with a remarkable trophy. In the light from her blazing consort *Tipperary* she saw an enemy preparing to ram, so she turned and met her port bow to port bow. High overhead the enemy's guns fired furiously, wrecking *Spitfire's* bridge and destroying her upper works and funnel. Lieut.-Commander Trelawny expected his ship to sink, and so threw overboard the steel chest of secret books. But she did not sink. Though lacking sixty feet of side-plating, she survived;

and she carried into port upon her forecastle twenty feet of steel torn from the dreadnought *Nassau*.

The work of the British destroyers that night outdid even that of the day before.

Early in the night the 2nd Light Cruiser Squadron met a similar German squadron. At 800 yards range the *Dublin* opened fire by searchlight. Switching hers on also, the *Southampton* attacked the *Frauenlob* and sank her with a torpedo. The *Dublin* was much damaged; she lost all her charts and navigating instruments and became temporarily a vagrant of the sea. The *Southampton* took fire; her midship guns' crews and all her searchlight parties had been wiped out. The action lasted fifteen minutes before the enemy drew off into the darkness. It put the last brilliant touch to the work of this squadron since the beginning of the battle.

In spite of such encounters, the German ships ultimately made their escape in the darkness. Thus the greatest naval action of the war had ended indecisively. The British losses were the more numerous. Five fine ships, three of them battle-cruisers, had been destroyed with nearly every soul on board, whereas no enemy vessel had suffered a like fate. The *Warrior* was taken in tow, but sank. The magnificent work of the destroyers and their severe losses had profited little in material damage to the enemy; yet they had played a great part in keeping the battle-fleet intact. Except for Evan Thomas' ships and the *Marlborough*, Jellicoe's battleships were quite unscathed. The Germans had suffered damage throughout their fleet and had lost one battleship, one battle-cruiser, and four light cruisers. It appeared that their ships were the less vulnerable and their projectiles the more deadly.

The spirited fighting of the scouting forces on both sides contrasted with the tactical struggle between the main fleets. Admiral Scheer's tactics were entirely evasive. Under the circumstances this was wise; nevertheless successful evasion is not success, even when you fight another day. This the German High Seas Fleet never did. It spent nearly three months in dockyard hands, then late in August made one last sally. At the approach of the British squadrons it withdrew. Hopelessly outpointed, the German Navy ceased to be a strategic instrument.

SUGGESTIONS FOR READING:

Naval Operations by Sir Julian Corbett, vol. III, pp. 316 *et seq.* *The World Crisis, 1916–18* by W. S. Churchill, pt. I, pp. 111–2.

Chapter XI: THE BATTLE OF THE SOMME

(See map on p. 113)

Rising by gradual terraces from the north bank of the river Somme and by steep spurs from its tributary the Ancre is a mass of rolling downland. The expanse of flattened summit was crowned here and there with woods. Below them nestled little villages in hollows under the crest-lines, as if sheltering their light timber and crumbling daub from the storms of Picardy. To the south-west, in the valley of the Ancre, lay Albert. Connecting it with Bapaume, seventeen kilometres away, a nearly straight road runs north-eastwards across the greatest width of the plateau. To the east in a narrow valley lay the smaller town of Combles. A battle unique in history was fought for the possession of these heights. Their southern and western faces had been converted into a vast fortress scientifically weaponed. During two years the most re-nowned army in Europe had given its ingenuity and labour to this work. It was expelled from this stronghold by civilian soldiers who learned whilst they fought.

All the Allies had agreed to attack their invaders during the summer of 1916; so before the end of 1915 plans were in the making to assault the German line north and south of the river Somme. But the plans underwent great changes. In-stead of 39 French divisions and 25 British assaulting a 48-mile front, only 5 French and 19 British divisions could be found to begin the work. The French had been drained of their strength at Verdun and the British had over-esti-mated their Army's growth. So the British front of attack was reduced to 15 miles, that of the French to 6 miles.

Since the 4th of June the Russians under General Brussiloff had been attacking with success on a vast front between
the Pripet marshes and the Roumanian frontier. On the
9th of June the Italians began a counter-offensive in the
Trentino, where the Austrians had attacked them in the
middle of May.

THE FIRST PHASE

On the 24th of June the guns opened the preparatory
bombardment, and continued it for eight days, 52,000 tons of
ammunition being fired from 1750 guns on a front of 27,000
yards. On July 1st at 7.30 a.m. the infantry of 11 divisions
of General Rawlinson's Fourth Army scrambled out of their
trenches between Maricourt and the Ancre near St Pierre
Divion. Between Maricourt and Fricourt the German first
line was overrun and by mid-day the village of Montauban
was captured. Meanwhile the ridge running westwards from
Montauban had been gained, and the village of Mametz at
its western end. Further west the enemy's line had been
deeply cut into between Fricourt and La Boiselle and between La Boiselle and Ovillers.

Northwards along the steep spurs below Thiepval heroic
fighting carried the terrific defences; often two belts of wire,
each forty yards deep, protected them. But in modern war
such costly heroism is its own undoing; the positions could
not be maintained. At Beaumont Hamel the success of the
attack was equally short-lived. North of the Ancre and eastwards along its valley similar successes were achieved, even
more ambitious in their gallant aims. Incursions into the
enemy's lines, miles in depth, took place; Grandcourt was
reached, Pendant Copse was rushed, Serre was stormed.
But in fortress warfare such dash is too easily quenched. Safe
in thirty-foot dug-outs in the chalk, many machine-guns and
numbers of the enemy remained unaccounted for in the heat
of the onset. Eventually some of our men returned, fighting,
as they had set out; but most were cut off. A subsidiary
attack was made at Gommecourt by two divisions of the
Third Army. It merely reached and occupied the enemy's
front line temporarily.

The French meanwhile, with their smaller force and greater experience, had made a considerable advance and taken 6000 prisoners at a light cost. This was a victory. Compared with the French, the British had failed. The military results of their action, including the 1983 prisoners taken, were small, judged by the scope of the undertaking without taking into account the expectations aroused. What counted was, however, to be measured otherwise. The ordeal of a vast attack, the first which the new British Army made, had left its courage undimmed in spite of appalling losses.

Assured of the temper of his troops, Sir Douglas Haig pressed his advantage in the Somme valley on the following day. Fricourt and Fricourt Wood were taken, and east of this strong counter-attacks were stopped. On the 3rd and 4th Bernafay Wood was taken, and hard fighting on these days at La Boiselle ended with the village in British hands. On the 5th Contalmaison was reached. Meanwhile the newly formed Fifth Army under General Gough was steadily engaging the enemy's front between La Boiselle and Serre.

It was now time to pause. The original military failure was showing signs of undergoing a direct conversion into a growing success. A breach six miles wide had been made in the enemy's first line, his strongest system of defence. A mile back he was struggling hard against continued pressure and had lost four well-fortified villages. The total of prisoners in the hands of the British had mounted to nearly 6000. The presence of the enemy in Contalmaison and Mametz Wood, however, made the resumption of operations on a large scale hazardous. These positions and two others on the flanks, north of Hardecourt and in the outskirts of Ovillers, were accordingly secured. The fighting for Contalmaison and Mametz Wood lasted three days before the village and the greater part of the wood were gained. The village was brilliantly taken three times before it could be held.

During this time the artillery positions had been advanced, and on the 11th a new bombardment began which lasted three days.

Whilst it was still dark on the morning of July 14th, British patrols broke cover and moved more than half a mile

AN 8-INCH HOWITZER BATTERY IN ACTION AT FRICOURT

towards the enemy's second line. The whole attacking force followed them and, with the aid of tapes previously laid out, formed up just below the crest-line where lay the enemy's front. At 3.25 a.m. an advance began which outdid all the gains of previous days. It tried the enemy so severely that he began to show signs of disorganisation shortly after noon. He was given no chance to recover. The infantry pressed on and drove him from the whole of High Wood except its northern corner. Cavalry was then sent forward north-eastwards, but unfortunately this move was a failure, just when success might have brought great results.

A more important crisis in the fortunes of the British Army in attack had not occurred since the Marne. The defensive positions remaining before it were incomplete and German reinforcements had not then arrived in any strength. Now the enemy began pouring in reinforcements and digging for his life. Had consolidation of the advanced positions and the effective use of artillery protection on this day been preferred to the glamour of a cavalry advance, the German awakening to their peril would have been too late. Ultimately the ground up to High Wood had to be abandoned in some depth on the 17th, and the wood was only won for us after two months more of dour struggle. The Army still had much to learn; but that it could both learn and, unfaltering, pay the price of knowledge none now doubted.

When the attack came to an end and the line settled down, a three-mile breach had been made in the German second line; three more village strongholds had been taken—Longueval, Bazentin le Petit, and Ovillers; Trônes Wood and the two Bazentin Woods were ours; and a footing in Delville Wood had been secured. Guillemont, Ginchy, and Pozières lay just in front. Like Delville Wood, they were to make Dominion military history in diverse ways then unforeseen.

The total captures since July 1st now amounted to 10,000 prisoners and 54 guns, apart from trench-mortars and machine-guns. Most valuable gain of all, six thousand yards of the southern edge of the plateau was firmly held. The first phase of this great battle ended not in exhaustion of spirit or even failure of resources, but solely owing to lack of military experience. The New Army had long since acquired skill in defence; it had lately attacked on a great scale with growing effect, though its efforts were often frittered away by lack of direction and faulty liaison between the various arms. However, one of the wider tactical aims of the battle was already achieved; the enemy made his last attack at Verdun on the 13th of July. By the 18th the enemy battalions on the battle-front north of the Somme numbered 138, as compared with 62 on July 1st.

The most inspiring element in the British success, the most full of hope for the future, was the superiority of the Royal Flying Corps over its enemy. This superiority profited the Army immeasurably, though invisibly, since the air war was waged far over the enemy's territory, and during the first stage of the battle hardly a German machine was seen.

During little more than two weeks' fighting the casualties exceeded 80,000. The military result achieved seems utterly lacking in proportion. It weighs hardly at all against the expense of the heroic spirit of the nation, the blood of its best youth, the tears of their beloved. The upturned gaze of endless columns of them passing into battle rested on the leaning Virgin of Albert. It seemed that she held out her Child to them.

THE SECOND PHASE

The change in the character of the fighting at this time was due in part to the enemy's realisation of the danger he was in, and in part to the weather. Low clouds, haze, and much rain spoiled the view for distance fighting, whilst heavy enemy reinforcements made frequent counter-attacks. Therefore the combat became extremely fierce and confused, and the state of the ground, much fought over during dull and wet weather, was indescribable.

Attacks with strictly limited objectives only were undertaken, with the idea of improving the British flanks before renewing the major offensive. On the right Delville Wood and Guillemont were taken and lost many times, wholly and in part, between the beginning and the end of this phase of the battle. The taking of Pozières on the left of the British attack was by contrast a clean-cut assault; it began on the 23rd of July and had gained the whole village by the morning of the 25th. Continuous progress along the Bapaume Road followed. The centre had got a footing in High Wood and climbed to the plateau between there and Longueval on the 20th of July.

But the right flank continued to be a cockpit, in which men were reduced to the direst extremity in their fight with each other and the churned and trackless earth. Through the sodden chaos of Trônes Wood communications ran towards the appalling destruction of Delville Wood and Guillemont. Slipping and floundering for hours at a snail's pace through mud and slime, long files of men went to and fro—carrying-parties with food, water, ammunition of all kinds, engineer and ordnance stores; forward observation parties with their wire and telephone equipment; stretcher-parties piteously burdened; reliefs bulky with arms and full pack and perhaps a parcel from home, struggling after the lightly loaded guide. Linesmen and repairing-parties worked everywhere, trying to make good the effects of the enemy's harassing fire on the communication trenches and the signal lines secured to their dissolving walls. On the roads behind, the confusion of wheeled traffic and marching troops beggars description.

Forward in the support lines the mouths of deep dug-outs gave out the close smell of crowds in hot, damp clothing. The greasy glissade into darkness, which often concealed the original steps, looked revolting even to a hurried seeker after safety. There were many of these, for the support trenches were chronically overcrowded and always subject to bursts of hurricane fire. The front trenches were mostly emerging from the destruction caused by some attack or counter-attack with all its dreadful consequences; the state of them was obscene, especially when they were newly captured. If death had a terror for the men who gave all for their country of their own free will at this period of the war, the terror surely lay in the world of foulness their dying gaze fell upon.

Day by day the routine work went on, in squalor and misery always. Men lived on, soaked with mud and beastly with vermin. Reliefs came and went; the front line filled up and the supports were crammed for attack after attack. Brigades disappeared "over the top" to the sound of every weapon within miles, from the chatter of the machine-guns to the clanging sound of heavy shell-bursts. In the event of success others followed to hold what had been won, and the gruesome work of repair began anew. Such fighting was never known before. Only once subsequently, on the Passchendaele Ridge, was it perhaps equalled in ferocity and hardship. The loss and the maiming of the best of the nation was terrible, but more terrible was the loss of touch with the simple, cleanly, comfortable ways of life. This begot an unforgettable misery, from the memory of which a man's nature must ever recoil shudderingly during the rest of his life.

Flanders has long borne the name of "the Cockpit of Europe"; but if there is one spot of its old blood-stained border-line which might assert a prior claim to the dreadful title, it is the few square miles around Guillemont. For here the whole armed strengths and military ingenuities of three nations concentrated on the solution of a comparatively small tactical problem. They solved it by the method of trial and error, each side exploiting every possibility in attack and defence and sounding the utmost depths of human misery in order to get the upper hand.

Bit by bit the Allied commanders unravelled the tangle of German defences; deed by deed the rank and file attained to a moral superiority over the enemy. By the middle of August Guillemont station was definitely in British hands, and on the 24th much ground was gained to the east and north of Delville Wood, which our men had long called "Devil's Wood", with reason. Finally in the first week of September, the whole battle front blazed up in a general attack and the 20th Division took Guillemont. On the same day Ginchy was reached. Three days of obstinate struggle followed, but Guillemont was held against all counter-attacks; meanwhile the ruins of Ginchy changed hands time after time. Another general attack was launched on the 9th of September, when the right flank of the battle line cleared in one great bound the obstacles which had cramped it. This carried the British line into Bouleaux Wood, overcame the resistance of Ginchy, and broke the enemy's next line of defence eastwards. At the same time the French advanced their line to Combles and Cléry-sur-Somme.

The struggle which the British Army waged for a footing on the heights from about Thiepval to near Combles had something of the character of the labours of Sisyphus. Painfully slowly and with many a slip backwards, but yet surely, the burden of Prussian "blood and iron" was thrust upwards and over the crest-line of these Somme spaces, till the gun-flashes betrayed for miles at night that the heights were won. The area gained in this phase was considerable and, from its commanding situation, of great importance. The cost of it was 104,000 casualties, raising the casualty rate to 18,000 a week from 5,000, the average for the Expeditionary Force. Notwithstanding, the "rifle-strength" of the Army at the end of August was 650,000, only 10,000 less than on July 1st.

THE THIRD PHASE

The British Commander-in-Chief now found himself in a position to undertake a more ambitious operation. A new weapon was ready for his use, the "Tank", so named for the sake of secrecy during manufacture; moreover, a great improvement in artillery tactics had been evolved in the "creeping barrage". At 6.20 a.m. on the 15th of September, after three days' bombardment, the Fourth Army infantry advanced to the assault of the third system of German defences. Forty-eight tanks were to have accompanied them, but about half failed to reach the field owing to breakdowns. Nine divisions went into action. The homogeneity of the Army is well illustrated, for two were regular divisions, one Dominion, three New Army, and three Territorial. Their spirit was advertised by the lad who carried forward into action a newspaper placard bearing in large type the legend "GREAT BRITISH VICTORY".

Many hours of severe struggle ended with the expulsion
of the Germans from High Wood. The possession of the mess
of craters and splintered timber had been won only at a great
sacrifice, but elsewhere progress was neither costly nor difficult. At 10 a.m. men accompanied by tanks were swarming
through Flers towards Gueudecourt. Morval and Lesboeufs
were also threatened. During the afternoon the attack was
taken up by two divisions of the right of the Fifth Army,
which drove the enemy out of Martinpuich and Courcelette.

This advance of a mile on a front of six miles was the
greatest success hitherto achieved in the Somme battle at
one effort; 4000 prisoners were taken. To add to the enemy's
increasing burdens in defence, the French at this time were
able to begin operations south of the Somme, attacking towards Chaulnes, so much had the pressure at Verdun been
reduced. Unfortunately bad weather came on and slowed
down the progress, though the operations were not dis-
continued. A successful attack opened the way to Morval,
where a redoubt called "the Quadrilateral", which had
barred the approach to the village, was stormed and taken
on the 18th.

The minor gains of the succeding days were the steps to a
further general advance. Accordingly on the 25th the
Fourth Army again attacked. Morval was carried, and
north of it Lesboeufs; Gueudecourt was approached, but
could not be stormed. Further west a half-mile advance
brought Eaucourt l'Abbaye within assaulting distance. The
fighting was deadly, because the infantry was insufficiently
trained to follow the barrage closely, and no battle-guide
but the barrage availed on ground so deceptive in its wasted
sameness.

On the following day a striking development of battle
organisation completed the work of the 25th before Gueudecourt. A tank, followed by bombers and co-operating with an
aeroplane, cleared a length of trench which was the main
defence west of the village. After a great many of the garrison
had been killed, the remainder, nearly 400 in number, surrendered. The village was then carried. This first beginning
of the combined tactics of the future, which were to be the

The Battle of the Somme

decisive factor in battle, was warranted by its effectiveness. Tanks had begun to justify themselves and the improvement of this arm was seriously undertaken.

The advance north of Combles on the 25th was equalled south of it, where the French took Rancourt and Frégicourt. Combles, now dominated from the heights on either hand, was evacuated by the enemy. Great quantities of stores and ammunition were found there in extensive underground galleries.

Whilst the enemy was still staggering under the blows of the Fourth Army and the French, he was assailed at Thiepval by the Fifth Army. This firm western bastion of the German defence was a maze of saps sited above the steep spurs which buttress the Thiepval Ridge in the valley of the Ancre. Soon after midday on the 26th the British infantry, assisted by tanks, began a methodical clearance of the enemy from his fortress. The fighting was very stern and lasted for a day and a half, the tanks playing an important part in it. Thiepval village was taken with 2300 prisoners, and counter-attack after counter-attack failed to regain it.

Since the 14th of September nearly 10,000 prisoners, 27 guns, 40 trench-mortars, and 200 machine-guns had been taken. Other evidence than this made it certain that the German resistance had been seriously shaken. Their trench system and the endurance of their troops had suffered grave damage. Their case was precarious, for of all the great fortress they had held on July 1st only the formidable bastion about Serre remained; and Serre was being surely turned. On their part the British found that their attacks were increasingly effective, whilst nevertheless their casualty returns were diminishing. It was clear that their confidence was maintained, their skill and battle-craft were growing. Favourable opportunities for the exercise of these attainments became fewer, however, as the season advanced.

The weather now began to interfere seriously with operations. Three days' continuous rain in the beginning of October made the conditions on the battlefield too difficult for the most determined spirit. Men and horses became exhausted in the mere struggle against mud and tempest;

sometimes in the front-line trenches only death could release men gripped by the devouring mud. The enemy was more fortunate, but suffered also, for a captured letter full of the horror of the struggle spoke of "the blood-bath of the Somme".

Early in October, trench by trench the ground north and east of Thiepval was taken. A larger-scale attack carried Eaucourt l'Abbaye and advanced the British line considerably east and west of the village. The enemy's military distress was now so obvious that both the French and British commands planned to strike blows from which they hoped for great successes. On the 10th of October a French Army commanded by General Nivelle recaptured forts Douaumont and Vaux at Verdun. The British Commander-in-Chief had in preparation a large-scale operation to reap the fruits of victory on the Somme and the Ancre. The moment was ripe; could he but take the last remaining defence-line covering Sailly-Saillisel, Le Transloy, Bapaume, and Grevillers before others were added to it, he might hope to advance more rapidly north-eastwards. The enemy's position before Arras would be difficult; he might be constrained even to retire thence.

The great general action was never fought. The weather got worse and worse during October, and only minor operations could be carried out. Ultimately the projected operation had to be whittled down to an attack on Beaumont Hamel.

For four days the weather had been dry and frosty, for two the British guns had turned the heights north and south of the Ancre into winking smoke-hazed beacons of high explosive. The assault took place at 5.45 a.m. on November 13th in dense fog. St Pierre Divion, attacked from the south, soon fell, and the prisoners taken there outnumbered the attacking force. North of the river the fighting was very heavy for two days. At the end of this time the troops, having shown great tenacity, had possessed themselves of Beaucourt and had got a firm footing on the crest of the Beaumont Hamel spur well to the east and north of the village. A series of strongholds, improved in accordance with the experience of the last few months and worked at for years previously, had been carried with great skill, the 63rd (Royal Naval) Division particularly distinguishing itself. This striking success was hardly achieved ere the weather set in stormy again. Had the grand attack, of which this was the fraction, been possible, far-reaching gains must have been effected, for at this time there was no "Hindenburg Line".

No eulogy of his troops by a general can surpass that of the British Commander-in-Chief in his "Somme Despatch" dated 3rd December, 1916. In language of perfect restraint he pays a tribute of praise to the Somme Army's deeds and sufferings which reveals the devotion of all to a praiseworthy ideal through great tribulation. The British casualties on the whole Western Front between July 1st and November 19th, were 463,000. The battle of the Somme caused 410,000 of these. During this period the total captures amounted to 38,000 prisoners, 29 heavy guns, 96 field guns and howitzers, 136 trench-mortars, and 514 machine-guns. The Commander-in-Chief could well be satisfied with the progress which the men he led had made as soldiers in a great military organisation. Ninety-seven German divisions had been needed, from first to last, to sustain their onset; of these 32 had been used twice and 4 three times. Moreover, decreasing losses and increasing captures of prisoners characterised the progress of the action.

As if to crown the Allies' achievements this year, a very complete defeat overtook the Germans at Verdun. In December General Nivelle recovered Caurières Wood in the Woevre, thus re-establishing the integrity of the Verdun defences.

THE RETREAT TO THE HINDENBURG LINE

The British position on the heights astride the Ancre lent itself to the making of echeloned advances up the valley. During the winter operations were carried out amongst the morasses on both banks, whenever the weather and the state of the ground permitted. The first step of the advance, made on the 18th of November, reached the high ground on the south bank overlooking Pys and Grandcourt. The next step,

Imperial War Museum Photo. Crown copyright

IN THE VALLEY OF THE ANCRE, 1916

delayed by the season until January 11th, crushed the enemy's remaining hold on the Beaumont Hamel spur. In successive stages of the advance during the next five weeks the Beaucourt valley was crossed, Grandcourt taken, and the enemy defences before Miraumont and Serre threatened. Finally the taking of the northern extremity of the Courcelette spur on the 17th of February rendered the German positions about Pys and Miraumont untenable.

During this time the British share of the line had been extended southwards to before Roye. Its length was now 110 miles, no one of which was ever quiet for long. Numerous raids provided much information, and about this time signs were revealed that the enemy intended to withdraw everywhere between Arras and the Aisne north-west of Rheims. The German Supreme Command, revived by the prestige of Hindenburg and the capacity of Ludendorff (Falkenhayn had been appointed to the chief command against Roumania), set about economising its men and providing for the recovery of their moral by taking up a newly prepared line of defence—the "Hindenburg Line".

Immediately after the British success on February 17th the Germans abandoned Pys, Miraumont, and Serre. Then their positions eastwards to Warlencourt and Gueudecourt were evacuated almost at once. By the 14th of March the withdrawal was general, and was being carried out with uncanny skill. Everywhere the Germans deceived their enemy as to the moment of their departure. As they retired, moreover, they destroyed roads, bridges, railways, buildings, trees, even the orchards of the peasant proprietors. They also left behind them booby-traps and delay-action mines. The pursuit was in consequence no headlong dash. Bridging, road-repairing, drawing charges, and laying railways had to be done before the artillery could be got forward and the heavy ammunition traffic which it requires begun. Meanwhile the infantry felt their way forward cautiously, with frequent skirmishes, and not until the end of the first week in April was contact with the outlying defences of the Hindenburg Line gained everywhere south of Arras.

Thus for the moment the chief anxiety of the German

Supreme Command ended. Yet, as has been since learned from Ludendorff's memoirs, they believed themselves in peril of defeat before the end of the year, unless unrestricted submarine warfare should save the situation.

SUGGESTIONS FOR READING:

The Irish Guards in the Great War by Rudyard Kipling, vol. 1, pp. 169–73. *The Old Front Line* by John Masefield. *A Subaltern on the Somme* by "Mark VII", pp. 150–1, 156–63. *The Somme* by A. D. Gristwood.

Chapter XII: WINTER 1916–17: A GENERAL SURVEY

THE events of the summer of 1916 had brought the German nation face to face with the possibility that ultimate victory might not be theirs. There had been no break-through in the main theatre of war, nor for the moment was there any danger that the Allies would break through the shortened line. But for the first time the German Army had been compelled to give ground before an enemy who had hitherto been far behind it in military preparation and experience and was now obviously catching up. Moreover the effects of the blockade of Germany were beginning to be felt; hunger and sickness were spreading among the civil population.

Though the outlook was dark, neither Germany's leaders nor her people could bring themselves to bargain with her enemies; but this moment was chosen to inform the government of the United States of the terms on which Germany would make peace, in the hope that the intervention of a neutral power might force the Allies to treat with her.

But the gulf between the two sides was now a moral rather than a political one. So far as the Allies were concerned, there was no desire to prolong the agony merely for the sake of fighting. There was military deadlock on every front. A stop-gap campaign was being waged by the imperfected British Army at awful cost. The Navy was carrying on a tantalising, sleepless, silent watch on the seas. Statesmen were failing under the strain, for the first Coalition Government had recently dissolved and Mr Asquith had been replaced by Mr Lloyd George as Prime Minister. Lord Grey had been succeeded in the office of Foreign Secretary by Mr Balfour. Lord Kitchener was dead, lost in the *Hampshire* on his way to Russia, which was now threatened with revolution. France was tired and given up to the idea of ending the war with one supreme effort—one only—in the spring. Roumania, which had joined the Allies in August, had been speedily over-run by a German Army under von Mackensen. England herself was finding that the new warfare jeopardised her island security and took non-combatants into its clutches, for there had been numerous Zeppelin raids by night and enemy aeroplanes had even bombed London in daylight. Yet to make peace with an unashamed and, as it proved, quite unshaken military autocracy seemed a wicked waste of all that had been done and suffered. Her treachery towards Belgium, whom she still proposed to treat as a prize of war, made it impossible to negotiate with Germany. Her latest terms were such as only a victor might dictate to vanquished foes, and by the end of December she learned that the Allies would have none of them.

Germany, disillusioned in her hopes of bringing her enemies to terms, now had recourse to her most formidable weapon against Great Britain. Submarine warfare had already proved a menace to the British command of the seas which was vital to the interests of all the Allies; but so long as the German Fleet had been liable to leave its harbours, their submarine strength had been divided between strictly naval operations and attacks on merchant-shipping. Damage to American shipping by "U boats" had almost caused a breach with the United States, only avoided by Germany's agreeing to certain restrictions on commerce-raiding. Early in 1917, however, she broke her pledges and began to use submarines ruthlessly against all shipping navigating the seas around the British Isles.

This was a direct challenge to the United States. Hitherto neither side in the European struggle had had much reason to hope for the adhesion of America, for though Great Britain had felt that a great nation descended from her own colonists could hardly side against her at such a crisis, she was learning that twentieth-century America is not a homogeneous community of English-speaking people. Moreover, British activity on the sea, as well as the submarine tactics of Germany, had caused embarrassment to the United States, and during the previous year Anglo-American relations had been acutely strained.

This latest move on Germany's part weighed down the scale in the opposite direction, and was speedily followed by damage to American life and property at sea. By the beginning of April 1917 the lengthy exchange of Notes between President Wilson and the fighting Powers had ended and America had joined the Allies.

British anxieties now found relief and financial difficulties were eased. But, though naval assistance in submarine-hunting was soon forthcoming from America, it was obvious that many months—perhaps more than a year—must elapse before American troops could take their place in the field; meanwhile the critical summer campaign must be weathered by the Allies on their own resources. And there had appeared in another quarter a cloud, at this moment no bigger than a man's hand but soon to darken the whole sky. In March the government of the Czar of Russia fell. At first the effects of this event were not foreseen, and some even thought that Russia would now fight with renewed vitality. None realised that within a few months the whole nation would be paralysed by revolution and that masses of German troops and material would be released for employment on the Western Front. It was a merciful Providence that brought one great ally to our side at the moment of another's collapse; but the loss was to make itself felt so long before the gain as to bring the Allied cause to the brink of disaster.

SUGGESTIONS FOR READING:

Twenty-five Years by Viscount Grey of Fallodon, vol. II, pp. 113, 127.
Foundations of the Science of War by Col. J. F. C. Fuller, p. 111 and note.

Chapter XIII: THE BATTLE OF ARRAS

(See map on p. 127)

THE plan of the 1917 campaign agreed upon by the Allies in November was doomed to change and then to failure. It had been prepared under General Joffre's direction, but in December both he and General Foch ceased to command in the field, having been severely criticised for the losses incurred in the autumn offensive. In Joffre's stead the French Government appointed General Nivelle, who had recently been brilliantly successful against the Germans at Verdun.

Under the agreed scheme, carefully proportioned tasks were assigned to each of the Allies. Nicely timed attacks of growing power on important objectives were to lead up to the main blows, which, it was hoped, would redeem the Belgian coast-line and break through the German defences elsewhere. But, encouraged by his recent experiences and impelled by the anxiety of the French people for a speedy and decisive victory, their new Commander-in-Chief decided on a bolder course. He prepared to exert the whole might of the French Army in striking a decisive blow at the earliest moment. Incidentally, an effort was to be made to give Nivelle the Supreme Command on the Western Front. This project was favoured by the British Prime Minister, Mr Lloyd George, but not by General Sir William Robertson, the Chief of the Imperial General Staff. So the British went on with their part of the originally agreed scheme.

Meanwhile the German retreat had added to the Allies' preparatory work and made the chances of success less favourable. General Nivelle's plan was the more gravely prejudiced. Sir Douglas Haig found it possible to adjust his arrangements to the change in the tactical situation without much trouble; but his hope of cutting off large numbers of the enemy south of Arras had gone.

The battle of Arras was begun on Easter Monday, the 9th of April. At 5.30 a.m. the British front threw up wave after wave of attacking infantry belonging to the First and Third Armies. They poured over the German line in the wake of a moving curtain of shell-fire, and soon after six o'clock the whole of the enemy's forward system was occupied from just north of Croisilles to almost the northern end of the Vimy Ridge, a stretch of fourteen miles. At 7.30 a.m. the attack, having reformed, stormed the German second line, most of which was carried also, though the Railway Triangle, due east of Arras, and a ridge just south of it held out. South of the Arras–Cambrai road the second stage of the advance was completed by noon. Neuville-Vitasse and Tilloy-les-Mofflaines were taken, and between these points a whole German battalion was captured at the Harp redoubt. Further south, St Martin-sur-Cojeul was taken. Though the resistance in the Railway Triangle was not mastered until 2 p.m., the general advance was resumed shortly after mid-day; it drove the enemy mile upon mile down the valley of the Scarpe, on the slopes of which two more entrenched systems were stormed and taken. To the north, on the Vimy Ridge, the enemy's third system was cleared, the hardest fighting falling to the 4th Canadian Division, who had to deal with deep underground tunnels occupied by the enemy reserves.

Progress at this rate is remarkable, having in view the fighting of the previous year. It would seem that what took a month to win in the battle of the Somme and a week in the battle of the Ancre required but an hour on this stormy Easter Monday. Material improvements, more heavy guns, higher training, and greater experience made the difference. Among the material improvements were a new fuse for high explosive shell, the gas projector, and new types of tanks and aeroplanes. The fuse detonated on the lightest touch without forming a crater, so that the resulting shell-burst raked the neighbourhood with splinters; and in the preliminary bombardment, which lasted six days, 2880 guns fired 88,000 tons of ammunition. For the handling of the new gas weapon "Special Companies R.E." were organised; hundreds of gas bombs from trench-mortars were fired simultaneously into a crowded area of the enemy's front-line defences, and the dense and unexpected concentration of phosgene gas caused frightful mortality. That all these advantages over the weapons of the previous year could be used effectively shows how the work of the Army had improved in the time. A magnificent spirit prevailed among the troops, unimpaired by the campaign of the previous year or by the drawbacks to compulsory service. An increasing use was made of the special knowledge of men professionally trained in civil life. Rail transportation had been improved and augmented; the provision for and control of road traffic was worthy of great centres of population; shelter, heat, light, means for the preparation of food and the supply of water for concentrations of troops were forthcoming as required; personal cleanliness and sanitation were specially catered for.

So it was that the troops assembled for the action near Arras could be maintained in comfort till the blow was struck. Large numbers of them even lived in the labyrinth of deep caves under the ruins of the city, which had been joined up by tunnels and lighted by electricity. Hutted camps sprang up and a little army of Labour units was employed in erection and maintenance. Meanwhile the fighting troops were just as busy in the forward area on new construction of more direct military importance—gun emplacements, deep shelters, and saps. All these developments contributed to make the first onset at the battle of Arras the striking success it was; yet it failed to make good the design for the subsequent attack. The prolonged defence of the Railway Triangle spoiled this.

The critical juncture in the tactics of the battle lay in the relaying of the attack with fresh troops. Two fresh divisions were to pass at midday through the thinned ranks of the three which had made the initial assault in the valley of the Scarpe; and to cover and prepare their advance, guns had to be got forward to destroy the wire protecting the last completed line of the enemy's defences. Colloquially this went by the name of "leap-frogging". The principle in all its simplicity governed Xenophon's use of some of his troops fighting their way across the mountains of Kurdistan into Armenia. So great, however, is the contrast between this and modern fortress warfare that a comparison is hardly to be made. Enormous numbers of men, masses of material, and unwieldy weapons must go forward in order and strictly to time. The ways they must take, over ground reduced to the state in which years of sapping and shelling have left it, require rapid repair and preparation. The task is as great as it is delicate. Any hitch in the arrangements or their execution risks that worst of disorganisations which comes from within—all this apart from the chances of war.

It was only the chance of war which hindered the relaying divisions. The artillery advance to the neighbourhood of the Railway Triangle could not be made in time. The guns had to carry out their wire-cutting bombardment of the enemy's further strongholds from their original positions at extreme ranges. Accordingly the 37th Division, advancing south of the Scarpe, was held up by uncut wire before Monchy-le-Preux, and the resulting delay was not overcome in time to forestall the arrival of the enemy's reinforcements. Just north of the Scarpe there was no hitch and the last completed line of the enemy's defence was pierced. Elsewhere the Germans were giving ground under steady pressure.

Meanwhile three divisions of cavalry had been assembling east of Arras. Small bodies of mounted men were sent forward along both banks of the Scarpe, where they rounded up many prisoners and took some guns. A general advance of the cavalry, however, was impracticable. The breach in the enemy's defences was not wide enough, and the avenue on the northern bank which lay open to the mounted troops was commanded from the heights about Monchy, still in the enemy's hands. So the mass of the cavalry was withdrawn.

That evening the weather, which had changed during the day, actually broke. For many days it remained stormy, with heavy falls of snow. Movement and observation were sadly interfered with.

During the night heavy fighting continued south of the Scarpe. On the morning of the 10th the approaches to Monchy-le-Preux were won in spite of fierce opposition and the hardships of the time. The rest of the German third line was taken in a general advance soon after noon. Desperate efforts to overcome the resistance of the enemy in Monchy continued to be made, and it was decided after all to hazard the cavalry in a general advance; two divisions rode round Monchy whilst the third advanced along the north bank of the river. Their remarkable forlorn hope was shattered by machine-gun fire, and for days the approach to the village remained littered with their gallant remains.

On the 11th the tenacity of the 37th Division prevailed. Monchy on its conical hillock was taken. Further south, Heninel and Wancourt became the scene of stiff fighting. It had been planned to join hands east of these villages with two divisions of the Fifth Army. On this day these carried the Hindenburg Line about Bullecourt and penetrated deeply into the German positions. They withdrew when the Third Army's troops failed to reach them owing to the resistance at Heninel and Wancourt. These villages did not fall until next day.

Near the northern limit of the battle area an attack along the Souchez River carried "the Pimple" on the northern shoulder of the Vimy Ridge. This deprived the enemy of his last foothold on the high ground and all hope of regaining the heights of Vimy, so he withdrew some distance eastwards on to low ground, where he could fight on even terms of observation. In doing so he abandoned guns, stores, and ammunition, and evacuated many villages and the town of Liévin, south-west of Lens.

Meanwhile the German Supreme Command was hurrying troops towards the gap in the line, and all possible labour was employed to complete a line of defence east of the break. This defence, previously projected and surveyed, joined the Hindenburg defences to the La Bassée system, and was known as the "Drocourt–Quéant Switch". The Supreme Command spent an anxious time making good the German losses in men and material.

The arrival of strong enemy reinforcements showed in the fierce counter-attacks begun on April 14th. Monchy was their first and principal objective. Throughout this day the enemy strove fruitlessly to retake it from the 29th Division. Later, on the 23rd and 24th of April, Gavrelle was assaulted eight times, and on the 28th and 29th seven times more. At

Roeux the line swayed back and forth in bitter struggle for many days. At the price of untold suffering and heavy loss the enemy gained time for the completion and manning of the Drocourt–Quéant Switch.

Though there was now no hope of breaking up the enemy's defence east of Arras and gravely discomfiting him, the British attacks had to be continued for two reasons. Nivelle's great offensive on the Aisne was delayed by the weather and by French political dissensions, and a new British concentration was forward in Flanders, where the main campaign of the year was to be fought.

Some of the British attacks of the waning battle were real, some were dummies. The real ones rolled up the Hindenburg Line to a point seven miles south-east of Arras and took Wancourt Tower and the ridge east of Heninel. After twenty-four hours of the fiercest fighting in the whole war, Guémappe and the ground overlooking Fontaine-les-Croisilles and Chérisy were taken. North of the Scarpe Gavrelle, Arleux, Fresnoy, and Cité des Petits Bois fell after a similar struggle. In almost the last of these attacks the Australians took a thousand yards of the Hindenburg Line east of Bullecourt. For four days, from the 3rd to the 7th of May, the men of the 1st, 2nd, and 5th Australian Divisions held on to their gains unsupported. On the 7th a footing was gained in Bullecourt village by the 7th Division, but the village was not completely captured until the 17th. The Australians, open to attack from all sides during this fortnight, had performed a memorable feat of arms. It was not until the 16th of June that the section of the Hindenburg Line west of Bullecourt was captured. In the meantime Roeux had been finally taken, but Fresnoy had been lost.

The dummy attacks caused the enemy great excitement, during which he shot to pieces large numbers of lay figures worked by ropes and some imitation tanks in "No Man's Land". Sir Douglas Haig notes G.H.Q.'s embarrassment at being unable to deny German reports of the bloody repulse of great British attacks which had not been made. There was, however, one genuine attack, on May 3rd, which was an almost complete failure.

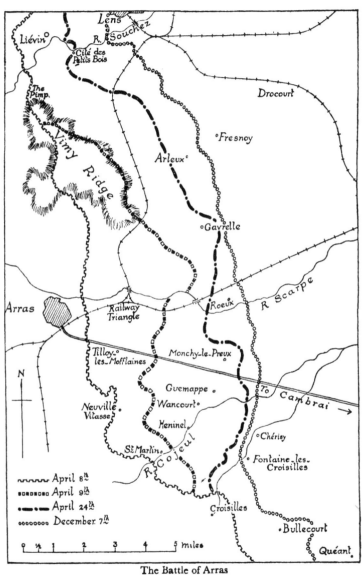

The Battle of Arras

The Commander-in-Chief summed up the results of all this fighting thus: "Our line had been advanced to a greatest depth of five miles on a front of over twenty miles. . . . A great improvement had been effected in the general situation of our troops on the front attacked and the capture of the Vimy Ridge had removed a constant menace to the security of our line". Nearly 20,000 prisoners, 257 guns, 227 trench-mortars, and 464 machine-guns were taken during less than a month's fighting.

These results were sufficiently heartening to a nation now persuaded to the "war of attrition". Nevertheless there were minds critical and unsatisfied that strategic success should be so elusive. There were, too, minds of an inventive turn busy on evolving means to overcome the strength of the modern defence. The fruitless hazarding of the mass of cavalry on the second day of the battle had clearly shown the strategic need of the moment. Their fatal vulnerability in spite of their mobility provided the key to the problem of satisfying this need. It was to unlock the ponderous armoury of the future.

SUGGESTIONS FOR READING:
The World Crisis, 1916–18 by W. S. Churchill, pt. I, pp. 282–3, 285.

Chapter XIV: SALONICA, PALESTINE, AND MESOPOTAMIA, 1916–17

(See maps on pp. 79, 176, and 138)

SALONICA, 1916

THE Allies' prospects in Macedonia suffered by trickery. In May 1916 the Greek garrison surrendered the fortifications of the Rupel Pass to the Bulgars after the merest formality of resistance. This greatly strengthened the enemy's defence and closed the one practicable line of advance into Bulgaria.

The increasingly unsympathetic attitude of the Greek Army and Court compelled drastic measures to limit their power to harm. Hitherto the Allies had exercised great forbearance, for the Greeks were in a painful position; now with the support of M. Venizelos, they forced the demobilisation of most of the Greek Army and the confinement of the remainder to the Peloponnese. Ultimately in the following year King Constantine was made to abdicate and M. Venizelos, who formed a government, was able to bring Greece into her proper place in support of her ally Serbia; thereafter an increasing army of Greeks strengthened the Allied line. Meanwhile, secure in the possession of Fort Rupel, the enemy was able during August to overrun the whole province of Kavalla.

All the summer the British troops and their allies were hard at work entrenching and road-making on a much larger scale than in the winter. The new front lay along the river Struma and traversed the Doiran foot-hills to the Vardar. The positions were everywhere inferior to those of the enemy, which had been chosen at leisure and fortified under German direction. Their line was extremely strong and it enjoyed splendid advantages of forward observation. The Allies were poorly served even by balloon observation, so deep and dark were the ravines in which the enemy gun-positions lay.

Nevertheless offensive operations were necessary in support of the Roumanian Army, which ultimately took the field on the 27–28th of August. So on August 10th the French and British started an attack, which was making good progress when the enemy turned the tables dramatically. He also was conscious that a military effort might influence Roumania's intentions and even neutralise her enterprise; so on August 18th he opened an offensive. With the connivance of the Greek frontier guards he surprised the Serbs on the Epirus front, took Koritza and Florina, and drove back the exile defenders to Lake Ostrovo. Simultaneously he completed his occupation of the Kavalla province, though he was rudely received in Kavalla itself by the guns of the Fleet.

The Allied effort was given a new direction as promptly as might be. First the French, then the two Russian brigades, and finally, in November, the 35th Italian Division were drawn off from the Struma and Doiran fronts to join in the fighting which won back Monastir. In this struggle the Serbian Army revealed magnificent qualities; its successful assaults turned line after line of strong defences in the rich plain before Monastir.

The British contribution to the campaign lay in maintaining an increasing length of active front. By the end of November our line was ninety miles long, from the mouth of the Struma to the Vardar at Macukovo. To tie down the two Bulgarian Armies opposed to them, the British progressively pushed across and up the wide levels of the Struma valley and, between September 10th and the end of October, took village after village in the direction of Seres and Demirhissar. The Macukovo salient was assaulted on the night of October 13th. Its German garrison was overcome and the position occupied, the raiders eventually withdrawing on the evening of the 14th. During October the first battalion of Venizelist Greek troops came into line.

In these operations the battle casualties of the Army were encouragingly moderate, but the sickness rate, mostly due to malaria and dysentery, was appalling. Sixty thousand cases of malaria were under treatment in base hospitals at one time in September.

The operations were successful in regaining a foothold in Serbia. The enemy was constrained to evacuate Monastir, which had for him a high sentimental value. But the victors were so exhausted that, though the enemy showed every intention of retiring on Prilep, it was impossible to maintain the necessary pressure. Thus no strategic advantage was gained; even the town itself lay under the scourge of the enemy's guns little more than two miles away.

The lot of the British Salonica Army was the least enviable of any of the Expeditionary Forces. Partly this was ill luck, partly it was poor leading. The section of the line held by the British was not a good or even a possible strategic take-off. This was no fault of theirs, nor was the lack of reserves necessary to the making of general attacks. But in these circumstances low ground dominated by the enemy and even more by disease-bearing parasites should have been shunned. To be only a part of a force of many nations, facing the least hopeful part of a position the force was too weak to take, holding a line it was never more than strong enough to defend, month after month pestered by parasites and prostrated by disease, is a wretched lot. But as on every other front, discipline was maintained spontaneously at the level the conditions required. To see the thing through became the only duty, and it was selflessly and cheerfully performed. The sorest trial of the troops was the contempt, too lightly spoken on many a lip, for their isolated, primitive task; for they fought, dug, and died of wounds or disease with distinction.

SALONICA, 1917

Roumania had been promptly crushed in the previous year, yet some sort of blaze had to be kindled in the Near East in 1917 to start the hoped-for conflagration on the Russian front without which the offensive in the west lacked an essential element. Accordingly General Sarrail ordered the resumption of the advance on Prilep. The British were to undertake the assault of the enemy's positions on the hills east, and particularly west, of Doiran; at the same time they were to make a demonstration along the Vardar. This was essentially the same plan which brought the campaign to a successful end in the autumn of the following year. Its result in 1917 was only a severe casualty-list. A more useless sacrifice of troops did not occur during the whole war.

Troops of the 26th and 22nd Divisions attacked on April 24th through barrages which the enemy was enabled to put down in anticipation, for it would seem that nothing had been done to prevent him getting information through his listening-sets. Moreover the British barrage had demonstrated the scope of their effort, and incidentally its inadequacy, at a rehearsal two days before. Still the infantry struggled gallantly up the slopes and through barraged ravines. Every slope was dominated from the next above and only tenable at impossible cost; and though a further assault on May the 8th was successful in reaching its objectives, these could not be held against persistent counterattacks. The fighting spirit of the troops appears in the bearing of Captain F. A. Durno-Steele of the Oxfords; he was twice or thrice wounded and had a leg shattered, but he sat on the enemy's parapet and threw bombs until he fell back dead. But all this availed nothing. Having advanced to the assault at 9.50 p.m. on the 8th, the troops held on out of sheer doggedness until the following afternoon. Then the order was given to evacuate the hill they clung to. Meanwhile the Allied hopes of disengaging Monastir had come to naught.

Towards the end of May, under cover of a demonstration on the Struma plain, the British troops were withdrawn to the heights overlooking it from the west. The Bulgars then sent a message that they were doing the same on their side and that the message would be their only demonstration. During the summer months No Man's Land on the Struma had a width of from twelve to twenty miles, reserved to the anopheles mosquito.

PALESTINE

During the latter part of 1916 the Eastern Force, with the Desert Mounted Column in its van, continued to push forward across the desert, while the railway advanced in its rear. On December 20th it reached its first principal objective, El Arish, which the enemy vacated without a blow; this offered the advantage of a harbour of sorts, to which supplies from the base could be brought by sea.

On January 9th, 1917, by capturing Rafa our troops reached the Egyptian frontier. Khan Yunus was occupied on February 28th, and early in March the Turks fell back and dug in on the line Gaza–Sheria, with Beersheba held as a strongly fortified outpost on their left or eastern flank. The British force was now on the border of the Land of Promise, with the desert at their backs. They had reached the Flanders of the Middle East, the plains of Philistia, on which the Jews had looked down fearfully from their fastnesses in the hills while the armies of Egypt from the south did battle with those of Assyria from the north and east.

There could be no further advance without a battle on a large scale. Our communications were precarious, with nearly 150 miles of desert, spanned only by a pipe-line and a single line of railway, which had by now reached Rafa, between the troops and their base. There was no port to help them with sea communications until they should fight their way at least as far north as Jaffa. To strike at Beersheba, and so reach the Turkish railway, would have brought their lines of communication for the last 30 miles directly parallel to the enemy's front—a most dangerous proceeding. Sir Archibald Murray therefore decided to attack Gaza. There were several further arguments in favour of this course. It meant fighting at shorter radius from rail-head, and with naval guns to protect the left flank. The water-supply would be less hazardous and the flat country more suited to the rapid advance of the railway.

Sir Charles Dobell's troops comprised the 54th (East Anglian) Division, 52nd (Lowland) Division, and the Camel Corps, with the Desert Column, which contained the Australian and New Zealand Mounted Division, Imperial Mounted Division, and 53rd Division (mainly Welsh troops), under Sir Philip Chetwode. The Turkish line was not continuously held. Gaza had a garrison of some 7000 and a number of isolated posts stretched as far east as Beersheba.

FIRST BATTLE OF GAZA

The plan of the battle was for the cavalry, advancing early in the morning of March 26th, to hold the country north and east of Gaza and prevent the arrival of reinforcements. The 53rd Division would follow them and attack the town from the south. The 54th Division would occupy the Sheik Abbas ridge, to protect their right flank and rear from the threat of Turkish troops advancing from the east. The main object of the attack was to cut off Gaza, occupy the town, and capture its garrison. Speed was of paramount importance, both because the attack was essentially a surprise and because until

Gaza was in our hands there would be no water for men or horses.

Failure was due to no fault in the plan nor to any lack of enterprise or stamina in the troops, who marched and fought without flagging throughout the whole of a blazing day. But, as was to happen subsequently on two most crucial occasions in the war, a heavy morning mist made the fortunes of the battle. The advance, in the success of which time was so vital a factor, was held up for two critical hours.

The two cavalry divisions reached their allotted positions north and east of the town, and the 53rd Division, after a costly attack over two miles of country almost without cover, had gained a footing on Ali Muntar and were threatening the approaches to the town from the south. It was now decided that the A. and N.Z. Mounted Division should turn over to the Imperial Mounted Division their function of guarding against enemy reinforcements, and themselves join in the attack on Gaza; and these troops were actually pressing through the cactus defences when night fell. The two hours of daylight which the morning mist had blotted out would have easily sufficed for the junction of the infantry from the south with the cavalry from the north and east, and the capture of Gaza. But darkness overtook the troops in a precarious position. The cavalry were thinly spread over a vast area and threatened by large bodies of the enemy moving south-westwards. More important still, they had had no water for their horses or themselves all day and there was none to be had north of the Wadi Ghuzze. To have clung on in the circumstances would have been a desperate gamble. The cavalry were therefore ordered to retire to the Wadi Ghuzze, and this necessitated the withdrawal of the 53rd Division. The troops had fought with the greatest gallantry and endurance, but the main tactical object of the battle had not been gained.

SECOND BATTLE OF GAZA

The Turks made extremely good use of an interval of three weeks. The British improved their position by bringing the railway up to Belah and the pipe-line to the Wadi

Ghuzze; but the enemy had dug and wired so energetically that he had by now an almost continuous fortified line from the sea to Atawineh Ridge. His two divisions in the line had been reinforced by three more and a number of fresh batteries. The great cavalry sweep, upon which the tactics of the first battle had hinged, was now no longer possible.

The second battle was a much more straightforward affair, and consisted simply of a frontal attack in two stages. The first stage was carried out successfully on April 17th. Tanks were employed and the enemy's first line of defence was taken, and during this day and the next was consolidated. For the final stage the main attack was entrusted to the 53rd Division (on the left or sea flank), 52nd (centre), and 54th (right). Tanks were again used and the supporting artillery supplemented by the French battleship *Requin* and two monitors. The rôle of the cavalry was to protect the open flank and make a containing attack on Atawineh. The attack was pushed with great vigour. The 54th Division gained its objectives on the right, but it ultimately became plain that the strength of the enemy position was so great as to preclude any hope of success except with casualties on such a scale as might endanger the position of the whole Eastern Force. In these circumstances the only sound policy was to break off active operations and resort to trench warfare, pending the arrival of reinforcements in men and guns.

On May 23rd and 24th a cavalry raid on a large scale succeeded in totally demolishing the Turkish railway running south of Beersheba.

MESOPOTAMIA

On every front the British Army had long been struggling against odds of experience and numbers, but only in Mesopotamia had it come near to disaster. The fault was a fault of policy, the failure purely administrative; but the state of the Mesopotamian Expeditionary Force was none the less grave.

Fortunately the publicity given the matter was not of a panic kind, nor did it err in excess. Accordingly the resulting changes proved as happy as any made to mend a failure in the whole course of the war. The most radical change made was the assumption of responsibility for the expedition by the War Office in place of the Commander-in-Chief in India. In consequence Lieutenant-General F. S. Maude took over the command in August 1916 and arrangements were made to provide him with the two essentials for his up-hill struggle. He was given without delay the force he needed to overcome the enemy; and he was assured material resources for a carefully organised campaign, special provision being made for the health of the troops.

Romantic figures are few among the higher leaders of the Great War. On the Western Front, Foch and Gouraud, Wilson and Harington; in the Middle East, Allenby and Maude—all these achieved military greatness, all were cultured men remarkable for other than military attainments, all were outstandingly proficient in knowledge of the use of modern weapons and were able to apply modern science to the needs of war. Between the brilliance of Allenby and Maude, both fighting the same enemy, there is a great contrast. Allenby, magnificent, forceful, looms gigantic in the mystic light of prophecy, power incarnate. Maude, simple, industrious, humane, martyrs his delicate genius in nursing to victory a broken, suffering remnant. It is possible that his fame will compare with that of Wolfe.

After the fall of Kut, the Tigris Corps, commanded now by Lieut.-General Sir G. F. Gorringe, had spent its remaining energies in taking the Dujailar Redoubt and clearing the south bank of the Tigris as far as the Shatt el Hai. Important as this success was for the future, the ill-provided troops were left weary and nerveless in the overpowering heat. In these circumstances, and with the floods out till late in July, nothing more could be done.

Following General Maude's assumption of the command the work of repair and reorganisation was taken in hand. It proceeded with miraculous effects, and in it the great gifts of the Commander-in-Chief and his real affection for the fighting man were apparent. In his despatch of April 10th, 1917, he mentions the "long hours and strenuous work" by the Commanders and Staffs and testifies that "sheer hard work and determination to succeed compelled success". Involuntarily he reveals the keen spirit which led them at every obstacle.

Three and a half months sufficed for this work of resurrection. Meanwhile the tactical overthrow of the maze of obstacles about Kut had been prepared also. Every ounce of effort was to be concentrated on pushing through to Baghdad; enemy adventures into Persia to the threatening of India would then be as well looked after as the pounds in the adage about pennies. Besides, the Russian forces in northern Persia hung on the flank of the invading Turkish Thirteenth Corps.

So on the 13th of December the Hai was crossed and the enemy on its left bank subjected during three weeks to a relentless pressure. Line by line his defences on the south bank of the Tigris were wrested from him. In operations of great complexity which went on until the middle of February the stubborn defenders were overborne again and again by the remarkable tenacity of Maude's troops, till by the 16th the moment had come to dislodge the Turk from his hold on the middle Tigris.

KUT RECAPTURED

It must have been a desperate hope that made the Turks cling to the Sannaiyat and reserve positions on the north bank once the British were masters of the south bank far above Kut; the menace to their communications grew with every action, and it only remained for the British to cross the river to command the Baghdad road. This they did at the southern extremity of the Shumran bend, aided by feint attacks lower down. Surprise attacks were made on Sannaiyat also, the first effecting a lodgment on the Tigris bank, the second capturing and holding two lines of the position. Fitfully and deceptively the British guns battered the remaining lines during the following days. Down-river lay the flotilla, adding to the clamour and awaiting the moment to steam through the long-contested reaches. Back and forth over these for many miles up-river the missile contest of many weapons hardly paused.

Daylight on the 23rd revealed three ferries at work across the Shumran bend. The uppermost crossing was a complete surprise; the other two were scourged by rifle and machine-gun fire till they were abandoned. But the one sufficed. By 3 p.m. the assailants had progressed a mile north from the crossing, just above which a bridge was being built. After a day of artillery battle over the bridge, the infantry of one

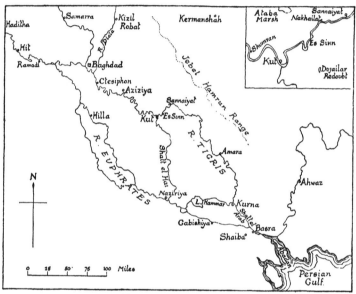

The Mesopotamian Front

division was across and that of another was crossing. Behind them waited the cavalry. During the day the third and fourth lines of Sannaiyat had been taken and, a favouring chance presenting, the fifth was secured before night.

On the following day, the 24th, the sixth line of Sannaiyat was taken without much opposition, and that evening the flotilla reached Kut. The Shumran fight was now absorbing the Turks' whole attention; yet for all the resistance they could make there, the position within the bend was being steadily cleared. Aeroplane reconnaissances showed the Baghdad road full of the retreating columns of the enemy. Against these the cavalry tried to break through, having crossed the Shumran bridge earlier; but they could not pierce the rear-guards, which clung to broken ground on each flank. Their effort was checked much as was that of the cavalry at Arras six weeks later. That night the remnant of the Turks withdrew.

In anticipation of pursuing in the morning, the troops in the Shumran bend were concentrated forward; starting early, they overtook the enemy eight miles on and harried him for two miles. Threatened by cavalry from the north and shelled by the flotilla on the river, he was eventually compelled to stand and fight the head of the infantry column of two divisions. On the following day the British infantry pressed on eighteen miles, to cut off more Turks. These only escaped by abandoning their guns and baggage. The flotilla was more fortunate; it fought an action with the Turkish flotilla and captured it. Among the prizes were the *Firefly*, abandoned disabled in the retreat from Ctesiphon, and the *Sumana*, lost at Kut.

As far as Aziziya the flotilla and the cavalry followed up the retreat and threw the Turks into confusion. There the pursuit was stopped in order that the lengthened communications might be reorganised and the rear Corps from the battle-field of Sannaiyat might close up.

THE FALL OF BAGHDAD

The Turks were given no time to stand on the well-maintained Ctesiphon position, and by March 7th contact was re-established with them on the line of the Diala. The first pontoons launched to make the crossing were riddled, but it is recorded that they floated down into the Tigris, where a number of wounded were rescued from them. At once the cavalry and some infantry of the rear Corps were transferred to the right bank of the Tigris and approached Baghdad from the south. During the 9th and 10th of March they pushed on, fighting continually, in difficulties for water and in blinding storms of dust. Meanwhile on the Diala in the bright moonlight of the 8–9th a party of seventy Loyal North Lancashires had crossed and for twenty-two hours held on magnificently.

Thus begun, the forcing of the river was accomplished at 4 a.m. on the 10th. It was bridged by noon. Thence the advance pushed over the high ground to the north-east of the city and Baghdad was entered from all sides on the 11th of March.

After the British entry into Baghdad, the operations of the Mesopotamian Expeditionary Force were largely those of an army of occupation. All that Sir Stanley Maude had designed came promptly to fruition. The Turkish Thirteenth Corps in Persia withdrew into Kurdistan, barely eluding the Russians thrusting down the road from Kermanshah to get contact with the British on the upper Diala. The Turkish Eighteenth Corps was thrust back up the Tigris beyond Samarra. The enemy forces on the Euphrates were driven off westwards beyond Ramadi. The security of Baghdad was complete before flood-time came; for eighty miles around it, north, west, and south, not a Turkish soldier remained.

The genius of Maude appears as much in the rehabilitation of a war-smitten land as in the breathless effort which rid it of the fount of its misfortunes. The general pacification of the country and the freeing of it from the oppressions of marauding chiefs and thieving nomads was firmly and quickly effected. Maude showed himself as skilled to use force with delicate restraint in appropriate circumstances as previously to display overwhelming power and inexorable determination. With pacification went hand in hand the encouragement of cultivation and the exploitation of natural resources in minerals. So successful was this work that Mesopotamia luxuriated in plenty and the Army became almost self-supporting in cereals and fodder. There was even some to spare for starving, anarchic northern Persia and for the wretched fugitives from Turkish cruelty in Kurdistan.

Contrast is the essential commonplace of war. The beginning and the end of the operations in Mesopotamia provide none the less a remarkable example—at first a heroic handful, maintained by a lengthening slender thread of supply; at last an army maintaining itself in great part on

Imperial War Museum Photo. Crown copyright

A DESERT ADVANCE IN MESOPOTAMIA

the plenty its presence made possible. A second contrast touches the sublime in its pathos. A departing Commander-in-Chief found it possible to praise, in the body of his final despatch, the medical officer who had attended him and his Staff at a time when the medical arrangements generally in Mesopotamia were scandalously defective. Sir Stanley Maude in his last despatch justly praises the care bestowed on the sick and wounded of the Army as a whole. Six weeks later, on the 18th of November, he died of cholera.

Lamented deeply by an Army whose deeds rank with those of the paladins, thus passed one of the greatest leaders known to modern times—not so much the head and front as the mind and soul of chivalry.

SUGGESTIONS FOR READING:
Revolt in the Desert by T. E. Lawrence, pp. 152–3, 157–60. *These Men, Thy Friends* by Edward Thompson (esp. pp. 156–8).

Chapter XV: THE BATTLE OF MESSINES

(See map on p. 153.)

IN the 1917 campaign in Flanders the immediate aim of the British was the possession of the high ground south and east of Ypres. The campaigns of the winter and spring had carried heights from which the enemy had long looked down on the Allies and which the Allies could not fully observe. Now that the southern flank was secure, it was time to improve the position in the north. Here, since the autumn of 1914, the enemy had been comfortably watching every movement of the Allies on the low ground. Perhaps from this he got the idea that he controlled the situation and need not bestir himself to seek further advantages. Marlborough in his time had acted similarly.

It was always in the mind of General Haig that during the fighting for an immediate objective such as the Somme uplands, the Vimy Ridge, and the Gravenstafel Ridge, the exhaustion or confusion of the enemy might offer an advantage which could be improved until it became decisive. In no case yet had the opportunity offered, or, if it had, been timely seized. The same turn of mind caused trench warfare to be waged with vigour by the British. It strove thus to maintain a moral superiority over the enemy whilst wasting his strength.

The methods of our French allies were different. Their trench garrisons were much less active and their general actions were begun usually with the idea of achieving a decisive victory. The different methods indicate the difference between the national characters.

Just at this period of the war each method in turn was searchingly tested, with grave consequences. The French Commander-in-Chief had gathered a great force of 1,250,000 men in three specially trained Armies on the Aisne. On the 16th of April they were sent forward to break the German line and sweep the enemy from France. The French nation's deferred hopes of ending the war were utterly dashed by the result. In fact the battle was not less of a success than was usual at this period—in a fortnight 45,000 prisoners and 450 guns were taken at a cost of 108,000 casualties; but it came so far short of expectations that the people fell into great depression of spirit. Portions of the Army became disaffected and there were some serious mutinies, though all news of these unhappy events was rigorously and successfully suppressed, and not even the British Army in France got wind of them. General Nivelle was superseded and General Pétain appointed Commander-in-Chief. Though he made certain concessions to the troops, he found himself unable to undertake the summer campaign as planned, in co-operation with the British.

Thus complete disaster threatened to overtake the Allies when Russia collapsed through revolution during the summer, and the long-drawn agony of Passchendaele became inevitable. In the beginning of the year the prospects of the British Army were very bright. Its numerical strength would reach its highest figure just when the gathering tide of experience and training could carry it at the flood to decisive success. But these prospects were to remain for ever a vision. When Russia failed and France weakened and Italy tottered, the British Army took a great grip of its foe and just held on, cost what it might. Most magnificent in its failure, it sustained the Allied cause unassisted through many months of peril. But before the vision faded, one blow of terrific power was struck.

The eastern slope of Kemmel Hill (in peace-time a holiday excursion for the people of Lille, Roubaix, and Tourcoing) looks down upon a tongue of high ground which divides the Lys valley from that of the Yser. The main ridge, on which Wytschaete stood, overlooks Ypres and Poperinghe, and from it a broad spur runs southwards to Messines and dominates Armentières. This ridge lay wholly within the outer German defences, and round its summit ran a second entrenched line. The third and fourth lines stretched north and south through, and east of, Oostaverne. These positions had to be wrested from the enemy, and with them Hill 60, in order to make ready the main British thrust further north.

When winter turned to spring, the restricted area of the Ypres Salient seemed more busy and crowded than ever. Carefully managed and well screened working-parties were always digging and carrying; one stumbled upon them everywhere, and it seemed that they worked the clock round. The work on railways, roads, water-pipe lines, buried cables, command posts, and dressing stations was pushed to the stage needed by the opening action, and as far beyond this, in the interests of the main battle, as the situation allowed.

Final dispositions were made in perfect summer weather; even the waterlogged shell-holes were alive with bright green frogs. Men, animals, guns, stores, and supplies were moved up to reinforce General Plumer's Second Army for the fight. Apart from thousands of specialist troops, the customary strength of the Army was raised from 12 divisions to 16, the field artillery from 800 to 1500 guns, the siege artillery from 400 to 800. The southern quadrant of the Salient and the country towards Kemmel was now opened up with many new sleeper-roads and light railway lines. It was packed full of men, weapons, and munitions; yet so clever was the arrangement that little sign of the men was apparent.

The munitions, stores, and supplies were everywhere in small heaps, but nowhere was a large dump to be seen. Guns lurked in every bit of cover, and every morning showed more "caterpillar" tracks between road and cover. Heavy trains of shrouded shapes on curious, long, skeleton bogies steamed up just as the dusk fell; loaded by the armament firms in England, they had crossed by the new Richborough train-ferry. Unsheeted in the dark at advanced railheads, the shapes crawled off their trucks into the neighbouring woods with the clang and clatter usual to tanks. Yet men told news of their coming in whispers.

A great gun-belt, four thousand yards in depth, grew on the narrow arc from Ypres to Armentières by way of Kemmel. Every hedge, drying-shed, homestead, and woodland echoed to the rhythmical cry of "Heave!" as the huge weapons were brought to bear. Sparingly and methodically they registered their targets, mostly through the eyes of the Air Service. But the growing weight and activity of the British artillery was equally opposed. Since the previous autumn, when the British infantry had heard with satisfaction that they might call for unlimited retaliation, the artillery war had changed. Until that time the field artillery alone had suffered much from counter-battery methods. Now devices of sound-ranging used by the Germans brought the heaviest and most distant weapons into the fray. The new-model battle began with back area "strafes" and artillery en-counters. A form of amusement favoured by Artillery Commands at this time was to select an enemy headquarters, railhead, or gun position, range on it every possible weapon, and so time a single discharge of each that a deluge of high explosive burst in one gigantic salvo on the target. During eight days the artillery worked itself up to the unparalleled fury it was to give to the battle. In this time 2374 guns, firing on a front of 17,000 yards, used 92,264 tons of ammunition. In addition 70 tons of gas were discharged in projectors.

At 3.10 a.m. on the 7th of June the action opened with a vast explosion. Nineteen mines along the front attacked were fired simultaneously; they represented years of work by the Tunnelling Companies in the laying, and their protection from enemy interference above and below ground had been an arduous task which cost many lives. In the grey of the early morning, nineteen great black pillars rose silently skywards with that unique, lazy lift which seems to set the laws of gravity completely at defiance. Then the rumble of a swaying earth-tremor was felt many miles around when these 470 tons of explosive utterly wrecked sections of the German defences and demoralised the neighbouring troops (the largest mine, that at Spanbroekmolen, formed a crater having a diameter of 140 yards).

As the mines detonated, the guns of the Second Army opened in a ring of white and crimson flame against the darkness and mists of the western and southern horizons. Moving and standing barrages, counter-battery and area "strafes", began with one great crash whilst yet the ground swayed to the impact of the mines. East and south over the entrenched lines, as the débris subsided, the British smoke-bombs whirled skywards, vortices of jewelled sparks which left billows of cloud now white in the coming dawn. An inferno of dull flashes lit them below. Over them rockets rose innumerable. A Cockney soldier looking back and forth said, "Blimey! Talk abaht a Brock's benefit!" He did not wait to say more, for at that moment some batteries of the enemy's artillery seemed to wake up. At the end of a few minutes they fell silent again, so thorough was the British counter-battery work. Only some six enemy batteries about Polygon Wood remained unlocated at the beginning of the action and gave trouble later.

The infantry assault was no affair of flashing bayonets and charging men; it was more like a lot of troglodytes steadily moving house, for the infantryman carried into the attack a formidable load besides his normal arms and equipment. Yet they went forward so steadily that only a few tanks could get into action in time for the earlier fighting. At 7 a.m. the New Zealand Division had captured Messines and two Irish divisions had fought their way through Wytschaete; here and at the White Château, near Hollebeke, the fighting was very fierce. The Grand Bois, near Wytschaete, had been cleared still earlier, and about midday the whole line south of the Canal moved down the eastern slopes towards the Oosta-verne line. The left of the attack moved steadily forward astride the Ypres–Comines Canal and the Menin railway, and over Hill 60. A hundred yards short of the limit of the advance ordered it was stopped by a great redoubt which the enemy had constructed in the spoil banks of the canal.

Meanwhile 60-pounder batteries were plunging forward through the chaos of Wytschaete and 6-inch howitzers, limbered to motor lorries, were passing the Lille Gate of Ypres to prepare the way through the Oostaverne line.

Twelve hours after "zero", at 3.10 p.m., two fresh di-visions assaulted the village and the line east of it. By evening the entire objectives had been gained with the exception of the strong-points in the spoil banks, and the south-eastern edge of Battle Wood, just north of these. The flanks of the attack—in the south, to the east of Ploegsteert, and in the north, on the Klein Zillebeke spur—had been secured by the exercise of valour and judgement. Seven thousand two hundred prisoners were taken; 67 guns, 94 trench-mortars, and 294 machine-guns were collected from the ground gained on this day of brilliant summer.

Though the enemy counter-attacked along the whole line on the evening of the 8th, he was repulsed everywhere. On the 14th the spoil banks, which still held out, were subjected to a bombardment now quoted as a classic of destructiveness. They then fell into British hands completely and the line was advanced to the edge of Battle Wood.

The overwhelming success gained in this strictly limited offensive shows well the striking-power which the Army had developed. An immensely strong position, $2\frac{1}{2}$ miles in greatest depth and nearly 10 miles wide, had fallen to it in a single day of perfectly timed advances. Details of the work done could be multiplied easily; let it merely be recorded here that the attack at Hooge in September 1915 had been opened on 500 rounds per battery and no more, that at Messines on 1000 for every gun, apart from huge reserves of ammunition and vastly greater gun-power. But first delay and then the troubles of our Allies were to clog and over-charge this magnificent weapon. The nation had given three years of toil and suffering and half a century's savings to perfect it. So perfect a weapon could not break; but the glorious success that should have been its portion, had fortune favoured, would now pass it by.

SUGGESTIONS FOR READING:

The 23rd Division, 1914–19 by Lt.-Col. H. R. Sandilands, pp. 150, 154.
The 47th (London) Division by A. H. Maude, pp. 98–102.

Chapter XVI: THE THIRD BATTLE OF YPRES

(See map on p. 153)

THE Flanders offensive was not resumed until the 31st of July. The plans of the Allies for the campaign of 1917 had mostly fallen through. The Russians had been unable to move in the spring; the Italians had been thrown on the defensive at Asiago in May; the French still suffered from the effects of the break-down of the Aisne offensive. The Italians, however, steadied their sensitive Trentino flank and then undertook a risky and costly advance over the Carso table-land towards Trieste. The Russians put forth one last heroic effort, beginning on July 11th, in which their generals Brussiloff and Korniloff achieved great successes in Galicia before the final collapse of all governmental authority. These successes affected both the Italian and Western Fronts, but the former more directly. General Ludendorff in his memoirs remarks that, had the last Russian offensive taken place in April or May, the German Supreme Command could hardly have "mastered the situation".

The British Army, resolutely seeking to carry out its allotted part, thus had against it almost the whole might of Germany and the undivided mind of the German Supreme Command. Even so it might have prevailed, but for delay in making all ready to begin the main attack at Ypres. This was due partly to the vastness of the preparations to be made on ground which the enemy still largely overlooked, partly to the policy of associating the hard-hit French with the work of freeing north-western Belgium. If the French Army did not recover, the Allied cause was as good as lost. So it was provided that the French First Army should relieve part of the Belgian Army and share with British troops in the victory which the British Commander-in-Chief had good reason to hope for. Unfortunately this relief took longer than had been anticipated.

One of the steps of the relief was the substitution of the British 1st Division for the French troops at Lombaertzyde. When only the infantry reliefs had been made, the Germans attacked, the two battalions to the east of the Yser Canal were annihilated, and the ground they had held was never recovered. This was a shrewd blow, for it added to the discontents of the time among the Allies.

Meanwhile, round Ypres, in a tongue of territory only two or three miles broad, there crowded hundreds of batteries, field and howitzer, whilst through the bottle-neck of the ruins countless troops and unceasing transport passed. The Germans had a potent weapon to hinder, though not pre-vent, these preparations in their new "mustard" gas, an oily fluid diffused from shells, which, with no warning save the characteristic smell, produced in a few hours terrible burns, loss of sight and voice, bronchitis, and pneumonia. Few died, but thousands were affected, and equally in the battery areas and the cellars of Ypres the "area shoots" of the German light batteries proved alarmingly effective. The heavy liquid lingered, often undetected, in the soil for many days, making it dangerous to dig in it, lie on it, or dump stores and rations, especially when the sun shone. To the many terrors of the soldier's life was added this insidious foe, only to be met with infinitely tiresome precaution and the discomfort of wearing respirators for hours at a stretch. The mark of the good soldier now was his "gas discipline".

After further postponements, July 31st saw the opening of the attack. A fortnight of preliminary bombardment ended at 3.50 a.m. with a discharge of incendiary shell and oil-drums. Behind a creeping barrage nine divisions of the Fifth Army went "over the top". The Second Army on the right and the French on the left advanced, covering the flanks. To do this the Second Army took La Basse Ville and Holle-beke and the ground north of the bend in the Comines Canal. The French even got beyond their objectives and occupied Bixschoote.

The Germans spared no effort to hold the high ground where it is crossed by the Menin Road. Though the right of the Fifth Army attack forced Sanctuary Wood, took Hooge, and occupied the Bellewarde Ridge north of this, it had to fight hard for every yard of its gains; and beyond lay a maze of entrenchments and "pill-boxes" making a citadel about the highest stretch of the Menin Road. Southwards they extended into Shrewsbury Forest, northwards they reached Westhoek. On this line the right of the attack was unable to make any impression. The summit had indeed been reached, but by no effort could it be crossed.

North of Westhoek the Pilckem Ridge held two systems of German defences. These were stormed and taken in turn. There was hard fighting at Frezenberg; the Pommern Re-doubt farther to the left made a prolonged resistance; south of Pilckem the breaking up of a counter-attack by a Prussian Guard battalion provided a grim struggle. Notwithstanding, the time-table of the advance was closely kept. St Julien and the crossings of the Steenbeek were secured by midday.

The last and most tragic shade of that perverse fortune which lay like a blight on the operations of the British at this period befel at this moment. The day, which had opened as brightly as the many preceding it, turned to rain. For two whole days rain fell heavily without ceasing, and for two more it poured at intervals.

The British soldier bore the personal discomforts with his usual growl. The chance of drowning helplessly as the water rose in some shell-hole was one on which he did not brood, though it was a fate which befel many wounded in these two days. But the battle plans were ruined. A colossal artillery power wasted itself blindly in making an impassable slough in front of the infantry it must needs protect. The move-ments of guns became almost impossible. Observation was obscured. The manoeuvres of tanks were very hazardous;

a few succeeded in crossing the awful desolation about Bellewarde Lake, north of Hooge, to assist the attack south of Westhoek, but others got mired and could never be extricated. Together with a bleached and tattered aeroplane, a few odd-length, palsied-looking tree trunks, fantastic coils of wire, screw pickets, and other half-submerged litter of a war of annihilation, they gave to the surroundings of the leaden-looking lake a brooding eerieness eloquent of disaster.

Except from their kite-balloons, the Germans no longer looked down upon Ypres. Thrust back on to a wide arc, they had lost over 6000 prisoners and in the north a great depth of their defences. Their counter-attacks had all failed to regain ground; but they had stopped the British advance along the Menin Road, the critical axis, and they had lost only 25 guns. If any further proof of the failure of the operation was needed, it was furnished a fortnight later. On August 16th, though the left of the Fifth Army reached Langemarck, its right suffered terribly at Glencorse Wood and along the Hanebeek.

The enemy had reorganised during the breathing-space which in part he owed to good fortune, and he now revealed a change in his defensive tactics. The virtue of his new dispositions lay particularly in their depth and their invisibility to both forward and air observers; consequently they were the more immune from artillery attack. Small infantry parties defended specially organised posts in shell-holes; they were supported by machine-guns in well-sited "pill-boxes". This system left over a large margin of strength for counter-attacks. Detailed instructions over the signature of Sixt von Arnim, commander of the northernmost German Army, were studied in every British division at this time; but all the study failed to produce a form of attack which could bring infantry through the forward defences in sufficient strength to carry the main position. The barrage protection required for this was not to be got. So a plan of attack was adopted based on thousand-yard advances. One was undertaken against Inverness Copse in the last week of August. At the end of six days of fierce fighting a pitiful remnant of the attackers held the western edge of the copse.

The war in the air surpassed all previous experience. The rays of the setting sun would often glint on the distant wings of many aeroplanes engaged in what went by the grim name of a "dog fight". In appearance it was more like an excited bowl of goldfish. Meanwhile, day in and day out, the "artillery planes" went about their task of ranging guns on hostile targets near the line, their course marked by the bursts of anti-aircraft shell; whilst long-distance machines flew far over enemy territory on bombing or photographic errands. In this enterprise the British showed more daring than the enemy by day, though the German bombing-squadrons were incessantly active at night. The Richthofen "circus" of enemy fighters, however, was much in evidence; and they were great "balloon-strafers". The kite-balloon had a special importance in this war of huge gun concentrations. On a day when there was much broken cloud about, the fast fighter would suddenly plunge out of a neighbouring bank on to the helpless gas-bag. A stream of smoking tracer-bullets set the gas in the envelope alight. As the wilting shape sank earthwards in a pall of dark smoke, two shining white domes floated slowly down; swinging to earth at the extremity of the cordage hung the two observers. The accompanying uproar was deafening as all the anti-aircraft defences tried to bring down the aggressor. As they were usually assisted by ambitious field gunners and anybody who had a rifle handy, it rained bits and pieces copiously for long after the "strafer" had got clear. One early afternoon in the middle of July the whole row of six kite-balloons between Poperinghe and Bailleul were in flames, their twelve parachutes all open below them, while the "strafer" ran the gauntlet successfully at a tremendous pace, dipping like a fieldfare.

In spite of all this activity, the offensive had been practically completely interrupted. Tactically a fresh start had to be made, and the preparations for this were not complete until September 20th. New communications to the front had to be built under unusual difficulties of the inclement season and the ceaseless artillery and air battle. Corduroy roads and light and heavy railways were constructed, although even the maintenance of a duck-board track was a precarious work, so easily could the enemy's kite-balloons pick out for destruction the few ordered arrangements which emerged from the waterlogged waste behind the British front. And the belt of war deepened; long-range guns by day and aeroplanes by night sought out the camps, concentrations, and communications of the forces converging on Ypres. The night sky was patterned with searchlight beams; luminous bullets white and red, slid up and down with astonishing slowness, yet in the strictest of linear successions, as bombers passed overhead. Frequently the explosion of dumps turned night into day.

The night of the 19–20th September was soaking wet. At dawn a thick mist shrouded everything. Through it, assaulting troops of eleven British divisions advanced on the Bassevillebeek, Polygon Wood, and the spurs of the Gravenstafel Ridge.

The right of the attack cleared Shrewsbury Forest, crossed the Beek, and fought hard for a footing on the Tower Hamlets spur. Inverness Copse was taken and the treacherous ground about the Dumbarton Lakes crossed, to the storming of Veldhoek and then of Polderhoek. The right of the Fifth Army carried Glencorse Wood and the Nonne Boschen. Along the Roulers railway two redoubts were stormed and the spur eastwards above Zevenkote taken. Farther north the troops cleared many farms in which were concealed "pill-boxes" and got astride the spur which rises to Gravenstafel. The left of the Fifth Army advanced a flank along the Staden railway. Altogether over 3000 prisoners were taken and a few guns.

The enemy soon showed his great concern for the positions he had lost. The artillery battle continued without rest for days and infantry counter-attacks were numerous, especially in the vicinity of the Menin Road. They were desperate on the 25th and 26th. Notwithstanding, on the 26th the right of the Fifth Army cleared Polygon Wood and advanced towards Broodseinde on the main ridge. Farther north Zonnebeke was taken and troops pushed on half a mile nearer to Gravenstafel.

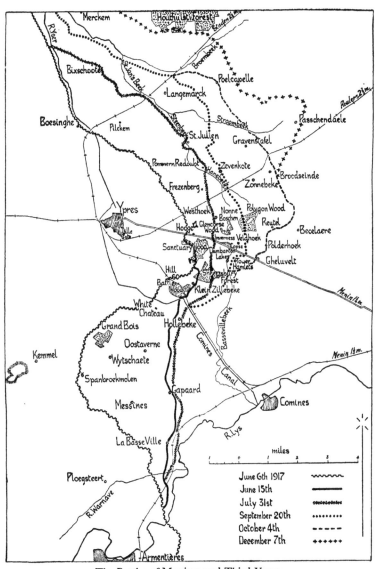

Merckem Houthulst Forest

R.Yser

Bixschoote

Boesinghe

Pilckem

Langemarck

Poelcapelle

Roulers 2½m.

Passchendaele

Stroombeek

St.Julien

Gravenstafel

Pommern Redoubt

Zevenkote

Broodseinde

Frezenberg

Zonnebeke

Ypres

Westhoek

Nonne

Polygon Wood

Boschm

Hooge

Glencorse

Reutel

Wood

Becelaere

Inverness

Veldhoek

Sanctuary Wood

Copse

Polderhoek

Dumbarton

Lakes

Tower

Hamlets

Gheluvelt

Hill

Shrewsbury

60

Forest

Battle

Menin ¼m.

Woods

Klein Zillebeke

White

Chateau

Hollebeke

Comines

Bassevillebeek

Grand Bois

Canal

Oostaverne

Kemmel

Wytschaete

Menin 1½m.

Spanbroekmolen

Gapaard

Comines

Messines

R.Lys

La Basse Ville

miles

0   1   2   3   4

Ploegsteert

June 6th 1917

R.Warnave

June 15th

July 31st

September 20th

October 4th

December 7th

Armentières

The Battles of Messines and Third Ypres

This seemed only to inspire the enemy with a greater fury to wreak upon the historic ground before Gheluvelt. On October 1st a concentration of artillery fire was turned upon it which had no equal in the experience of the 23rd Division. Through such a reeking deluge nothing could pass, not even a visual message; it is recorded that the "gallant little pigeons" failed. This increase of the enemy gun-power had doubtless been made possible by the collapse of Russia; yet it probably did not surpass that of the British barrages hereabouts. When the German infantry attacked, it was supported by aircraft sweeping low over the British trenches. Though many casualties were thus caused, the enemy was unable to regain more than a few yards of the ground he had lost, and that at an unimportant point.

The main German attack was to have followed this operation, on October 3rd; but owing to the unfavourable result it had to be postponed until the 4th, and even then it was forestalled. Ten minutes before it was due to take place, the appalling British barrage fell upon the unprotected German masses assembled for the assault. British infantry advancing with the bayonet overcame such resistance as remained, and over 5,000 prisoners were taken. Polderhoek Château was occupied, Reutel entered, and the Becelaere–Broodseinde road crossed at one point. North of this the crest of the main ridge was passed; the crossings of the Stroombeek were forced, in spite of the deep going after the night's rain; and tanks assisted to storm Poelcapelle, the western half of which was secured. Along the Staden railway a specially important point of high ground securing the flank was gained.

A position had thus been won which the British Commander-in-Chief would have been content to organise for winter defence. But in spite of the lateness of the season, its inclemency, and the impracticable ground, and in spite of the pressing need that he should rest his troops, he was compelled as much by our own danger as by the duty and debt we owed our exhausted allies to press on. The German scheme of defence had not failed, but it had brought great suffering and hardship on the defenders. Losses which

General Ludendorff has since acknowledged to be "enormous" had had to be made good by drawing heavily on the Eastern Armies. It was of the first importance, therefore, that the German Supreme Command be allowed no quiet to arrange the ordered transport to France of the masses of troops which Russia's pitiable fate set free. Moreover the French were slowly recovering their spirit and, having gained a victory at Verdun in August, were to undertake operations on the Aisne towards the end of October. The enemy's attention must be diverted from there, and if possible from the Italian advance across the Carso, until the onset of winter defeated military endeavour generally.

Accordingly, on the 9th of October British infantry were moving again on the rain-soaked slippery soil towards the enemy's remaining strongholds; these were the Passchendaele Ridge and Houthulst Forest. On the left the French First Army advanced also.

The enemy was driven up the western slopes of the main ridge from the villages, farms, and strong-points there situated. Poelcapelle was cleared in spite of fierce opposition. Along the Staden Railway strong-points were methodically reduced. The Guards and the French splashed and floundered through the floods along the Broembeek and drove the Germans back into the forest from the numerous hamlets and farms about its edge. Over 2000 prisoners and a few guns were taken. Simultaneously a distinct little operation freed the village of Reutel from its last German occupants.

During the war twenty-seven awards of the Victoria Cross were made for brave deeds by officers and men of the 29th Division. The sixteenth was for heroic work in taking blockhouses along the Staden Railway on this day. Company Sergeant-Major John Skinner of Pollokshields belonged to the 1st K.O.S.B., and since the day the battalion had landed on the Gallipoli Peninsula he had seen much of war. He wore the Distinguished Conduct Medal, twice earned, the Military Medal, and on his left sleeve eight gold wound-stripes. On this day the advance of his company was stopped by three "pill-boxes" from which streamed machine-gun bullets. Skinner and his company officer engaged them with their rifles and silenced two of the guns. Then on his own initiative the C.S.M. stalked the pill-box on the left, got behind it, and threw bombs into it. The garrison surrendered. The next he dealt with by pushing bombs, from the side, into the machine-gun embrasures. Sixty prisoners, six machine-guns, and some trench-mortars were thus taken by him single-handed.

Shortly afterwards Skinner was given leave to England to receive the Victoria Cross from the King. Returning for the front, he fell sick at Folkestone and was sent to hospital. He recovered promptly, but to his surprise was ordered to Edinburgh for duty with the reserve battalion of his regiment. He still had his return leave-warrant in his pocket, however, and determined to use it. Back in France, his disobedience was condoned; he excused himself as having a bet with another warrant-officer on who would first get the ninth wound-stripe. The sequel, the noblest climax of this warrior-life, was reached during the winter. The ninth wound was Skinner's last. He went over one morning at dawn to bring in a man crying out in No Man's Land and was instantly killed.

The ground was daily getting worse and the weather remained uncertain; as the troops assembled to attack again, at dawn on October 12th, rain streamed out of the inky blackness, and it continued throughout the day. On the right certain gains were made up the western slopes of the rising ground north of the Roulers Railway. Then an order to stand fast was given on account of the weather. In the centre the order to break off the action seems to have been effective only because the valleys were rendered impassable. On the left the 4th, 17th, and Guards Divisions gained all their objectives along the Staden Railway. In all over 1000 prisoners were taken and a notable feat of endurance was performed.

The whole front and its approaches had now become a vast quagmire where men sank waist-deep and animals were drowned. The difficulty of getting forward stores and supplies and of getting back the wounded was at times insurmountable. Sanitation was hopeless, so great was the amount

December 1917

June 1917

PASSCHENDAELE BEFORE AND AFTER BOMBARDMENT

Imperial War Museum Photo. Crown copyright

of wreckage. Withal the two artilleries ceased not to roar their defiance at each other with undiminished violence. Truly it was cheaper to attack than merely to hold on; but attack was impossible, for men could hardly drag themselves forward. This was the supreme tragedy. A magnificent artillery arm had been built up, trained, and supplied by a widely national diligence incomparable in the pathos of its endeavour. Through a fateful turn of the weather it brought about its own discomfiture. So yet another item of experience had to be built up into the science which was to carry not this Army, but its successors, to victory over the same ground a year later.

The Flanders front might not rest, even though to take but the whole of the Passchendaele Ridge was now impossible. An improvement in the weather allowed of further operations beginning on October 22nd. East of Poelcapelle and in the Houthulst Forest an important advance was made, in which the French Army took part.

On the 26th the weather was again doing its worst. In spite of heavy rain, with consequent flooding of the low-lying ground, a small hill south of Passchendaele was captured. Meanwhile Gheluvelt had been entered and Polderhoek Château retaken; it had been lost in a counter-attack some time previously. A similar end overtook this later thrust, for in the face of a counter-attack the ground gained was abandoned. One of the contributory causes of the failure was the choking of the British rifles with mud picked up in the advance. During the day the French secured the crossings of the St Jans Beek. By the 28th of October, working with the Belgian troops on their left, they had driven the enemy from what was called the Merckem Peninsula, a product of the inundations.

The activity at Ypres had sufficiently occupied the enemy's western Armies. On the 22nd and following days the French reduced the salient of Laffaux, near the Aisne, and took the Chemin des Dames. The combined effect of both the western Allies' efforts failed, however, to hinder the Germans reinforcing the Austrian Carso front. Fearing that their Austrian ally was on the point of collapse under the onslaught of the

Italians, the Germans had sent at first two, then more, divisions from the Russian front to the Carso. This reinforcement turned the tables there. The Italian Second Army had become disaffected through the absorption into its ranks of a large proportion of recently drafted munition-workers, who regretted their former high wages and unusual luxuries. On October 26th at Caporetto this Army broke with the loss of 10,000 prisoners and many guns. In three days this disaster had endangered the Italian Third Army, and the Germans and Austrians were advancing steadily through Venetia towards the Tagliamento, taking many more prisoners and much material.

Not on this account only was the action before Passchendaele resumed. Sir Douglas Haig intended to strike soon at a part of the Hindenburg Line near Cambrai, which he knew to be weakly held. Secrecy was essential, and part of the shroud of secrecy could best be woven about Passchendaele.

On October 30th the outskirts of the village of Passchendaele were reached. On November 6th the village was taken and the ground north-west of it along the main ridge secured. The closing action of the offensive followed four days later. By dint of stern fighting under the worst of weather conditions further ground was gained northwards from Passchendaele.

The total captures since July 31st amounted to over 24,000 prisoners, 74 guns, 941 machine-guns, and 138 trench-mortars. The appearance of the long columns of prisoners, passing from time to time, bore out General Ludendorff's statement that the effect of the Flanders fighting on the moral of the German Army was disastrous. The physical exhaustion of the prisoners made their march very slow and they had the air of animals tamed by terror into apathy. In all 78 German divisions experienced what these men had gone through.

Victorious engagement had followed victorious engagement. The price of victory had been paid over and over, generously; yet ever the fruits of victory were withheld. At each renewal of the battle all knew that the fruits of victory could not be gathered. Yet none faltered. The heroic endurance displayed was not only beyond hope of reward but even quite apart from hope. It was a deed of faith. Though the official title of the battle has been staidly chosen, the agony of a nation knows it by the pregnant name of "Passchendaele".

SUGGESTIONS FOR READING:

The Irish Guards in the Great War by Rudyard Kipling, vol. II, pp. 166–8.
The 56th (1st London) Division by Major C. H. Dudley Ward, p. 164.
The Tunnellers of Holzminden by H. G. Durnford, pp. 1–13.

Chapter XVII: THE BATTLE OF CAMBRAI

(See map on p. 163)

IT is possible that a new era in military history opened on November 20th, 1917. On this day a great battle experiment in the use of tanks was put through with a measure of success. Much thought and great personal sacrifice on the part of the Tank Corps had gradually made this arm reliable. Experience with the earlier "Marks" of these weapons had developed inventiveness and improved their handling in action. The combined operations of tanks and infantry were studied at "battle-rehearsals". A Tank School came into being, appropriately at Agincourt, where, the play has it, the Dauphin and the Constable of France wagered on horses and armour on the eve of the battle.

The position attacked was that part of the Hindenburg Line which lay between the Scheldt Canal at Banteux and the Canal du Nord excavation north-east of Hermies. This battle-ground offered three advantages. Firstly, the going for tanks was firm; previously they had always fought over contested ground often bottomless after heavy shelling. Secondly, the enemy's strength before Cambrai had been to some extent sacrificed in order to provide resistance in Belgium. Lastly, an initial success would open the way to the crossings of the Sensée; if the crossings could then be gained, the enemy's communications to the Arras front would be in jeopardy, and a retreat would be forced upon him as extensive as that after the battle of the Somme.

The movements of the British troops to Italy at this time conveniently masked the concentration of others in the Third Army area under General Byng. The secrecy with which the arrangements were made was profound, and the attack came as a complete surprise to the enemy.

There was no preliminary bombardment or registration of artillery targets. As the November dawn broke, a great fleet of 340 tanks lumbered forward over the British line, obscured in billowing clouds of smoke. The guns opened fire at the same moment. They were in greatest concentration on the immediate front of the attack, but on all the front south of the River Scarpe artillery, gas, and smoke demonstrations were made. The infantry of 6 divisions followed the tanks. The latter crushed down the German wire entanglements and then patrolled the Hindenburg trenches, destroying machine-guns and compelling the garrisons to shelter underground. The infantry passed through the gaps in the wire and cleared the enemy from his dug-outs. Meanwhile the enemy's artillery had been greatly hampered by the smoke.

By half-past ten that morning the Hindenburg Line and the Hindenburg Support Line, incorporating the defended villages of La Vacquerie, Ribécourt, and Havrincourt, had been broken through on the whole front assaulted. But the village of Flesquières in the centre of the Reserve Line held out; the tanks advancing up the hill to it were knocked out by gun-fire. The sole survivor of one German battery, an officer, served a gun single-handed and disabled several tanks. He was eventually killed at the gun, and because of his gallantry our men tried to identify his body—but in vain.

Elsewhere the divisions were pressing on north-eastwards through driving mist, and the cavalry now moved up behind. The right of the advance, reinforced with a fresh division, secured the crossings of the Scheldt Canal at Masnières and Marcoing. But when a tank tried to cross the bridge at Masnières, bridge and tank fell into the canal; the bridge had been damaged by the retiring enemy. North of Masnières, Noyelles was taken, but the artillery advance on the right of the attack was delayed by congestion on the roads behind. North of Flesquières the 62nd (West Riding) Division brilliantly captured Graincourt, and to the left of this the Hindenburg Line was being rolled up northwards. But between Noyelles and Graincourt there was a deep bay in the British line due to the continuing check at Flesquières. Moreover the destruction of the Masnières canal bridge delayed the cavalry, which was to sweep eastwards on to the enemy's communications. Thus the enemy was given time to man his defences about Rumilly.

During the afternoon a squadron of the Fort Garry Horse got across the canal to the south of Rumilly by a temporary bridge. Piercing the German reserve defence line, it charged and captured a battery and then dispersed half a battalion of infantry. In this dashing work most of its horses were killed or wounded; so the squadron defended itself where it lay, and at nightfall it withdrew with its prisoners.

The check on the Flesquières Ridge now began to slow the advance to right and left. Yet cavalry reached Cantaing and the 62nd Division completed a 4½-mile fighting advance by entering Anneux. This performance bears comparison in mere distance with any advance on the Western Front up to this date; as it was made over a renowned system of fortifications, its merits are unapproached.

Next day at 8 a.m. Flesquières was taken. At 10.30 a.m. infantry, tanks, and cavalry began to move northwards across the wide valley to Fontaine-Notre-Dame and Bourlon —alas, too late. The enemy's resistance was now stiffening, and though the line of the Bapaume–Cambrai road was reached and the village of Fontaine secured, it was found impossible to penetrate Bourlon Wood. Even tanks failed in this. At Noyelles and at the crossings of the Scheldt Canal desperate fighting followed. East of the Canal, before Rumilly, the enemy fought obstinately, determined to give time for his reinforcements to arrive. Luck had indeed favoured him in this already, for quite by chance a division from Russia had begun detraining at Cambrai on the day of the attack. Battalion by battalion, it was posted in the Rumilly sector of the reserve defence line on arrival. On the left also the advance was now stayed before Moeuvres.

At this stage the advance had covered an average depth of $4\frac{1}{2}$ miles and a greatest depth of nearly 6 miles on a front of more than 10 miles; and the captured guns were significantly numerous. The time allowed in the calculations of the Staff for the appearance of enemy reinforcements was up. But as signs were reported which indicated that the enemy might withdraw, it was decided to assault the Bourlon Ridge. Success in this would be the beginning of greater successes; not to attempt it left no alternative but to retire to the Flesquières Ridge.

On the 22nd a preparatory move was made by the Queen's Westminsters of the 56th (London) Division, after nightfall. They stormed Tadpole Copse, a strong-point in the Hindenburg Line just west of Moeuvres. The enemy on his part was not idle on this day; he retook the village of Fontaine-Notre-Dame.

On the 23rd, infantry and tanks tried to push on through Fontaine and Bourlon Wood. The resistance was most determined, and though the wood was captured, it was not found possible to maintain a footing in Bourlon village to the north of it or in Fontaine. Tanks, it is true, roamed about the streets of both and did great damage to the enemy, but without advantage to our infantry.

The combatants now became locked in another of those awful struggles so characteristic of this war. In sleet and rain for days the swaying lines were tossed to and fro by the clamorous, bloody tide of battle. Fontaine and Bourlon and the intervening wood, riven and gas-soaked, became merely the scene of the fight. Its one object was to break the enemy, flesh, blood, and nerve. After four days of this, the shattered 51st and 40th Divisions were relieved by the Guards and the 62nd. Part of the 13th East Surreys (40th Division) lay in Bourlon village fighting on, beyond relief; two days elapsed before they could be succoured. A temporary and very limited success in Fontaine and Bourlon brought this succour, and also many prisoners. All the while a similar

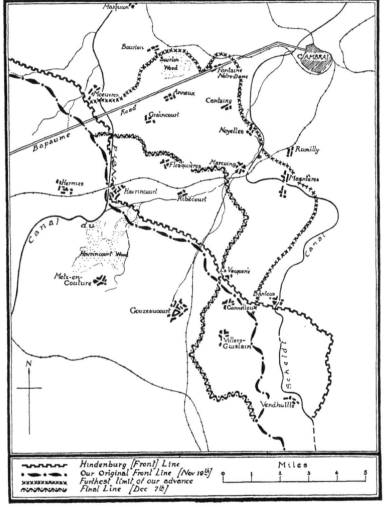

The Battle of Cambrai

combat raged at Tadpole Copse, where the 56th Division was able to maintain itself.

It was now plain that the Bourlon Ridge could only be gained by a different form of attack. During the preparation for this two days passed in comparative quiet, whilst reliefs were made and captures disposed of. These amounted to 10,500 prisoners, 142 guns, 350 machine-guns, and 70 trench-mortars.

But the project never materialised. On the 28th and 29th of November the enemy was busy registering artillery targets and moving troops on the new front and south of it. On the 30th, between seven and eight o'clock in the morning, five German divisions and portions of two others attacked between Masnières and Vendhuille, the southern haunch of the salient. The shortness of the preliminary bombardment deceived the defenders more than its great intensity harmed them. The surprisingly sudden infantry assault, aided by low-flying aeroplanes, pierced the British defence at once. About Masnières and just south of it no lasting impression was made on the 29th Division; around Vendhuille the 55th Division gallantly fought off all assaults that day. But in the centre, though islands of resistance about gun-positions and machine-gun posts put up many a staunch fight, the defence was penetrated.

The disorganisation was in fact serious. The slopes west of Gouzeaucourt began to be covered with fugitives, many carrying breech-blocks and similar essentials. The tide was turned, however, by the arrival of the Guards Division from Metz-en-Couture, where all roads met, about 2 p.m. The last of them had only recently left Fontaine and the Bourlon positions, caked with mud and having that air of neglect and exhaustion which follows hard fighting. When they counter-attacked at Gouzeaucourt with all the dash of fresh troops, it was noticeable that every man was brushed and polished as if for a march up the Mall. The stream of fugitives from the lost positions, seeing this, forgot their haste. Already three wildly cheering batteries had passed them going into action; these were the 235th Brigade, R.F.A., whose guns were to cover the Guards' attack. The enemy was thrust out of Gouzeaucourt; but he could not be dislodged from Gonnelieu.

Three battalions of tanks, which had been moving off to refit, returned to the field at this time. They were too late to support the attack, but they helped to strengthen the heroically extended line. Later the cavalry reinforced the right of the Guards and a fresh infantry division their left. The crisis in this part of the field was over.

But the enemy's main assault fell upon the northern face of the new salient. It did so at 9 a.m., two hours later than that on the south-eastern face and just when the effect of this was at its most serious. Before dusk five heavy attacks had been made, in one of which were eleven waves of German infantry. The shock was borne by three British divisions in line from Fontaine-Notre-Dame to Tadpole Copse, the 47th, the 2nd, and the 56th. Lines of enemy infantry crossing the crests of the ridges east of Moeuvres were raked by machine-gun fire, and one mass which broke through down the southern slopes between Bourlon and Moeuvres was swept out of existence by short-range artillery fire.

The enemy's artillery was busy too. Following his usual custom at this period, he was saturating the undergrowth of the wood at Bourlon with gas. The consequences to the 19th London Regiment, holding the right of the wood, were wholesale blinding. Six hundred strong at the beginning of the action, ultimately it numbered only seventy. The 17th Royal Fusiliers lived up to the standard their 4th Battalion had set in the beginning at Mons. The devotion of a platoon which fought to the last man saved an advanced company when the German attack broke upon it. As fine an end befel a company of the 13th Essex, which was isolated by the first attack west of Moeuvres. At 4 p.m. the officers and N.C.O.'s held a council and sent back two runners to say that they had determined on "no surrender". Their gallant fight was heard all that night. A similar fight raged round three advanced posts held by the 1st Royal Berks. The traces of it appeared two days later when the posts were retaken; the German dead were heaped around and upon the British, quite concealing them. The remaining posts in the Berkshires' forward line beat off the enemy, though long out of touch with supports. Such parts of the insecure northern face of the salient as were lost at any time during this day of costly fighting were promptly regained and held. Three staunch divisions bore the weight of seven in attack, and at the end of the day they remained unshaken.

There remained no hope now of taking the Bourlon Ridge and Moeuvres; a withdrawal to the Flesquières Ridge was therefore ordered. After a quiet day on December 4th the withdrawal began. It was completed, with some fighting, on the 7th, and the Hindenburg defences provided excellent shelter.

Thus a belated venture with tanks well-nigh brought about the results which the Allied commanders had originally planned for in the campaign of 1917. The experience gained was of the greatest use in the advance to victory in the following year, by which time the tank had established itself as an indispensable weapon of offence. Nevertheless the narrow failure at Cambrai nearly turned to disaster just because the new use of this weapon was so very successful; the fatigue of co-operating prostrated the infantry, whilst the irresistible power of tanks impressed the troops with too great a trust in them. In other ways too the use of these strange weapons was a delicate matter. Their presence complicated the problem of traffic, the leading of infantry, and the use of artillery. Every added complication is another opportunity for the germ of inertia. This fatal malady was the cause of the disaster among the ravines about Gonnelieu on the 30th of November.

The Cambrai battle will always remain one of the most dramatic episodes of the war, for it provides a signal example of the success of a well-organised attack annulled by swift and equally well-organised counter-attack.

SUGGESTIONS FOR READING:

The World Crisis, 1916–18 by W. S. Churchill, pt. II, pp. 346–8.   *The 29th Division* by Col. J. F. C. Fuller, p. 173.

Chapter XVIII: ITALY AND PALESTINE, TO MID-1918

(See maps on pp. 169, 176 and 237)

ITALY

THERE is a marked contrast between the fortunes of the troops on the Western Front and those of the British divisions which spent the last year of the war in Italy. These escaped the vicissitudes under which the Armies in France and Belgium suffered every ill but failure. It was their fortune to be used against comparative weakness, and thus they got the chance to acquire a finish denied by events to their comrades in France. Their culminating achievement is one of the greatest feats of the war; their technical perfection reveals the British Army at its finest.

On the 26th of October, 1917, the Austrians, reinforced by six German divisions, broke through the Italian eastern front near Caporetto on the Carso. By the 29th the Italian Second Army was in utter rout. Though the Italian Third Army extricated itself finely from serious jeopardy on the sea-flank, the total losses of the Italians reached 250,000 men and 700 guns. Riots broke out in Italy as the enemy invaded it from the east.

Immediately five French and five British divisions were sent from France to assist the Italians, a transfer of troops during the progress of critical operations on the Western Front which was highly creditable. Sixteen days after Caporetto the Italian front was momentarily steady on the line of the river Piave, while French and British troops were moving towards it through the tide of Italian soldiery ebbing sullenly westwards. The railway journey down the valley of the Rhone and along the Riviera had been an enchantment to men fresh from the desolation of Flanders. The inhabitants had greeted them warmly and the British residents had provided little luxuries for them at the stations. Later, on the line of march and in billets, the fine discipline of the British troops and the kindliness of officers and men made, as usual, a profound impression. On November 20th General Sir Herbert Plumer took command of the British Army in Italy, and shortly afterwards H.R.H. the Prince of Wales joined the Staff of the Fourteenth Corps (7th, 23rd, and 41st Divisions).

When the French and British divisions began to relieve the Italians, they defended the right bank of the Piave east of Monte Grappa. The Eleventh Corps (5th and 48th Divisions) remained in reserve, being grouped with a French and an Italian Corps in readiness to counter any attempt by the enemy to break through the mountain front. The position of the defenders from Monte Grappa westwards was a delicate one; it was the vulnerable flank of the Piave line.

On the bastion of the Montello, overlooking the wide river-bed, the British Fourteenth Corps relieved an Italian Corps in the first week of December. The sector had a length of 10 miles between Nervesa and Rivasecca, the enemy's front line being a thousand yards away on the other bank. Beyond lay the Venetian Alps. The defences in use by the Italians had first to be converted to the more elastic system evolved on the Western Front, so the troops found plenty of work, if little fighting. Very soon, however, patrols began crossing the swift river-channels to seek out the Austrians. This called for great endurance.

An unusually delayed first fall of snow occurred on December 13th. This relieved an anxious situation on the mountain front, but it added to the hardships of patrolling on the river front. The method of this was for a man, stripped and liberally oiled, to swim the first deep channel with a rope. He then dragged over a boat containing the patrol clothed in white smocks and gum-boots. Wading through the further swift channels men were often swept away, and the devotion of their comrades alone saved them. Success in this hazardous and trying work was always hardly earned.

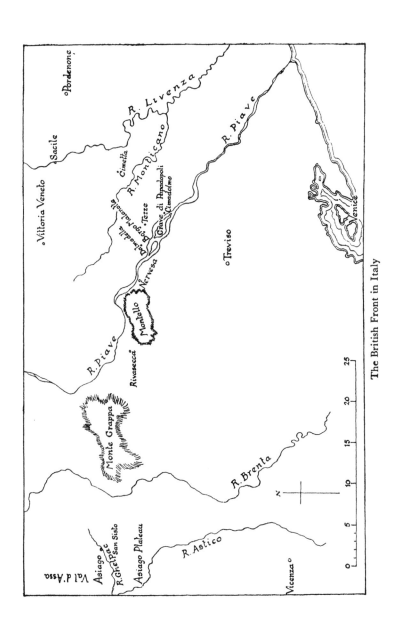

The British Front in Italy

Not unnaturally the first British success was in the air. On Christmas Day an enemy aerodrome was sought out and bombed. On Boxing Day twenty-five of the enemy returned the compliment; of these, British and Italian airmen shot down eleven without loss.

On January 27th, 1918, the British line was extended farther down the Piave, the 5th Division taking over 8000 yards of front from the Italians below Nervesa. By the middle of February the whole Italian front was tranquil. The British casualty lists, never long, had been shortened by profitable work on the defences, notwithstanding that shelling by heavy guns and air bombing continued severe. The spirits of the Italian troops had miraculously revived. The six Prussian divisions had left Italy for France; accordingly the 5th and 41st Divisions and three French divisions returned to the Western Front during March.

In the middle of March the remaining French and British divisions were withdrawn from the river front and transferred to the mountain front, where they took over part of the defences of the Asiago plateau, a position of great importance and difficult to defend. The relief of an Italian by a British division on the plateau was consummated at a headquarters luncheon to the music of an Italian band. The Austrian gunners added three large shells to the function, the only three fired in a month. It is a Teutonic custom to chorus "Ein, Zwei, Drei" in honouring important toasts. The band may have had difficulty in classifying the production of the interpolations; wind or percussion, however, they accorded soloist's privileges to the second and third.

An Allied offensive by French and British forces on the mountain front was planned for the spring, but it was continually put off. About April 20th an Austrian offensive began to be expected, but it did not materialise until June. On the 15th, just when all was in readiness for an assault on Asiago, the Austrians advanced in an attack on the whole of the 75-mile front between the river Astico and the Gulf of Venice, and of the 50 divisions assembled for this offensive, 16 were concentrated against the portion occupied by the French and British divisions. Reliable information of the enemy's intention had been received on the previous day. In addition, night patrols saw the enemy concentrating during the preliminary bombardment, which had opened at 3 a.m. All forward telephone wires were soon cut; it had been impossible to bury them deep in the rocky ground.

Like their allies three months earlier, the Austrians were favoured by thick mist. This and the absence of telephonic communication hampered the artillery defence; so the enemy onslaught at 7 a.m. was not broken everywhere by the fire of the infantry. Taking advantage of the woods before the British right and left centre, the enemy made lodgments in the front line. That on the right was small, but reached out to the San Sisto ridge, the key of the British position; that on the left was more considerable and put four batteries of guns out of action.

Valour was not wanting at need, however. Whether the potential hero is never far to seek or the hero is drawn to peril as to a lode is an eternal question. Two instances, one favouring each view, occurred to save the Allied front on this day.

Lieutenant J. S. Youll, 11th Northumberland Fusiliers, was out with a patrol when the attack opened. He sent back his men and remained to watch developments. When forced to return, he was unable to reach his own division; he therefore reported to a company of the division on the left. After the assault he found himself with a few details on the flank of the enemy's incursion. His little party was surrounded and being fired into by a machine-gun from the rear. He charged the gun and killed the crew himself; then, turning the gun on the enemy, he killed many more. And he was not content merely to defend; he collected men and attacked successfully three times, but, being unsupported on the left, he had to withdraw his party on each occasion. Awarded the Victoria Cross, he fell in fight at Vittorio Veneto five months later.

Lieutenant-Colonel C. E. Hudson, D.S.O., M.C., commanding the 11th Sherwood Foresters, became aware that the enemy had reached the crest of the San Sisto ridge in front of him. Collecting a mixed company from his headquarters and from an Italian trench-mortar battery, he drove the Austrians headlong from their hold. Following them up, he found the front line in the possession of a crowd of others. These held up their hands and an officer made to surrender. One of the crowd then threw a bomb, which killed this officer and severely wounded Hudson. He could not get up, so he rolled to a trench and fell in; but before he would be carried off to have his painful injuries cared for, he gave directions for the prosecution of the counter-attack. These were followed and the line was restored. The Victoria Cross was conferred also upon this hero of many gallant exploits.

In the forward area on the left, which had been infiltrated by the enemy, isolated remnants struggled gallantly on through the day and night, and their tenacity gave time to build up the defence anew on switch-lines connecting with the second line. The power of the enemy's thrust was finally broken, and on the morning of June 16th the whole of the front line was recovered in a counter-attack.

At a comparatively small cost the French and British had inflicted a severe defeat upon the enemy. But peril arose in another quarter. The Austrians had crossed the Piave to the Montello, and further down stream. They took 10,000 prisoners and pushed their success during the subsequent days. However, on June 20th the river rose in flood behind them. The Italian reserves were well handled; counter-attacking at this juncture they completed the Austrian disaster. Thus the British and French were saved the difficulties of a withdrawal from the Asiago plateau, where they had so firmly maintained themselves.

During the summer the British gave the enemy no rest. Raids were frequent. Out of the line in the area for rest and training the divisions exercised in this and more ambitious forms of attack. Whilst the British were adding to their training and moral, the Austrians were losing heart.

PALESTINE

On June 28th, 1917, Sir Edmund Allenby, from the Third Army in France, succeeded Sir Archibald Murray as Commander-in-Chief of the Egyptian Expeditionary Force.

Only on the coastal sector, and for a short distance, were the opposing lines within striking distance of each other. But it was upon Beersheba, at the other end of the line, that Allenby decided to deliver his main attack. The defences here were less formidable and offered a chance of success at far smaller cost. The capture of Beersheba would enable the British to use their superiority in cavalry in a wide sweeping movement which would threaten to roll up and envelop the Turkish line and thus force the enemy to evacuate his strongly fortified right flank; moreover, the comparative inaccessibility of Beersheba to our troops would make an attack there the more unexpected by the enemy.

This main attack on the right was entrusted to the Twentieth Corps (General Chetwode) and the Desert Mounted Corps (General Chauvel). But a secondary attack was to be made at the same time by the Twenty-first Corps (General Bulfin), which lay in close touch with the enemy opposite Gaza. As was intended by Allenby, the enemy mistook this attack (which they expected to be accompanied by a landing of troops further north) for the main attack, and had therefore concentrated their resources behind Gaza.

Since July considerable reinforcements had been received by the enemy on this front. The railway (metre gauge) had been extended to Beit Hanun, just north of Gaza, with a branch to Huj, and large supplies of ammunition and other stores had arrived. His defences had been strengthened until they constituted an almost continuous line as far east as Sheria. So it was evident that the Turk intended to stand upon this line. On our side strenuous training and the most elaborate preparations were necessary for the operations over the country south of Beersheba, which was practically waterless and quite devoid of good roads.

THIRD BATTLE OF GAZA

The operations opened with a week's bombardment of Gaza, daily increasing in intensity and assisted from October 30th onwards by the guns of one cruiser, two gunboats, two destroyers, and four monitors. On October 28th the concentration for the attack on Beersheba began, the

53rd and 60th Divisions leading, the 74th and 10th in reserve. The Desert Mounted Corps moved south of these in their broad sweep to the east. All standing camps were left intact in the Belah area, a move·that successfully misled the enemy, who reported that there were "six infantry divisions in the Gaza sector, deeply echeloned".

During the night of the 30–31st, the Twentieth Corps and Desert Mounted Corps moved forward to their positions of deployment under a bright moon. A preliminary attack of the former had by 8.30 a.m. gained the enemy's outer defences and enabled the guns to move forward for wire-cutting in the main positions. The attack proper began at 12.15 p.m., and by 1.30 the main positions south of Beersheba had been captured by the 60th and 74th Divisions. The Anzac and Australian Mounted Divisions, after marches varying between 25 and 35 miles, had reached their objectives in the hills 5 miles east of Beersheba at 8 a.m., and now had an almost level plain between them and the town. The high ground commanding this from the north was secured with some difficulty, and troops attempting to cross the plain found progress difficult. "In the evening, however, a mounted attack by Australian Light Horse, who rode straight at the town from the east, proved completely successful. They galloped over two deep trenches held by the enemy just outside the town and entered it at 7 p.m. About 2000 prisoners and 13 guns were taken. This attack laid open the left flank of the Turkish position for a decisive blow."[1]

The Twenty-first Corps' assault on Gaza, which was principally intended to draw reserves towards the coast before the attack on Sheria, was now fixed for November 2nd. Umbrella Hill, a formidable outwork, was captured by a preliminary operation at 11 p.m. on the 1st. The main attack, at 3 a.m. on the 2nd, secured nearly all its objectives, including Sheikh Hassan and the south-west defences, and successfully attained its tactical end. Six hundred and fifty prisoners and 3 guns were taken, and several fierce counter-attacks on the Sheikh Hassan position were repulsed with great loss.

[1] Allenby's Despatch, December 16th, 1917.

Our right wing pushed forward slowly through difficult country during the next three days, and desperate counter-attacks near Khuweilfe, intended to throw out of gear the elaborate mechanism of the offensive, were driven off. A group consisting of the 53rd and Yeomanry Divisions and the Camel Corps was formed to protect the right flank and hold in check the Turkish Seventh Army, based on El Khulil (Hebron).

By the evening of the 5th the British were ready for the second and decisive stage of the great battle which had begun at Beersheba. The Yeomanry opened the attack by storming the left flank of the enemy's position. The 10th and 60th Divisions attacked at noon after a march of nine miles, captured the strongly entrenched positions of Rushdi and Kauwukah with 600 prisoners and several guns, and reached Sheria station. Mounted troops took up the pursuit and pressed on towards Huj, with the result that when the Twenty-first Corps made their final assault on Gaza next day they found that the garrison had withdrawn. A force was immediately pushed along the coast as far as the mouth of the Wadi Hesi to prevent the enemy from using this water-course as a line of defence.

In one of several successful cavalry actions on the 8th the Worcestershire and Warwickshire Yeomanry charged and broke up an enemy rear-guard near Huj, capturing 12 guns in the face of a stout resistance. The Turks were now in full (and often disorganised) retreat, and the scope of our pursuing columns was limited mainly by the difficulties of supply.

During the 10th and 11th the advance became slower and the stiffening resistance indicated that the enemy was making a great effort to stand on a line which would protect the only railway that connected Jerusalem with the north and her ultimate sources of supply. The hot wind (khamsin) which blew during these two days was a great discomfort, especially to troops and horses so severely tried by shortage of water. But the Desert Mounted Corps captured Esdud (Ashdod) and held a line stretching south-east thence to Arak el Menshiye.

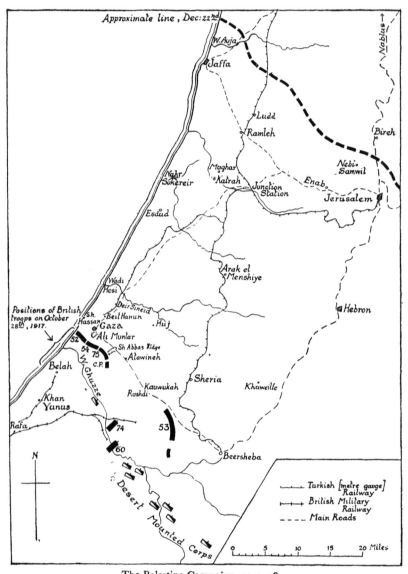

The Palestine Campaign, 1917–18

The fighting troops were now 35 miles in front of railhead, and the forwarding and distribution of supplies and ammunition was no easy matter. By the morning of the 13th, however, all preparations were complete for assaulting the enemy's positions covering the railway. These were favourably sited on high ground running from Katrah to Mughar; but a great feat of arms was performed by the 52nd Division, who, aided by a dashing charge of the 6th Yeomanry Brigade, captured the position with 1100 prisoners and three guns. This attack was crowned by the occupation of Junction Station early next morning and the capture of two undamaged locomotives and much rolling-stock—a most valuable acquisition. The enemy's troops were now separated into two bodies, of which one was retiring northwards between the railway and the sea, and the other eastwards on Jerusalem. General Allenby's despatch recorded that

in fifteen days our force had advanced sixty miles on its right and about fifty on its left. It had driven a Turkish Army of one cavalry and nine infantry divisions out of a position in which it had been entrenched for six months, and had pursued it, giving battle wherever it attempted to stand. Over 9000 prisoners, 80 guns and 100 machine-guns, and large quantities of ammunition and other stores had been captured.

We had now secured a useful landing-place for stores in the mouth of the Nahr Sukereir.

Ramleh and Ludd (Lydda) were taken on the 15th, and Jaffa (Joppa) was entered unopposed on the following day; but further advance northwards was out of the question until the railway could be brought up closer to the fighting area. There would be a certain risk, too, in such an advance till we could secure our eastern flank by establishing a footing on the Nablus (Shechem)–Jerusalem road. This, therefore, provided the next objective. Since it was important to avoid any fighting in or near the Holy City itself, the point aimed at was Bireh, ten miles north of Jerusalem. Possession of this would isolate Jerusalem from Nablus and the main bulk of the Turkish forces.

The hill country, through which the advance must now proceed, contained many positions such as a few troops could easily hold against many, and the one main road (from Jaffa to Jerusalem) crawled for four miles through a narrow and precipitous defile which might well become a death-trap.

The Yeomanry, supported by the 52nd Division, moved through the hills north of this main road towards Bireh, while the 75th Division, with a right flank-guard of Australian Cavalry, pushed up the road, capturing Enab (Kirjath-Jearim), ten miles west of Jerusalem, on November 20th. This advance was one of very great difficulty and hazard, with extremely few gun-positions available, and in the course of it the Gurkhas made great use of their experience of mountain fighting. Heavy rain set in, which made the advance of guns and transport most arduous, while this and the rapid fall in temperature which coincided with the rise in altitude was a severe trial for troops in summer clothing and without blankets. On the following day a brigade was pushed out from Enab towards Bireh. There was no road for wheeled transport and the enemy guns commanded all tracks, but the Nebi Samwil ridge was in our possession before night. We had thus reached the furthest point of Richard I's advance more than seven hundred years earlier.

The enemy were now well placed and resisting stubbornly, while the nature of the ground prevented our artillery from giving any adequate support to the infantry attacks. It therefore became evident that a pause for reorganisation would be necessary before the positions guarding the Nablus–Jerusalem road could be forced. Our line was consolidated, and the 60th Division relieved the 75th, which now returned to the coastal plain.

Rain, which had now fallen for some days, continued to add to the difficulties of transport. Camels were of little use on the wet ground and an army of donkeys was collected to supply troops in the line. The Turkish railway, for which a couple of engines had been brought from the Soudan, was now used, but could deal with only 100 tons a day. Road construction and improvement were tackled with great energy. During the last week of November fierce enemy counter-attacks were made all along the line, with especial violence on the Auja and at Nebi Samwil, but our line held fast.

THE CAPTURE OF JERUSALEM

Fair weather favoured the early stages of the preparations against Jerusalem, and the 53rd Division, which with the Twentieth Corps cavalry was advancing from Beersheba to threaten the enemy's position from the south, had reached a point 10 miles north of Hebron by December 6th. Three days' heavy rain, which began on the 7th, jeopardised the preparations, but in spite of this the gallant attack of the 60th and 74th Divisions carried all its objectives. By the evening of the 8th these divisions held a line close to the Nablus road and within a mile and a half of Jerusalem. The advance continued next morning and a position was taken up across the road, four miles north of Jerusalem. The Turks had withdrawn under cover of night, and at noon the city was surrendered.

On December 11th General Allenby made his formal entry into Jerusalem on foot by the Jaffa Gate. Thus was an Arab prophecy fulfilled, that when the Nile flowed into Palestine (it was conveyed thither by the pipe-line), the prophet from the west, Al Nebi, should drive the Turks from Jerusalem. A proclamation was made in seven languages, announcing that order would be kept in the holy places of the three great religions, which were to be protected for the free use of worshippers.[1]

Certain minor operations involving an advance of some six or seven miles on each flank were now necessary in order to stabilise our line and leave a sufficient margin of protection for Jerusalem on the right and Jaffa on the left. These were completed by the end of the year, and it was possible to settle down to the important work of improving communications over the conquered area.

On December 26th and 27th determined efforts were made by the enemy to recapture Jerusalem. Not only were these

[1] *A Brief Record of the Advance of the Egyptian Expeditionary Force* (H.M. Stationery Office).

attacks withstood by the 53rd and 60th Divisions, but the
10th and 74th counter-attacked with such vigour that by the
end of the operations the Turks had been driven back an
additional seven miles.

Before any further advance northwards on a large scale
could be considered, months must be spent on road and
railway construction, the accumulation of stores, and the improvement of water-supply. In the meantime, in order to
make the right flank secure, it was decided to drive the
enemy beyond Jordan. Such a move would secure in addition control of the Dead Sea and a suitable base of operations for raiding the Hedjaz Railway in conjunction with
our Arab allies. The great difficulty of this operation lay in
the nature of the country over which the advance had to be
made. The ground slopes steeply to the Jordan valley and is
intersected by narrow and precipitous "wadis". The slope
is not continuous, but broken by a series of ridges affording
strong defensive positions to the enemy. The nature of the
terrain is illustrated by the fact that one battery of field
artillery took thirty-six hours to march eight miles.

The 53rd and 60th Divisions began the attack on February
19th. The fighting was extremely fierce and was marked by
a great increase in the volume of enemy machine-gun fire;
but by the 21st Jericho had been occupied and the banks of
the Jordan reached. Further operations, carried out early
in March, were necessary to push our front, again over very
difficult country, as far north as the Auja. We thus gained a
sufficiently wide frontage on the Jordan to give us a safe
jumping-off ground for the important raids that the high
command had in contemplation.

During January useful operations had been carried out
by the friendly Arabs under Emir Feisal on and near the
railway south-east of the Dead Sea. It was partly to damage
the railway and partly to support these Arabs by drawing
northwards some of the troops opposed to them that raids
against Amman and Es Salt were carried out. A still more
important aim was to draw Turkish troops from west to
east of Jordan and mislead their High Command as to the
direction of our next main attack.

Operations against Amman opened on March 21st, 1918 (a notable date on the Western Front). Amman is some 20 miles east of Jordan, and there is an ascent of 4000 feet in 12 miles to be made before reaching the plateau on which it is situated. The British force consisted of the 60th Division, the Anzac (Mounted) Division, the Light Armoured Car Brigade, and other details. Heavy rain had fallen during the three preceding days; the flooded Jordan was extremely difficult to cross (in the face of considerable opposition) and the state of the tracks greatly hampered movement. The enemy was thus enabled to anticipate our final attack by moving reinforcements and guns to Amman. The rain continued, and our men had to advance under the greatest difficulties and hardships. Nevertheless by the evening of the 24th the 60th Division had occupied Es Salt. On the 27th the Anzac demolition parties reached the railway; a bridge was blown up north of Amman and considerable damage done to five miles of line south of the town. But the enemy were by now too strongly placed to allow of our permanently interrupting the line, as we had hoped, by destroying the viaduct and tunnel. On the 30th strong enemy reinforcements had come up, and the order for withdrawal was given. By April 2nd all troops had recrossed the Jordan except those holding a bridge-head at Ghoraniye.

As a result of the raid, Arab troops were enabled to harass severely the weakened Turkish garrison at Maan, to the south, and to damage the railway in that neighbourhood.

After costly and unsuccessful attacks upon our Ghoraniye bridge-head, the enemy took up a strong position at Shunet Nimrin, some five miles east of Jordan. The Es Salt raid, of which the first object was to cut off and capture the forces holding this position, was planned for the middle of May. But when the Beni Sakr Arabs volunteered to co-operate in any attack of ours, provided it took place before May 4th (their supplies would only last till this date), it was decided to alter the date to the beginning of the month. Unfortunately the help of the Arabs did not materialise and the main object of the raid was in consequence not achieved; but nearly 1000 prisoners were taken, and a Turkish document reports that the Commander and Staff of the Fourth Army, whose headquarters were at Es Salt, were within one minute of being captured. The enemy's apprehension of a large-scale attack east of Jordan was further increased. This produced a most valuable result. The Turkish Armies were henceforward dispersed into two large groups separated by a most serious obstacle in the River Jordan. Each group imagined itself to be the target for our next attack and therefore magnified its difficulties and increased its demands for reinforcements and munitions. This led to much friction between the Turkish Army Commanders and the German Commander-in-Chief, Liman von Sanders.

During April the 52nd and 74th Divisions and many Yeomanry Regiments were despatched to France; twenty-four further British battalions and a number of siege batteries and machine-gun companies subsequently followed these. Their places were gradually taken by the 3rd (Lahore) and 7th (Meerut) Divisions from Mesopotamia and other Indian troops, many of whom were as yet without experience in war and needed further training. It was thus necessary to stand on the defensive for a considerable period and refrain from anything in the way of major operations.

SUGGESTIONS FOR READING:
The 23rd Division, 1914–19 by Lt.-Col. H. R. Sandilands, pp. 266–8.
With the 48th Division in Italy by Lt.-Col. G. H. Barnett, pp. 72–3.
Revolt in the Desert by T. E. Lawrence, pp. 276–7.

Chapter XIX: THE GERMAN OFFENSIVE ON THE SOMME

(See map on p. 191)

By the beginning of 1918 Great Britain was faced with a serious situation. The Russian débâcle had freed a million and a half of enemy troops, additional heavy guns, and much ammunition for use on the Western Front. Military assistance from America still needed time to materialise. Meanwhile, with German submarines still dangerously active, and London, now the heart of the Allied war organism, threatened in its activities by the raids of Gotha aeroplanes, the man-power of the British Armies was being exhausted.

Thus impelled, the Government, though haltingly, overhauled the Military Service Acts and prepared to reinforce the depleted Armies. The difficulty of the work was considerable. To take men from essential war industries, such as munition-making, ship-building, and coal-mining, would be indirectly to court military disaster. To deplete agricultural labour, the merchant navy, and the professions on which the now precarious welfare of the community depended appeared most hazardous; intense effort must be maintained in the face of threatening starvation. Nevertheless a fresh sorting of duties was as unavoidable as it was urgent. To decide to do what was safely possible was not all; to get the decisions carried out properly and fairly was almost as difficult. The means were devised under the Ministry of National Service, controlled by Sir Auckland Geddes. Statistical records of the population, their occupations and fitness for military service, were the foundations upon which it set to work. It called up men for military service as they were required. It examined the ways of "diluting" skilled labour and essential services. It took advisory control of the women's auxiliary war organisations formed for nursing, welfare, transport, and clerical duties on the lines of communication and at the bases, and of the drafting of women into industry. Considerable reserves of power were made available by dint of constant small readjustments of vocation which left the people unruffled, their labours unhindered.

During the winter troops were passing in endless trainloads westwards through Germany and Belgium. Their time otherwise was spent in careful preparation for the work that lay before them. On arrival in France they were massed opposite the centre and right of the extended British front, which, stretching to Barisis, south of the Oise, had now a length of 125 miles, and none of it inactive. Favourable weather was awaited.

Behind the British right and centre, formed by the Fifth and Third Armies, lay the area devastated by the enemy in his retreat to the Hindenburg Line early the previous year. Within it communications were poor and, in the south, lines of retrenchment practically non-existent. For the purpose of a sustained defence much work required to be done. The training of the troops in defence, on new principles, was almost equally urgent. It was not possible to undertake both tasks with effectives thinned by fighting, considering also the shortage of reinforcements, the longer line to be held, and the needs of Italy. Much therefore remained to be done when the storm broke on March 21st, 1918.

The attack had long been forecasted with definiteness. The British Army talked about it, and, of course, jested about it, particularly with a certain old steam-roller driver busy on the Albert–Bapaume road. He always bantered back that he was making ready for their retreat and that he would be better off than they when it came. He was. When the time came, he set off down the road and no traffic control could stop him—he passed the western outskirts of Albert under full steam about dusk!

A few minutes before 5 a.m. on the 21st of March the enemy's bombardment opened on the whole front of attack from the Oise to the Scarpe. Moreover, as if to warn the whole Western Front that its hour had come, he sent his heralds farther afield. East and north-east of Rheims and between the La Bassée Canal and the Comines Canal he made great artillery demonstrations; rail-heads were picked out and many peaceful "back areas" elsewhere awoke that morning to the explosion of long-range shells. He bombarded Dunkirk from the sea; but for thus flouting the Dover Patrol he was to pay on St George's Day, a month later.

After nearly five hours of shelling the German infantry advanced to the assault in serried waves. No less than 40 divisions attacked the eastern face of the British line north of Moy; 6 more advanced across the marshes south of this; 18 others made the decisive thrust against 16,000 yards of the northern face of the Somme front. Altogether a strength exceeding the whole of the British Army in France attacked on a 54-mile front from the Oise to the Sensée. The British Fifth Army had 11 divisions in the line, covering 30 miles; 3 more and 3 cavalry divisions stood in reserve. The Third Army had 8 divisions in the line, covering 24 miles of the front attacked, and 7 in reserve.

A thick white fog obscured the enemy's movements, and the defending infantry's "S.O.S." signals were accordingly unperceived. Later the day was warm and bright, conditions which had prevailed for some time. Thus the attackers were favoured. They met with resistance on the line of the British outposts, but in the majority of cases surrounded and isolated these. Some of the outposts were relieved by counterattack, notably those at the haunches of the Flesquières salient, where the enemy was early held up. Others were still sending wireless reports of the greatest value after nightfall. The weight of the heaviest German onslaughts crushed the forward defences in places, however. Here the main defensive positions were penetrated during the day, but the bulk of the defenders, fighting gamely, steadily withdrew. Swinging back under the greatest of the pressure, they took the advancing German infantry in flank as they assaulted the succeeding lines of the battle zone. Into these the reserve divisions moved up. It was thus that the 24th Division at Le Verguier and the 21st at Epéhy prevented the enemy from breaking the line at a very critical time.

That night, the right of the Fifth Army had been pressed back towards its flank on the Crozat Canal, the centre had been indented deeply beyond Savy, and its left lay back west of Templeux. The centre of the Third Army had been driven in with a deep bay in it at St Léger. Yet the enemy was still satisfactorily contained everywhere; his first impetus had been checked with loss. The Flesquières salient had become much more pronounced; it was therefore expedient that the three divisions within it should withdraw. This they began to do during the night.

When the vigour of the action was renewed on the 22nd, the same misty conditions prevailed as on the morning before.

There was fierce fighting for the crossings of the Crozat Canal. Though the enemy got over at several points, he was thrown back everywhere but at Quessy; even here he got no further than Tergnier. It is recorded that the destruction of the bridges was delayed until the enemy was close upon them. One officer, when his firing-circuit failed, lit the instantaneous fuse of the demolition charge with a match. He escaped miraculously.

Against the centre of the Fifth Army the enemy was now thrusting terrifically hard and air reconnaissance later showed great masses following up the advance. The British line was thinning perilously as it stretched out towards Beauvois. However, north and south of the danger-point the defence was firm at Coulaincourt and Fontaine-les-Clercs. All day on the 21st and all day on the 22nd the 1st Royal Inniskilling Fusiliers held out at Fontaine-les-Clercs, the retirement of the troops on their right leaving them enveloped. A small party was sent back at 3 p.m. on the 22nd and succeeded in getting through; the remainder fought to a finish, repulsing the enemy time after time.

On the 22nd the Third Army just held the enemy. Though St Léger was lost and the bay in the line was deepened to beyond Croisilles, the progress cost the Germans dear. But the Fifth Army was now "all in", and the pressure upon it never relaxed. Its right wing clung to the line of the Crozat Canal. For its left wing to stand and fight east of the Somme was to stake all on one high hazard. No supports remained on which to retire and reform. So the rear line of the battle zone was abandoned and the prepared positions of the Peronne bridge-head were not defended. The troops passed through them to the crossings of the long northward reach of the Somme. With rear-guards constantly in action, they withdrew throughout the night and during much of the following day, the 23rd.

On the 23rd the enemy forced the whole length of the Crozat Canal. In the forest lands to the south-west of it the fighting was confused and bloody. At Ham the Germans found a gap in the line, pushed through it, and crossed the

Somme. North of Ham their every approach to the river was shattered by artillery fire.

During the night of the 22nd–23rd the left of the Third Army was withdrawn to the line Henin–Fampoux. Its left flank never budged afterwards. Pivoting on this, the line of the Third Army swung back on a wide arc and reached Ytres. Throughout the whole of the day the enemy dogged its dangerous heels. Five and six separate attacks were made on the front about Vaulx-Vraucourt and all were repulsed. Critical situations arose elsewhere and were resourcefully grappled with. The right flank of the Army was uncovered by the prolonged withdrawal of the Fifth Army through the Peronne bridge-head; but the enemy was held at bay in brilliant actions about Four Winds Farm and east of Rocquigny. Beugny was magnificently held by the 9th Welch Regiment, and the rest of its brigade was thereby enabled to disengage and withdraw. At Mory a gap which had opened during the night was closed during the day. Desperate fighting, however, continued here, and on the 24th the village passed into the enemy's possession. The German efforts to get forward south of Arras were supremely courageous. General von Below's Army fought so stoutly that it had ceased to have any offensive value by the following day. Before a single machine-gun post west of Henin lay four hundred German dead.

But the flank formations of the Third and Fifth Armies were now quite out of touch, and the enemy, with his usual resource, found the weakness and got through, in spite of Rocquigny being most stubbornly held against him from sunrise until the afternoon, and in spite of the devotion of a portion of the South African Brigade isolated north of Cléry-sur-Somme. The South Africans fought until only a hundred men remained unwounded. The troops at Rocquigny extricated themselves.

That day the enemy occupied Combles and pushed on to the high ground about Morval, overlooking the old Somme battlefield. To the south the sadly thinned left wing of the Fifth Army was making a last stand. To the north the right wing of the Third Army was actually fighting its way back, though heavily engaged in front and brokenly exposing many a flank. From dawn onwards the line of the Somme south of Peronne was attacked in great force. The river was low and the marshes along it unusually dry. At Pargny and at Ham the enemy was able to add to his hold of the left bank and thence to get forwards, but only to meet determined resistance and to be stopped by a counter-attack west of Ham. Next day, however, the northern section of the river line had to be abandoned owing to the retirement of the right of the Third Army.

Southwards, towards the Oise, the Germans reached Chauny and were approaching Noyon. Near Cugny a squadron of the 6th Cavalry Brigade fought a remarkable action. It charged to the relief of some heavily engaged infantry, broke through the line of the attackers, sabred many, and took a hundred prisoners.

It was at this critical stage of the battle that reinforcing divisions, mostly drawn from the First and Second Armies, began to come into action. The advanced troops of four divisions pushed straight into the fight on arrival, and strove gallantly to redress the balance. The 63rd Machine Gun Battalion, with twelve guns in Lesboeufs, expended 25,000 rounds on the masses of the Germans about Morval and gained time for their division to take ground to the right of the Third Army. The 15th Cheshires and the 15th Sherwoods went similarly to the support of the Fifth Army and made an effective counter-attack. The other divisions helped to cover the retreat from the Somme crossings and delayed the enemy's progress from Ham and Pargny. Along the Oise, divisions of the Third French Army were coming into line on the deepening flank. This isolated the British Third Corps, which passed under the French Army Commander.

Thus steadied, the retreat entered upon its last stage across the Somme battlefield. Change and contrast can never have been more marked. The shell-swept slough of a year and a half before had been visited by the magical hand of spring. For a summer it had shone with masses of flowers—poppy, mayweed, cornflower, and agrimony. It was now clothed with their luxuriant remains and with laid, rank grasses. Its gaping, sodden wounds had smoothed and dried.

Those who had known these teeming acres and dwelt there dangerously felt the touch of age as they crossed them again. Faces and deeds half forgotten returned to mind, and with them came associations reaching ludicrously back to civil life. Old landmarks were lost. Lives had been lived and laid down that once gave character to them. Those who recollected had become veterans in the oldest of professions; they felt as if they had never practised any other. The intense passion of the former struggle was gone. The solid effort of 1916, its seething chaos and high-strung pitch of courage, had no counterpart in this. The scattered, casual, deadly encounters blazed and died along a gallant broken line. Its segments recoiled through a swarming, lurking infiltration which swayed it this way and that in bickering flame. It was as if the very earth, inured to war, no longer felt the shame of it as hitherto, drawing it underground. Instead she feverishly flung aside the veil of the morning mist and in the early spring sunshine flaunted her subjugation, spurned by the feet of armies.

From this period onwards it was clear that the enemy aimed at severing the French Army from the British, south of the Somme. To this end he pressed his attack relentlessly towards Montdidier, where the French were detraining. At the same time he strove to reach the high ground beyond Gommecourt and Bucquoy across the Ancre. The degree of his success may be judged by the resolve of the French Commander-in-Chief, General Pétain, to retreat, if forced, on Paris independently of the British. On the 24th he informed Sir Douglas Haig of this, who promptly wired the information to the Chief of the Imperial General Staff, Sir Henry Wilson. The consequences were momentous, as will be seen.

The second contributory aim of the Germans only just failed of accomplishment. The neighbourhood of Mory, Sapignies, and Behagnies continued to be the scene of a desperate struggle. There was also stiff fighting just north of the Somme on the right flank of the Third Army, now extended thither. Between, the line opened perilously at the junction of the Fifth and Fourth Corps. Taking full advantage of this, the enemy passed the Ancre north of Miraumont on the 25th and climbed towards Gommecourt and Bucquoy on the 26th.

The right of the Third Army was then ordered to fall back to the west bank of the Ancre, where other forces were at hand. These were just in time. Enemy machine-guns were thick in Colincamps. A section of field guns disposed of them, galloping into action and firing over open sights at close range. This gave the reinforcing troops time to deploy in the gap between Beaumont-Hamel and Bucquoy. Accompanied by light tanks, they retook Colincamps and finally stopped the German offensive there. This was the first occasion that light tanks—"whippets", as they were called—were used in action.

Unfortunately the retirement of the Third Army to the Ancre was too generally carried out. The right should have rested on Bray-sur-Somme. It withdrew beyond this, and when the mistake was discovered had reached Sailly-le-Sec. The Fifth Army was to pay wearily for this. It was too tired to march, but if only its battered remnants could be got together on a sound defensive position it was still capable of holding the enemy. Of the two essentials for this, a good position and some few troops already in occupation of it on whom to retire, the second was not forthcoming. Though the front south of the Somme had passed under command of the French, their divisions were not yet in sufficient strength, and it was no longer possible to send British divisions south of the river.

Such expedients as the situation allowed of were improvised. Their pathetic insufficiency does not detract from the steadiness and good order prevailing behind the changing battle-line; their effects remain the glory of the fighting troops employed. At Liancourt, west of Nesle, on the 25th the Germans were pushing through in force between the parted flanks of the Eighteenth and Nineteenth Corps. The situation was extremely critical. There arrived in buses from further south the 61st Brigade, 20th Division. Previous fighting in

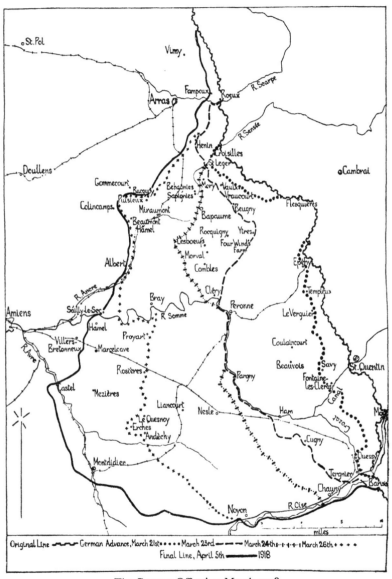

The German Offensive, March 1918

support of the 36th Division had reduced it to 450 rifles; notwithstanding, it contained the enemy and made possible the withdrawal of the division to which it belonged. A force which can only be described as motley was collected by the Chief Engineer of the Fifth Army, General Grant, and this was posted in the old Amiens defence line, Mezières–Marcelcave–Hamel, south of the Somme. It was made up of stragglers—mostly siege gunners whose guns had been taken—details, schools of instruction, and specialist Army troops such as tunnellers, surveyors, and Canadian and American Engineers. Towards the line which they took up the remnant of a fine Army retired, painfully but stubbornly.

On the 26th it stood to fight on the line Le Quesnoy–Rosières–Proyart. A vigorous German thrust south-westwards from Nesle succeeded in penetrating to Erches, between the British right and the French left. Two British divisions, relieved by the French on the previous day, hurried back to mend the break. They fought finely at Andèchy, holding it until the afternoon of the 27th. North of the break, at Le Quesnoy, a part of the 61st Brigade, numbering 100 officers and men all told, under Capt. E. P. Combe, the Brigade Major, defied the enemy from dawn until 6 p.m. The survivors, eleven in number, retired with honours such as few gain in war and many pay for.

No finer battle in a modern sense was ever fought, for the ideal that each man should lead himself must almost have been attained. Withal the fatigue on both sides was extreme. Opposing detachments often marched in full view of each other—when one lay down to rest, so did the other; when one fought, the other countered. A higher degree of devotion under extreme hardship can surely never have inspired the partisans of two conflicting ideals, identically circumstanced.

The supreme ordeal of the gallant Fifth Army was, however, yet to come. On March 27th their exposed left flank about Proyart was turned from across the river west of Bray. The Third Army's mistake had betrayed their hard-tried comrades in the moment when final success must otherwise have rested with them—Amiens would then have been saved from injury and the all-important railway thereabouts from interruption. As it was, a minimum of ground along the river was conceded. The troops held every foot elsewhere against the fiercest pressure. The 20th, 30th, 24th, 66th, and 8th Divisions, and of the last the 2nd Devons and 22nd Durham Light Infantry (Pioneers), made this ill-starred day glorious. On their right the French were forced back and the enemy reached Montdidier.

On this day Albert fell into German hands, but attempts to debouch from the place were stopped and the enemy lost heavily. During the months that followed the German front line lay in the western outskirts of Albert, and the cathedral with its famous leaning Virgin was demolished. It had long been said that when the precarious image fell the end of the war would come. The end was indeed coming, though not the end which then seemed likely.

One day more the Fifth Army dragged its tired limbs westwards, till it rested on the slopes crowned by Villers-Bretonneux, where it stayed the tide of conquest, 10 miles from Amiens. The command of it then passed from General Gough to General Rawlinson. The French continued to be pressed back down the valley of the Avre towards Castel. On the 28th, however, the storm-centre had shifted to the valley of the Scarpe. At 3 a.m. a furious enemy bombardment began and lasted until 7.15 a.m. Then five German divisions, three of them fresh, attacked the two divisions on the extreme right of the First Army, north of the river. Four others attacked the two divisions on the extreme left of the Third Army, south of the river. Eleven more assaulted the British front as far south as Bucquoy. Three more were held in readiness to carry the Vimy Ridge on the 29th.

The attack was expected and precautions had been taken. The morning broke clear, and the enemy's preliminary concentrations were found promptly by the British guns. The great violence of the artillery battle on this day tested the British gunners severely. One incident out of many shows how they rose to the occasion. In a 6-inch howitzer battery, as the action proceeded, all the detachments were destroyed, and every gun but one. The four remaining officers kept this gun in action until two of them were killed and the two others wounded.

Along the 56th Division's front "the bulk of the forward posts were obliterated".[1] Nevertheless, when the German assault came, it met disaster. About Roeux, on the north bank of the Scarpe, six lines of the enemy advanced in almost close order. Old 15-pounder guns concealed near the front line fired on them at point-blank range with terrible effect, whilst everywhere machine-guns in the remains of the out-post line took them in flank and rear. Still the survivors came on and with great courage began to cut by hand the wire before the British positions. At this they withered away. The remnants of British advanced troops disputed every yard of the German advance. All along the line southwards to Puisieux the story of costly defeat was repeated. There is a dreadful irony in the fact of a prisoner taken on this day carrying six days' rations, two blankets, and a spare pair of boots. What an orgy of inspections must have heralded his setting out! Yet for him Charon's penny even would have been superfluous kit.

For yet another week the enemy kept up his attacks, particularly about Arras and south of the Somme. But, hampered by poor communications across the old battlefield, his exhausted divisions made little advance and gained no advantage. The third of the great German incursions into Picardy had ended, by the narrowest margin, like its prede-cessors without decisive result. Its indirect consequences indeed laid the foundation of victory for the Allies.

On the gate-posts of the Hôtel de Ville at Doullens is in-scribed in English and French: "In this Hôtel de Ville on the 26th March, 1918, the Allies confided the sole command of the Western Front to General Foch. This decision saved France and the liberty of the world". Present at the urgently convened meeting which made this appointment were the Commanders-in-Chief of the French and British Armies, General Pétain and Field Marshal Sir Douglas Haig; the Chiefs of the respective General Staffs, General Foch and Sir Henry Wilson; M. Clemenceau, and Lord Milner.

[1] *The 56th Division* by Major C. H. Dudley Ward, D.S.O., M.C.

M. Poincaré presided. Its act was confirmed at Beauvais on April 3rd by General Bliss, Mr Lloyd George, and M. Clemenceau, representing the American, British, and French Governments. The original meeting was the direct result of Pétain's message to Haig that, if forced, the French would retire independently on Paris. It examined the urgent problem of the use of reserves. It satisfied itself that the British line north of Arras had been levied upon to beyond the danger point and that the French reserves were being brought up slowly and inadequately, considering the gravity of the peril. It convinced itself that the liaison between the two armies was failing and that a common purpose hardly existed. The conclusion arrived at commended itself to all present. It marked what has come to be regarded as the turning-point of the war.

Thus a common peril had served to unite the Allied armies and to free the army leaders of political worries; and it had providentially braced the politicians to face the situation in their own sphere. The long ordeal of 1917, with one national army morally disintegrating, had been ended. Though both armies were now deteriorated under the mental and physical strain of individual national effort, they would, united, exceed the sum of their failing strengths. Poor suffering France could rise still to her chosen watchwords, Equality, Fraternity, Liberty. The union of the Eastern and Western German Armies had given the enemy moral advantage, but the effect had failed to be immediately decisive. The Allies had now taken a similar step—too late, but not hopelessly so.

SUGGESTIONS FOR READING:

A Fatalist at War by Rudolf Binding, pp. 203–21. *The World Crisis, 1916–18* by W. S. Churchill, pt. II, pp. 408–12. *The Somme* by A. D. Gristwood, pp. 142–5.

Chapter XX: THE GERMAN OFFENSIVE ON THE LYS

(See map on p. 202)

THE news of the German advance in Picardy was received in England with consternation. The moral stimulus of successful fighting, whatever the cost, can do much to deaden a people's hunger. But now it had failed. Happily Lord Rhondda had just extracted order out of chaos in the rationing of food supplies; otherwise the strain might have proved too great. As it was, reassurances were necessary. Unfortunately, for years the loss or gain of a little ground had made the illusion of defeat or victory. Everyone had forgotten that victory only follows the complete collapse of the enemy; that to give ground may be, as at Bannockburn, the only way to victory. The loss at a blow of more ground than, in the aggregate, had been won by the British Armies since their reconstitution was the impressive fact of the moment. It was impossible to explain it away.

Statesmen found a ground for public optimism in the appointment of General Foch to the Supreme Command. They repeated emphatically that all the losses of men and material in the recent battle had been made good, and they mildly pressed the need for a further extension of the scope of the Military Service Acts. Examined in detail, the grounds of these reassurances were less satisfying. On the outbreak of the offensive some 80,000 men on leave were recalled; 80,000 others, under nineteen years, were sent overseas forthwith, though there was reason to believe that the physical strain would be beyond their powers. That the spirit of these boys subsequently justified the step in a wonderful way cannot excuse the circumstances of their drafting.

Munitions were promptly replaced and work on new reserves set forward as quickly as the strike bogey allowed. Parliament's labours in legislating a new "comb-out" of men from industry for the Army were completed with unusual despatch. It was proved again that the heart of Britain was sound, if her methods were muddled. One instance may be given. A South Wales colliery band was turned out amid shouts of "Come on, fellers, let's go an' enlist!" The manager failed to stop the march by urging the pressing need of coal for France; only the persuasive obstinacy of the Recruiting Officer was effective in getting the men to return to the coal-face till sent for.

Reinforcements numbering 160,000 served in some measure to restore the numbers of the B.E.F. But time also was needed to rest and re-form its shattered divisions. Out of 58 of these, 46 had been engaged in severe and prolonged fighting between the 21st of March and the 5th of April. No rest, however, was vouchsafed them. It was General Foch's policy to use spent troops again and again, in order to save his reserves; the agony they endured was the price of ultimate victory.

A new blow had been visibly preparing for some time along the river Lys, and the unusually rainless spring offered early opportunity for it to be struck. It was preluded by thirty-six hours' gas bombardment, which changed at 4 a.m. on April 9th to mixed gas and high explosive. At 7 a.m., in fog, the enemy's assault began against the front between the La Bassée Canal and the Bois Grenier and fell first upon the left brigade of a Portuguese division, which was to have been relieved that night. The Germans broke through. The flanks of the British divisions right and left of the Portuguese were turned, though both formed defensively towards the break, and the interval was covered promptly by cavalry and cyclists. Behind these, two British divisions deployed, but failed to restore the line in the north about Laventie.

Near the La Bassée Canal the enemy was held. The 55th (West Lancashire) Division had for some time occupied this vital sector, which covered Béthune and the coalfield behind. They had been carefully trained in every detail of the prepared defence scheme and practised by means of frequent alarms; so that when the Germans attacked in a dense fog their momentary success was turned into failure by hand-to-hand fighting. Over 700 prisoners, indeed, were taken, many of them being trapped in a tunnel. The 55th Division yielded no ground to the repeated attacks in the succeeding week, and their courage and tenacity in this greatest defensive feat of the latter part of the war held the Germans cramped within narrow bounds.

The enemy reached the line of the river Lawe and the river Lys by evening. He even secured a bridge-head about Croix du Bac, having crossed the Lys on the heels of the retiring defenders at Bac St Maur. Elsewhere he was thrown back from these rivers with great losses.

The night was hideous with the clangour of artillery battle and the insidious menace of gas. At dawn on the 10th the Lys was forced at Lestrem and Estaires, and a struggle of the fiercest kind was waged among the streets and houses of Estaires. British machine-guns in the upper storeys raked the attacking troops on the opposite bank of the river, and the houses had to be destroyed by shell-fire before the enemy could make good his footing. The Germans then pressed on to Steenwerck, with guns well forward. The semi-sanctity of guns was a thing of the past; in this the richly munitioned modern armies set a new standard. It paid best at times to fight a weapon to the last and then destroy it.

The enemy now found it needful to extend the front of his attack. Shortly after dawn on the 10th he advanced towards the high ground about Messines, Wytschaete, and Hollebeke. Recoiling to the Wytschaete crest, the defence held firmly on, and no impression was made on the British line at Hollebeke; but Messines was lost in the night after a day of stern struggle. Armentières, now in a deep and narrowing salient, was evacuated that night with commendable steadiness. The bridges over the Lys were all destroyed.

The battle front now extended from the La Bassée Canal to the Comines Canal. Enemy attacks on its whole length next day, April 11th, found the unmended weakness east of Merville. The thin British line could not stretch at a tactical need without gaping here and there; it was under extreme tension. So the enemy entered Merville and providentially fell to looting the place, for hunger already had its edge fretting the belt of the German soldier. The defenders withdrawn just west of the town perceived the disorder; fires broke out and revelry resounded.

A little to the north of Merville the weight and impetus of

the German attack carried it beyond Neuf Berquin and within half a dozen miles of the important railway junction of Hazebrouck, where reinforcements were due to arrive.

North of Steenwerck, for the most part, the enemy paid dearly for small gains. Ploegsteert Wood, however, passed wholly into his hands, with other ground about a mile in depth towards Nieppe. Here and at Messines and Hollebeke the Germans had been met with the bayonet. But the defenders were too few to be wasted on a jig-saw line of salients and re-entrants; consequently that night a withdrawal to the slopes east of Neuve Église was effected, and the troops took up a line from near Steenwerck to Wytschaete. Not only were they precariously few on the northern wing of the defence, but they were only precariously reinforceable by drawing piece-meal upon the garrisons of the salient east of Ypres. The enemy forces on the other hand were in great strength; moreover they were used in desperate fashion.

Notwithstanding that he had been checked and his plan to spread his flanks foiled on the 11th, the enemy thrust hard towards the Hazebrouck railhead on the following day. The 12th of April was a day of critical struggle unsurpassed in gravity during the whole four years of the war. In a special order Sir Douglas Haig solemnly conjured the troops to rise to the occasion; he frankly acknowledged "Our backs are to the wall". To British soldiers he could not have used a more potent rallying-cry.

Such reinforcing divisions as could be found, including one withdrawn from Italy, were arriving, but twenty-four hours must elapse in detraining them and deploying them in support. The troops in battle had almost all recently come through exhausting experiences on the Somme. They were resisting an attack which in concentrated fierceness outdid even the offensive against the Third Army about and south of Arras. Individuals among our tired men lost heart. Deprived of their leaders and pitilessly harried from position to position, they lost cohesion. Numbers wandered aimlessly away, taking no notice of anybody or anything, even their own safety. But yet there remained a sufficiency of dauntless men to mark the day with heroism.

Day had not dawned when the enemy began a serious diversion in the southern part of the battlefield. A sudden attack broke the British line about Pacaut and made to cross the La Bassée Canal. Two batteries of the 255th Brigade R.F.A. were retiring from the canal, but seeing the seriousness of the threat, each battery got a gun into action within five hundred yards of the bank. Meanwhile a party of gunners dashed back with rifles and held a drawbridge. The enemy was checked and from this moment the tide turned against him in this part of the field. The arrival here of reinforcements from south of Arras, battle-worn already as they were, gave the defence the necessary strength; the huge numbers of the enemy had henceforward no other effect than to increase his casualties. West of Merville the defenders gave a little ground, but then stood firm.

The critical area was about Vieux Berquin. South of the village the 4th Guards Brigade of the 31st Division, and north of it two brigades of the 29th Division, hung on to their positions. The tenacity they showed is almost incredible. Little parties of men fought completely surrounded for most of two days. It is related of one such party that the last man of it left alive held off the enemy with his rifle for twenty minutes till he was killed by a bomb—this was Private Jacotin of the 3rd Coldstream Guards. And these men did not rest satisfied with defending; they attacked.

The 4th Guards Brigade began by attacking. With ten companies in line, it may be said to have attacked a whole German Army in depth; machine-gun fire and guns at point-blank range could not stop it. Having thrown back the Germans, it held 4000 yards of front with both flanks unsupported. This line was attacked in turn about 4.30 p.m. after a tremendous bombardment, but without success. Twice on the morning of the 13th the enemy was again repulsed. Then he brought forward field guns to point-blank range and destroyed the trenches of the left company of the 4th Grenadier Guards, the left of the Brigade. The survivors fought back to back, surrounded. Of a company of the 2nd Irish Guards sent to their relief, only one N.C.O. and six men answered that night. At 6.30 p.m. eighteen sur-

vivors of the Grenadiers left their trench and charged with
the bayonet. Fourteen survivors returned to the trench, now
a mile within the German lines. Just before night they
charged again for the last time. The one injured survivor
escaped from the enemy's hands twenty-four hours later.
The 29th Division to the north of the 4th Guards Brigade
made a fighting retirement of 6000 yards in three days and
nights.

Finally, in little parties, the remnants of these troops
crossed the line of the 1st Australian Division between Nieppe
Forest and Meteren, which had been fortified since the de-
trainment of the division at Hazebrouck early on the 13th.
On this line the German advance on Hazebrouck was
stopped. By self-sacrifice for which no praise is too high the
Guards had again saved the situation.

The enemy command had allowed "I would" to act the
bully to "I dare not" in rushing on Hazebrouck through a
bottle-neck of low ground. Yet great efforts were made to
spread the flanks of the attack. On the afternoon of the 12th
the fighting at Neuve Église became fiercer, and continued
all night. Next day it was extended south of Bailleul and
Meteren. By then the Germans had gained a foothold in
Neuve Église, only to be ejected from the place before noon.
They had suffered great losses; yet they came on again that
day, to find the defence cleverly withdrawn to the Ravelsberg. On the morning of the 14th the enemy was again
cleared out of Neuve Église by bombing, but it fell into
German hands later that day. The Mairie, held by a party
of the famous 2nd Worcesters, resisted until 2 p.m. Thanks
to this dogged valour, the enemy made but a little gain on
his northern flank. At the very moment of success, too, his
hopes of pushing out his southern flank were dashed; a
counter-attack drove the Germans back from the canal
drawbridge near Pacaut.

The atmosphere during these days of intense struggle
appears dark, but now and then some jest threw its cheerful
beam across the darkness, like Jessica's little candle. When
pigs die no comets are seen, usually; but the death of one
near Merris lit the sky with battle. Some of the 29th Division

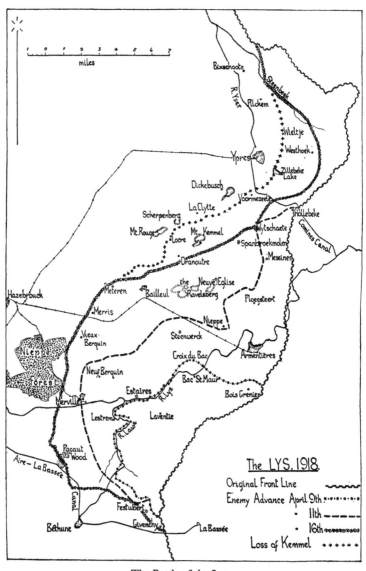

The Battle of the Lys

heard its dying squeal in a farm through which they had just retired. They returned, captured the farm, and "avenged" the pig.

To provide defenders for the lengthening Lys battle-front, Sir Douglas Haig shortened his line east of Ypres. The troops in the Salient were gradually withdrawn until on April 15th they held the Wytschaete Ridge, Westhoek Ridge, and the line of the Steenbeek. These moves were also designed to spoil any enemy plan to extend the scope of his operations northwards. Possibly as a result, the only operation undertaken by the Germans was against the Belgian right. It aimed at Bixschoote on April 17th and failed, the Belgians taking 700 prisoners.

About this time the new unity of command began to show results; General Foch moved French troops northwards behind the British. The enemy, evidently convinced of his error in thrusting with his crowded centre, proceeded to try for more elbow-room. On the 15th, using four fresh divisions of quality and more artillery, he assaulted the Ravelsberg. Having succeeded in gaining its eastern end, the Germans worked westwards along it. That night they entered historic Bailleul, cradle of Scottish kings; but in the blazing town the hungry German infantry found all too little food. The British line was then withdrawn to the lower slopes of the Kemmel range, between Meteren and Dranoutre.

Bent on improving this small advantage, the enemy delivered many local attacks on the 16th, most of which were repulsed. One, however, gained Meteren and the other took Wytschaete. Counter-attacks by both British and French failed to regain either place permanently. Next day the enemy tried to take Kemmel Hill. With eight divisions, seven of them fresh, he launched a great attack on a front of 21,000 yards. Despite every effort, backed by great gun-power, it failed, a result which testifies to the inexhaustible spirit of the much-enduring British troops.

Foiled in the north, the enemy tried now to free his southern flank. The German shelling was terrific, but only at Givenchy and Festubert did he make even a temporary gain, and of this he was quickly deprived with great loss.

For a week after this no great attack was made in the north. But the German position in the low ground along the Lys was obviously one that must be either improved or abandoned, as it was completely overlooked from the high ground on either hand, about Béthune to the south and Kemmel to the north. The enemy command chose to seek salvation in another attempt to take Kemmel Hill. Success would cover their right and dominate the defence to the north about Ypres. Unfortunately for the Allies, the Germans did succeed.

On the 21st of April French divisions had relieved the British between Meteren and Spanbroekmolen, due east of Kemmel. On the 25th, after a sustained shelling with gas, this front and that of the British eastwards as far as Hollebeke was assaulted about 5 a.m. Seven German divisions attacked and five of them were fresh. The French were pressed back to the lower slopes of Mont Rouge and the Scherpenberg and the enemy established himself on Kemmel Hill. The British right was turned; in spite of gallant resistance, the line was forced off the Wytschaete Ridge on to the Ypres-Dickebusch flats. That night the Allied line ran west from Hill 60 by Voormezeele to La Clytte. But it was secure. Forthwith the salient east of Ypres was narrowed still more on account of its newly imperilled communications. From Voormezeele the line was established towards the west end of Zillebeke Lake and thence to Wieltje and Pilckem.

Hope must have surged strongly in the German breast. After a day of small actions the enemy tried to force his way to the Scherpenberg on the 28th, the front of the attack extending from Locre to Voormezeele. In spite of the heaviest losses, assault after assault was made, only to fail. The most determined came on in mass with bayonets fixed, and British infantry went out to meet them with the bayonet and overcame them. Next day, April 29th, was the last of the battle of the Lys. The French in a counter-attack re-took Locre.

The German thrust on the Lys front had involved the Allies in a new peril, for it became a direct bid for the Channel ports and there were moments when it seemed that this prize would be won. But the German Higher Command made the mistake of allowing what was designed as a minor operation to develop into a major one. Temporary successes led them to thrust more and more troops into an ever-deepening salient, and when at length the Allied line held firm, the cost at which the enemy were obliged to hold their gains proved ruinous.

THE ATTACK ON VILLERS-BRETONNEUX[1]

Since the Allied line had steadied along the Avre and the Ancre, the Germans had made many attacks north and south of the Somme. Disappointed with the results of these, the enemy undertook a more serious operation. On April 24th he attacked the high ground about Villers-Bretonneux with four divisions supported by tanks. Tank met tank for the first time in war. The British "whippets", notwithstanding, did deadly work against the enemy's infantry, and south of Villers-Bretonneux the British heavy tanks stopped the enemy's advance. Villers-Bretonneux, however, fell to the Germans with a strip of ground north and south of it some three miles long.

The gain was not long held. An attack at 10 p.m. on the same day drove back the Germans and at dawn on the 25th the remnant of them was surrounded in the village. The 13th Australian Brigade in the centre greatly distinguished itself. The whole operation, planned and carried out within twelve hours, was brilliant work. The local advantage lay with the side holding the height of Villers-Bretonneux. Moreover, possession of it was essential to the resumption of the Germans' progress down the Somme valley, the most direct method of separating the British from the French. To be deprived of their gain with such swiftness and decision made the Germans' successes on the Somme and the Lys appear of doubtful value. This augured ill for them. They were sacrificing themselves in thousands for gains that did not amount to decisive victory. So far as the British front was concerned, they had failed; neither skill nor power were

[1] See map on p. 191.

wanting to its guardians at the end of a month of tremendous battering.

SUGGESTIONS FOR READING:

The Irish Guards in the Great War by Rudyard Kipling, vol. II, pp. 199–207. *The 29th Division* by Col. J. F. C. Fuller, pp. 188, 196, 198. *The Spanish Farm* by R. H. Mottram, pp. 192–208.

Chapter XXI: NAVAL OPERATIONS, 1917-18

THE return to ruthless submarine warfare early in 1917 was not on a small scale, for the Germans had nearly ten times as many of these craft as they had had in 1915. Notwithstanding, the peril to England did not stand to that of 1915 in ratio of the strength of U boats. Never for a moment had the needs of the country for defence against submarine depredations been lost sight of. Anti-submarine entanglements had multiplied in the straits and bays; new destructive appliances had been devised and perfected; new means of detection had been brought to a high degree of accuracy.

The Straits of Dover were entirely closed to shipping and boomed. The North Channel was obstructed with an ingeniously laid out net barrage, and many of the island fairways about the north and west of Scotland were similarly closed. Those left open held risks for the submarine almost, if not quite, as great as that of the entanglement. The hydrophone and depth-charge were the new agents in this. To the listener with hydrophones on the shores of these channels it was possible to follow the sound of passing submerged propellers and to locate them even up to a distance of twenty miles. Depth-charges could then be fired at the spot indicated or dropped by fast vessels sent out in chase, and the resulting explosion was fatal to submarines within a radius of a hundred yards.

The decoy-ship also was employed with varied stratagem. The most usual variety was for the crew to set about abandoning the vessel. Under fire of the submarine this demanded a high courage from the "mystery-ship's" company. If the submarine unwarily approached its "prize", side-screens were dropped, revealing concealed guns, whose crews speedily submerged the U boat for the last time. Then the fugitive boats' crews returned or their remnants were rescued. Soon enemy submarines saw in every "tramp" a possible decoy, on which they wasted valuable time and ammunition.

All these methods of defeating the submarine peril were developed with extreme secrecy and increasing success. But their development took time, and before the defence had gained the measure of the attack, the Allies, and Great Britain in particular, suffered grave anxiety and heavy losses.

ZEEBRUGGE

To mitigate the rigours of the submarine campaign Sir Roger Keyes, Vice-Admiral commanding the Dover Patrol, designed to deprive them of advanced bases on the Belgian coast. Ostend, Blankenberghe, and Zeebrugge are connected with Bruges and Antwerp by canals. At Bruges there was a strong concrete-covered submarine dock, as it were a nest of young sticklebacks. To prevent egress, the mouths of the canals at Zeebrugge and Ostend must be blocked. The scheme depended on the weather, the direction of the wind, the treacherous Channel tides and their relation to the hours of darkness. It was minutely detailed in phases, like a trench raid. No less than 163 vessels were under orders for it, exclusive of covering-forces in the North Sea.

After two false starts due to sudden changes of wind and weather, the expedition sailed again for Zeebrugge on the afternoon of April 22nd. Fast motor-boats blanketed the heavily gunned coast defences with smoke; aeroplanes went up into the rainy darkness to bomb them; monitors shelled them with heavy shell from far out at sea. Under cover of this the *Vindictive*, a light cruiser specially armed and appointed, the *Daffodil* and the *Iris* (Mersey ferry-boats) ran the gauntlet of the batteries on the Mole of Zeebrugge and brought up alongside the Mole to land stormers. Simultaneously Submarine *C 3*, filled with explosive, was run in among the piers of the railway viaduct which joined the

Mole with the shore. Meanwhile destroyers and motor-boats invaded the anchorage and attacked the quay-side shipping with gun and torpedo.

From midnight for an hour an incandescent inferno raged in the cold glare of searchlights. The feverish gunnery of the nearer batteries alongshore and on the Mole was countered by the fire of heavy trench-mortars on the deck of the *Vindictive* and by two 3-inch guns in her foretop. *C 3* went up in a sheet of flame and rent a great gap in the viaduct. This made the Mole inaccessible to enemy reinforcements. Fighting for a footing there were men of the landing-parties from the *Vindictive*, which was kept pushed against the Mole by the *Daffodil*; her men ashore fought with bomb, rifle, and bayonet among the sheds, wired defences, and shipping below. Above the parapet of the Mole, swept by shell and splinters, the upper works of the *Vindictive* were dissolving in fragments; twice her foretop was wrecked, and when at last its guns were silent all in it had been killed or wounded. The *Iris* could not make fast. Two young officers landed from her; one jumped to the parapet from a swaying scaling-ladder, the other dropped from a derrick. Both died fighting whilst they tried to moor their pitching vessel.

At the height of this disturbance three concrete-filled block-ships steamed out of the smoke off the end of the Mole, engaging the batteries there as they passed. The first was damaged in charging the entrance boom; the other two passed her, entered the canal, were swung fairly across it and sunk. The damaged ship meanwhile had dragged her grounded stern over the mud, and the bottom was blown out of her as she lay across the entrance channel. The use of the canal by submarines was impossible from that moment.

Motor-launches and destroyers followed the block-ships to take off their crews. The hazard was extreme, but 166 all told were thus rescued from the three ships—there ought not to have been so many to rescue, but certain spirited men had refused to be taken off as arranged, before the ships went into action. Another motor-launch picked up the disabled dinghy in which the two officers and four men from *C 3*, all wounded, had rowed away after igniting fuses.

Imperial War Museum Photo. Crown copyright

BRITISH BLOCK-SHIPS IN THE ZEEBRUGGE CANAL MOUTH

Further gallant rescue work fell to the destroyer *Phoebe*. She and her consort *North Star* attacked the Mole batteries to draw their fire from the rescue-boats. In this work the *North Star* received vital damage. Twice *Phoebe* secured her with a hawser and enveloped her in smoke, only to have the hawser cut by the enemy's fire. Then she tried to push *North Star* out of danger. But *North Star's* course was run; she was sinking. So her crew were taken off, even a last man who appeared on the derelict's deck as *Phoebe* was steaming away.

Near 1 o'clock in the morning the stormers were recalled to the *Vindictive* and the ships withdrew into the smoke. Unawares the *Vindictive* carried away with her a large fragment of the Mole parapet which had lodged aboard her. In the dawn of St George's Day she appeared like a ship afire as she made for Dover, for her riddled funnels were wreathed in flame.

In the words of Captain Carpenter's signal, "the dragon's tail" had been given "a damned good twist".

THE MERCHANT SERVICE

During the years of the war there were lost by enemy action 2774 merchant ships, of which the British share amounted to 2197. In spite of the increasing risks, no lack of crews to maintain the busy war trade overseas was ever experienced. Many acts of gallantry were recorded; death, wounds, and sufferings from exposure of crews in open boats were borne with patience and without loss of spirit. A characteristic distinction invests the memory of Captain Fryatt, a shipmaster of the Harwich service. Following the Admiralty instructions, when threatened with destruction by a U boat he sent his ship the *Berlin* at her to ram her. His action saved his ship. But for this the Germans planned his capture, took him later, tried him, and shot him.

It speaks well for the seamanship of the merchant service that a system of convoy could prove of the greatest profit during the last two years of the war. Wherever it was possible, great companies of ships of all kinds and speeds other than the very fast were shepherded together under the escort of fast warships. Steering zig-zag courses in formation and without lights at night was trying work, and its success was remarkable.

The adventures of submarines and the endurance shown by their crews during the war were among its wonders. But there was a limit. Perhaps the most troublous thing for the enemy crews was the suppression of all news of the capture and destruction of U boats. There was reason enough for this apart from its moral effect. But as the total of losses grew and none could say how they befel, the German crews bade despondent farewells on leaving on the long course "north about" to face the risks of the Western Atlantic. Finally the men of the High Seas Fleet mutinied. Their motives may be gauged from the fact that the lost U boats numbered 216 at the end of the war.

SUGGESTIONS FOR READING:

"*Q*" *Ships* by E. Keble Chatterton.   *The Blocking of Zeebrugge* by Capt. A. F. B. Carpenter.   *The Dover Patrol* by J. J. Bennett ("Jackstaff").

Chapter XXII: THE GERMAN OFFENSIVE CONTINUES

(See map on p. 16)

THE war, as it drew to its end, became a colossal burden under which the world writhed. The senses of the individual found it overwhelming. It numbed them; equally now it paralyses descriptive narrative. The business of war filled the world. Material and human resources, drawn to it from all the earth, were squandered on its vast battlefields in furious excess. Distant and primitive peoples were broken in to its confusions; North Africans and Indians early, and, as time went on, the coloured races of the West Indies and of West, South, East, and Central Africa, the Egyptian fellahin, the whole race of Arabs, the Burmese, the Annamese, and the Chinese became used to its labours and cruelties.

The struggles of Teuton and Turk during the summer of 1918 resemble nothing so much as the flurry of a grounded whale. The Slavs had sunk in the welter; the Latins were too exhausted to wade in and make an end; the Anglo-Saxons and the peoples they had assimilated were warily husbanding their remaining resources and watchfully awaiting signs of weakening in the frenzied struggles of the antagonist. The stranded leviathan must not break away. Fresh Anglo-Saxon spirit and strength was to come from the New World, but it was urgent now that this support should not be delayed.

The plans to bring it were laid. Ships and shipping had not been the life of the British nation for nothing during the centuries of its growth. Fleets of passenger-vessels began plying under convoy between the eastern seaboard of the United States and the western ports of Britain and France. Only one troop-ship was lost at sea by enemy attack and the loss of life was comparatively trifling. This great, minutely organised maritime adventure, bringing American troops to Europe in 1918, was the culmination of Britain's mastery of the sea and was the peak of her naval effort.

By the month of May the American Field Army was pouring into France at the rate of 50,000 a week. In order to economise shipping, arms and transport of French and British pattern were furnished it, and its leading divisions straightway began their war-training with the French and British Armies. Meantime, whilst the enemy was making his final drives against the French front during the summer, a steady flow of reinforcements reached the diminished British Army. Gradually the shattered divisions were built up again and reserves adequate for the scheme of defence were apportioned. A reorganisation of all the expeditionary forces was ordered, and troops returned from Italy, Salonica, Egypt, and Palestine to the Western Front. Whatever the temptation to dissipation of strength earlier in the war, it was clear now that concentration was the paramount strategic need.

The lesson of the retreat on the Somme was respected, and the British defences and communications were steadily improved. Five thousand miles of new trenches, reserve systems of shelters, battle headquarters, machine-gun posts, entanglements, gun-positions, signal lines, dressing stations, tank traps, and surface-drainage pits were constructed in the narrow tract remaining between the front and the coast. The vital lateral railway threatened at Amiens, Béthune, and Hazebrouck was improved by the laying of 200 miles of broad-gauge switch tracks.

Meantime the artillery and air war on the British Front reached a pitch of violence never before maintained, particularly at night. The Germans were compelled to cease air operations against England in order to make an effective reply to the Allied air offensive in France. The last raid on London occurred on Whitsunday, 1918. The night sky of Flanders at this time was an unforgettable spectacle. On humid nights the sounds were weird. A great shell fired from Wervicq could be followed by ear throughout its journey to St Omer. The thud of the gun that fired it, the whisper, moan, rumble, and bluster of its career, its fading reverberations which dying ended in a far-distant groaning tremolo of a burst.

Raiding and patrolling along the front increased. The Australians showed special initiative in this work, but everywhere it was boldly done and began to yield a great harvest of prisoners. In July the Germans opposite the 56th Division, south of Arras, set up on their parapet a board on which was chalked "Please don't raid us any more". This ascendency over the German infantry presaged successes to follow. About midsummer limited offensives brought gains of ground important both to the British defence and to contemplated offensives.

Outwardly the war had taken on a new character. The forward areas were deceptively quiet and deserted by day. Movement began at dusk and everything was still by dawn. The busy hive of 1917 was a doubtful memory. Camouflage was everywhere, was everything. Out of all sorts of shapeless chrysalids unremarked by day there emerged at dusk the sinister, hard-outlined "imago" of some great weapon, vehicle, or dump of carefully cleaned shell. The night traffic on the roads was of a steady continuity and orderliness such as no city in the world could boast up to that time. Main roads bore quadruple lines of it and a block was a rarity. The pavé roared the night through. By day every house-wall along the roads sheltered quiet groups of British, Dominion, and American troops, engaged in adjusting with the help of "Crown and Anchor" the disparities of their rates of pay.

Though the British front was little disturbed, the northern end of it remained long under threat. Vast preparations being made against it after the capture of Kemmel were visible to air observation and photography. The threat never materialised in action. Notwithstanding, British troops had yet to face another German attack.

THE NINTH CORPS ON THE AISNE

Five divisions which had suffered severely during the fighting on the Somme and the Lys were temporarily detached for "rest" to the French Sixth Army. They arrived on the Aisne, very weak in spite of their new drafts of young soldiers, and three of them shortly took over the defence of fifteen miles of line north-west of Rheims. The confidence of the French in the lasting quiet of this front proved to be misplaced. Hardly a fortnight had elapsed when on the 27th of May the enemy opened an offensive against Duchêne's Sixth Army. Twenty-eight German divisions with tanks supported the attack; it drove in 35 miles of the front north-west of Rheims.

The attack was a complete surprise. The Germans took the Chemin des Dames from the French early in the day and they then proceeded to force the Aisne and the Vesle. But the resistance of the unfortunate British divisions, four of which were now engaged, was firm. Glorious instances appear in the conduct of the 2nd Devons and the 5th Battery, 45th Brigade, R.F.A. The former gave ground literally foot by foot till not a man was left. The battery fought its guns until they were disabled; then the remaining gunners were assembled by their officers and led in a counter-attack on the swarming German infantry. Few outlived the day. The Devons were cited in an Order of the Day by the French and their colours decorated with the "Croix de Guerre", and a similar distinction was conferred upon the Battery. The honours were well earned. The line of these tried troops was never broken, though their numbers were depleted by casualties and exhaustion to such an extent that when the last of the five divisions of the Corps was deployed the whole force was formed into one weak division. Two of the divisions were broken up, a tragedy which the survivors always mourned. One of these, a young subaltern of Dominion birth, remained for long the sufferer by one of war's grimmest touches of humour. Wounded and unconscious in a Casualty Clearing Station in Champagne, his "case-card" was inadvertently exchanged with that of an officer whose wounds proved mortal. Late in June he had failed to resurrect himself to the satisfaction of "Records" and the Army Pay Department. He was on his way up from the Base to rejoin, hoping still to find someone to vouch for his identity.

The enemy's advance up the valley of the Ardre against the British gradually slowed, and on May 31st was stopped. Elsewhere the Germans added to their gains and reached the north bank of the Marne between Dormans and Château Thierry, and along the Aisne they pushed on to the edge of the forest of Villers Cotterets. The British defence maintained its resistance during the following days; the enemy's culminating efforts against it at the Montagne de Bligny on June 6th made no impression.

The enemy now began a new battle. On the 9th of June he moved against the French line between Noyon and Montdidier and subsequently advanced steadily south-westwards. He followed this up on the 15th of July with assaults east and south-west of Rheims. Both attacks were expected and, though both gained ground, the military results of neither were such as the Kaiser and von Hindenburg, present in the neighbourhood, looked for. However, the passage of the Marne was won and the German line advanced south and west from the Oise. But French, American, and Italian troops subdued all efforts to continue the progress towards Rheims and Compiègne. The high-water mark of Germany's military fortunes had now been

reached. The contemplated offensive in the north was delayed and the thirty divisions waiting there in reserve under
the hand of the Crown Prince Rupprecht were never
launched. They had ultimately to be dispersed in the effort
to withstand the blows, now imminent, which the Allied
leaders had been steadily preparing for some time.

SUGGESTIONS FOR READING:
The World Crisis, 1916–18 by W. S. Churchill, pt. II, pp. 452–3. *Out of my
    Life* by Field-Marshal von Hindenburg, pp. 358–64.

Chapter XXIII: THE ALLIED COUNTER-OFFENSIVE

(See maps on pp. 16 *and* 216–7*)*

THE strain on the French front had become very great
during July. The eight French divisions in Flanders were
therefore withdrawn and transferred to strengthen it, and
responsibility for keeping a reserve of four divisions behind
the Franco-British junction about Amiens was assumed by
the British Commander-in-Chief. Further, at Marshal
Foch's request, four British divisions were spared for use
under the French command. Marshal Foch was about to
make his first great counter-stroke, which is as much the
practical military turning-point of the war as the Doullens
decision appointing him to the supreme command must be
regarded as its administrative turning-point.

The need of the moment was undoubtedly great. But that
the British line could be depleted to the extent of sixteen
divisions whilst awaiting attack by Prince Rupprecht's
thirty was as much a compliment to our Army as it proved a
well planned piece of strategy on the part of Foch, who seems
to have gauged exactly the situation of the enemy in July,
1918. Preserving his positions about Rheims and Soissons,
he allowed the enemy to press on southwards over the Marne
and westwards over the Avre, to the point of exhaustion.

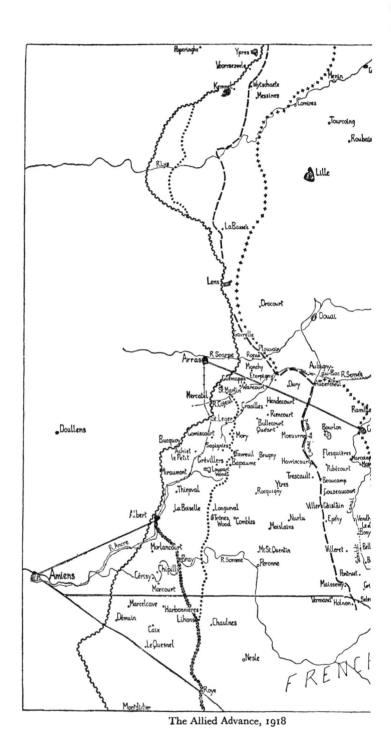

The Allied Advance, 1918

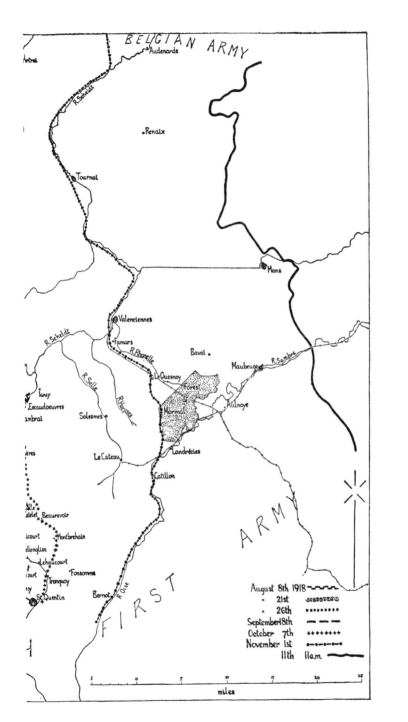

BELGIAN ARMY

Audenarde

R. Scheldt

Renaix

Tournai

Mons

Valenciennes

R. Scheldt

Famars

R. Rhonelle

Baval

R. Selle

Le Quesnoy

Maubeuge

R. Sambre

Kouy

Escaudoeuvres

ambrai

Solesmes

R. Harpies

Forest

Mormal

Aulnoye

Le Cateau

Landrécies

Catillon

lle

atelet Beaurevoir

icourt Montbrehain

llenglise

Lehaucourt

ourt Fonsomme

ny Tronquoy

R. Oise

St Quentin

Bernot

FIRST ARMY

August 8th 1918

21st

26th

September 8th

October 7th

November 1st

11th 11 a.m.

5   0   5   10   15   20   25

miles

Then, using every man the Allies could muster for battle, he struck in overwhelming strength at the great Marne salient. He pricked it like a bubble and made the Germans on the Avre look over their shoulders at his approach to their tenuous communications. Though American, Italian, and British troops all took part in the action, the main force was French, and fast tanks of French manufacture gave it its crushing quality.

THE SECOND BATTLE OF THE MARNE

When this blow fell on them the Germans were struggling for certain tactical advantages indispensable to their further advance. Some were fighting actually with their backs to their main objective, trying vainly to thrust back the Italians to Epernay. The main front of their battle was at grips with the American First Corps, 6 divisions each of a strength of 27,000 men, at Vaux, Fossoy, and Château Thierry.

No gun fired to give warning. From the eastern edge of the Forest of Villers Cotterets swarmed scores of "Moustiques" —the little French tanks. Before them for the last time the tide of German invasion turned. That day, July 18th, it receded 8 miles; 16,000 prisoners were taken and 500 guns.

To the British were assigned the important tasks of attacking at the haunches of the great salient, to the southwest of Rheims and before Soissons. The enemy was already in retreat from the Marne when the British divisions struck in on the flanks. Two advanced astride the Ardre on July 20th and the other two began their struggle for the high ground about Buzancy on the 23rd. In both directions steady progress was made, and on the 28th the Montagne de Bligny was retaken. An advance of over four miles in ten days of continuous fighting had yielded 1200 prisoners. On the other flank the final objective was reached four days later after a fierce struggle. The American Army in this action gave "convincing proof of the high fighting quality of its soldiers".[1]

[1] Supplement to Haig's Despatches.

The French victory at the Marne had rendered perilous the Germans' extended line at the limit of their last push south-westwards. The Allies' strategy now prepared a new blow at the communications to this salient, this time from the north.

Early in August the First and Second Armies began very actively to do things which seemed to portend an attack on the Germans in the Lys salient. Reinforcing troops appeared and were identified by the enemy in the line at Kemmel; tank concentrations and combined training were unmistakable from the air; medical arrangements were ostentatiously added to. Meanwhile, with ponderous stealth and the most painstaking care the Fourth Army was reinforced and its line extended across the Amiens–Roye road. Thence it ran north to Morlancourt. Night by night the woods, villages, and all other cover became more and more crowded with troops. Before dawn all sign of their movement had passed. Last of all, the tanks, 400 in number, the Cavalry Corps of three divisions, two special brigades of motor machine-gunners, and a cyclist battalion moved up by night marches, and the attacking troops took over the line.

At 4.20 a.m. on the 8th of August the artillery opened a devastating fire. Simultaneously the Fourth Army infantry left their trenches and attacked. Many enemy batteries never had the chance to fire a shot; they were overwhelmed. A complete surprise had been sprung. A shroud of thick mist favoured the first steps of the operation, and perfect co-operation between the infantry and the ubiquitous tanks carried the attack irresistibly to the first objective, Démuin–Marcelcave–Cérisy. After two hours on this line the advance was relayed by infantry, cavalry, light tanks, and, on the Amiens–Roye road, the motor machine-guns and cyclists.

A sweeping success followed, and at dusk an advance of nearly 7 miles had been made. The village of Chipilly, north of the Somme, was the only hold which the Germans kept for long that day; but they were ousted from it after a stern struggle. The combined fighting of all arms was magnificent. During the night cavalry and armoured cars pushed on eastwards beyond the line Caix–Harbonnières–Morcourt. At dawn on the 9th Le Quesnel was taken and the consolidation of the position captured was thus completed.

These were the results of the initial effort. As soon as its earliest move was assured, the French First Army, placed for the purpose under Sir Douglas Haig, was ordered to the attack. At 5.5 a.m. on the 8th it began to pivot on Montdidier, swinging its left along with the British line. By the end of the day over 16,000 prisoners and 400 guns had been taken, with great dumps of ammunition and provisions. Little wonder that General Ludendorff considered the 8th of August the "black day" of the war. No victory on the Western Front since the beginning could compare with it in material results. Amiens and its vital railways no longer lay at the mercy of the enemy's long-range guns, a strategic gain of great value.

That night the enemy was hastily blowing up dumps and hurrying all his transport eastwards to the Somme. On this rout the tireless aeroplanes, inexorably pursuing, found many targets.

During the following days the victory was improved. The front of the advance was extended to include the French Third Army, on the right of the First. Montdidier fell on August 10th. By the 12th the enemy had been forced from the long salient he had held on the Oise, a vast loss which caused his troops great dejection. The Allied advance was stayed on the 13th on a line running from Roye to Bray, at the threshold of the old Somme battlefield. The British had advanced 12 miles and the total of prisoners taken by them alone had increased to 22,000, with over 400 guns. Thereafter only enough activity was maintained on this front to dissemble the intention of the British Commander-in-Chief.

Such a resounding deed of arms as the battle of Amiens had effects more lasting than the material and strategical ones mentioned. Following closely on their unnerving defeat at the Marne, it shook the moral of the German Armies;

more, it raised that of the Allied Armies. The British, with 13 infantry divisions, 3 cavalry divisions, and one American regiment, had defeated 20 German divisions. The French had known again the inspiring march, each step of which freed more of their beloved country. From this time the enemy was thrown on the defensive, his last and dearest hopes of victory shattered. He withdrew from his advanced positions about Serre and prepared to abandon the Lys salient.

THE BATTLE OF BAPAUME

The strategic objective of the British at this stage was the line St Quentin–Cambrai. As a result of the last action the German front between Roye and Arras formed a great salient to Albert, the most vital part of which was dominated by the plateau about Bucquoy, south of Arras. Here the ground was little damaged and therefore good for the use of tanks. The forthcoming battle was intended to be the main British effort in the campaign of 1918. The end in view was the recovery of the ground ceded during the retreat in the spring; more could hardly be hoped for after the toilsome struggle of two years. The losses expected in forcing the enemy back to his main defences, the Hindenburg Line, would make the British Army incapable of further effort in 1918. In 1919 it would play a subsidiary part; the American millions were looked to for the decisive onslaught. It was with this prospect that the battle of Bapaume was begun.

The first two moves were designed to give a firm take-off for the main attack and to confuse the enemy's expectation of this. They succeeded after a stiff fight. At dawn on the 21st of August, in thick fog, 5 divisions of the Third Army advanced north of the Ancre on a front of 9 miles. The enemy's resistance was very obstinate and was only overcome by the spirit and tenacity of the attackers. After heavy fighting about Achiet-le-Petit the line of the Arras–Albert railway was gained. The reorganisation of the attack proved a delicate matter, so ragged had the advance become owing to the enemy's stubbornness. The second of the preliminary attacks took place next morning. Three divisions of the

Fourth Army with some tanks took Albert by envelopment and advanced across the Bray–Albert road.

The main attack began at 4 a.m. on the 23rd with the capture of Gomiecourt. By 4.45 a.m. the whole of a 33-mile front from Lihons to Mercatel had closed with the enemy. The Fourth Army astride the Somme fought hard for its gains and steadily added to them; south of the river the slaughter of the enemy was exceptionally heavy. Against fierce attacks the Ancre was forced opposite Thiepval and the crossing maintained for exploitation. North of the Ancre the Third Army made rapid progress towards the Arras–Bapaume road and began closing on Bapaume from the north-west. The enemy's defence now became much disorganised; he had lost 5000 prisoners and many guns. Moreover along the Ancre the Germans stood in a perilous salient.

The Third and Fourth Armies pressed their advantage. The attack was reopened at 1 a.m. on the 24th, and the high ground between Bray and La Boiselle was won. By a faultless manoeuvre of one of its Brigades and the gallantry of another in crossing the Ancre, the 38th Division brilliantly contributed to the taking of the heights of Thiepval. Miraumont fell after a dogged defence lasting three days. This cleared the way to Loupart Wood and Grévillers. Between Sapignies and Mory resistance was maintained, but the Guards reached St Léger. The Mercatel spur having been cleared thus, a beginning was made of rolling up the Hindenburg Line eastwards; Croisilles and St Martin-sur-Cojeul were taken.

There followed five days of hard fighting. Determination remarkable in an army which had suffered so much in a year was shown in the lasting heat of its onset. The supply of the infantry infiltrating the enemy's positions called anew for ingenuity. Tanks loaded with ammunition and other stores followed the infantry attack closely, and boxes of ammunition were parachuted from aeroplanes on to the actual fighting-line. Without respite the enemy was driven across the old Somme battlefield. Heavy counter-attacks by fresh German divisions at Trônes Wood and Longueval did not avail to stem the ebb-tide of defeat. Combles fell on the 29th, early. On this day Bapaume was evacuated, a gallant thrust having reached Favreuil, slightly to the east of north of the town, on the 25th. Further north, with amazing dash Riencourt was reached; in the maze of this part of the Hindenburg Line the fighting was chaotic and most difficult. Ultimately, as on a previous occasion, the miserable ruins of Riencourt proved untenable.

These were the immediate gains made in the fighting, and there soon accrued to them the fruits of a sound strategic conception. On the 26th Roye was entered by the French. The Germans then retreated on the whole front between the Oise and the Somme. By the 29th the French were again in Noyon and with the British Fourth Army they occupied the left bank of the Somme from Nesle to Peronne.

The later steps in the advance of the Third and Fourth Armies had been hard fought. The German machine-gunners were most difficult to dislodge; they held out to the end with complete devotion. Yet the British, victory in their eye, pressed on relentlessly. They even crowned their work with two successes which prepared further victory. On the night of the 30th–31st August the 2nd Australian Division in a bloody fight brilliantly took Mont St Quentin, which dominates Peronne. At the other end of the fighting line Bullecourt, Hendecourt, and Riencourt were captured. In between, the Third and Fourth Armies, heavily engaged all along their front, made steady progress. On September 1st Peronne was evacuated by the Germans.

The battle of Bapaume launched the Allies fairly on a career of victory. In ten days 23 British divisions had driven 35 German divisions right across the old Somme battlefield, the most favourable ground possible for machine-gun defence, and had taken 34,000 prisoners and 270 guns. Moreover the spirit of the German troops had suffered great depression. The line of the Somme had been turned by the fall of Peronne. The Hindenburg Line had been lost west of Quéant, where it connected with the Drocourt switch-line. North of Bapaume the Germans had been forced back miles across the southern tributaries of the Scarpe.

The enemy was driven to take stock of his heavily taxed resources. In consequence he abandoned the Lys salient, having removed the vast collection of stores and ammunition accumulated there for the offensive. The sufferings of the German troops in this salient had been terrible, as vast cemeteries testified. The British artillery concentration about it was relentlessly active. It was said that no German artillery observer on Kemmel Hill lived to do more than six tours of duty. Till the spring of 1918 the graciousness of Kemmel's cloak of trees had refreshed millions of war-strained eyes; now it looked bleak and poverty-stricken, but more massive and upstanding than before. So were the troops who returned to it early in September, when the enemy abandoned it. Both had suffered and hardened and grown greater to one end; together they had broken thrust after thrust for the English Channel. The invader would soon be out of sight of Kemmel. The Channel ports were now safe beyond peradventure. But the flowers of the forest were withered.

The gains in the battle of Bapaume were so remarkable that operations with a wider scope could be contemplated. Already the strategic aim of the campaign of 1918 appeared likely to be accomplished at less cost and in a shorter time than the most optimistic hopes had dared deem possible. The German Army had revealed in the field a weakening which was to be mortal to its fortunes. Actually the state of the great enemy host was in some respects miserable; how it bore up under its falling fortunes is matter for a certain pity and much amazement. The German soldier's confidence in himself and in his leaders was shaken. He had seen his comrades sacrifice themselves in thousands since the 21st of March, and the victorious faith in which they had died seemed to have died with them. It had been superlative; it had sustained the army's strength in spite of famine and elemental material needs. All were poorly fed for campaigning—so poorly that even the suffering inhabitants of the occupied territory took pity on them at times and gave them food. It is therefore no wonder that the repute of the German soldier was not what it had been. Yet, having borne a crushing defeat, they gathered strength to exact the full price of victory from the Allies.

On the other hand, victory was once more perfecting the British fighting-machine. Its weapons were plenteous and always improving, and the skill and spirit of the troops, in spite of physical deterioration, were steadily rising. The revelation of all this in the recent battles had exceeded the most sanguine expectations. In consequence the British Commander-in-Chief altered his views and planned a more rapid overthrow of the enemy. During the later stages of the battle of Bapaume the Germans had recovered in a measure from the extreme confusion and disorganisation caused by the first onset. They resisted tenaciously on the line of the Somme south of Peronne and clung to the high ground between Nurlu, Rocquigny, and Beugny. They were striving to get a respite during which to reorganise their ravaged formations and marshal them to the shelter of the Hindenburg Line. It was therefore imperative that no time should be allowed for the enemy's failing spirit to recover from the last blow before he was again assailed.

THE BATTLE OF THE SCARPE

The operations had reached a stage which called for a further extension northwards of the attacking front. A new enemy flank had become exposed, within which lay the northern end of the Hindenburg Line. The enemy's hopes of maintaining an ordered withdrawal depended on making the best possible use of its defences. The plan to deprive him of this resort had long been laid, and ere the battle to the southward was allowed to die down, it was ready in detail. Fresh troops had been assembled for its execution; their imminent onslaught would ease the situation further south and their success would end the resistance there. Economy of time, material, and fighting-power would thus be achieved. Nevertheless the operation was extremely formidable.

It was still dark on the morning of August 26th when the German positions astride the Scarpe were assailed fiercely on a front of $5\frac{1}{2}$ miles by troops of the First Army. The weight of the British artillery fire was crushing; the barrages were supreme; the counter-battery shoots devastated the enemy gun-positions. The infantry attack was supported by tanks and great numbers of low-flying aeroplanes. It was successful everywhere. The dominating height on which had stood Monchy-le-Preux was carried before noon. South of this the enemy had by then been driven from Wancourt and Guémappe. North of the river Roeux was reached. On the following day the same troops added greatly to their gains. When their effort ended on the 31st, the Cojeul and Sensée rivers had been crossed and Eterpigny taken. North of the Scarpe, Roeux, Plouvain, and Gavrelle had fallen.

The operations of the First Army, thus successfully opened, were not allowed to pause. At dawn on September 2nd the southern end of the immensely strong defences which linked the Hindenburg line at Quéant with those of Lens and La Bassée was assaulted. The front of attack extended some eight miles. Immediate success crowned a faultless scheme, which was exploited by the infantry with astonishing dash. Strongly posted as the Germans were, they were overwhelmed by the power of the British blow. The fighting for all arms was severe, particularly in the labyrinth of fortifications making the junction of the two lines of defence about Quéant. The result was a glorious achievement against positions of unique strength. Late in the day the machine-gun defences along the reverse slopes of the Dury ridge proved a troublesome obstacle, but they were cleared and the seal of victory set on this work of the First Army. An advance of 3 miles on a front of nearly 8 miles had been made. In the two operations 16,000 prisoners and 200 guns had been taken.

But this was not all. The Third and Fourth Armies had engaged the enemy on the same day as far southwards as Peronne. At first the Germans resisted with the energy of despair. This failed, however, before the spirit of victory which moved their assailants.

On this day a company cook won renown. Company cooks did not usually find themselves beckoned by anything more imperative than a harassed sanitary officer. Their days, as long as they lasted, were spent in some sooty corner of a filthy trench or fly-blackened ruin. Thence they supplied troops in the line with six hot issues of food in the twenty-four hours. In one such corner at Larch Wood, near Ypres, during 1917, the cooks on three consecutive days were wiped out to a man. In their dingy service dress the men who followed the "cookers" always gave the impression that the British Army would never lack "salt". So it proved on this 2nd of September. During his company's advance it was this cook's duty to carry a bag of precious rations. But when the company's advance was checked by machine-gun fire, near Moislains, a greater duty beckoned him. He dropped the rations, rushed the British barrage, shot two of a machine-gun team, bayoneted a third, and disabled the gun. Discipline forbade that he return to recover his ration-bag, but it is related that he then took thirty-seven prisoners and "relieved them of much useful property", after which he was able to hand over a bag of rations to his platoon commander. So Private Jack Harvey, 22nd London Regiment, was awarded the Victoria Cross.

That night, the 2nd–3rd September, the enemy hastily evacuated his positions opposite the First and Third Armies. He took refuge on the line of the Canal du Nord, from Peronne to Ytres, and north of this along its continuation to the Sensée—only, however, to resume his retreat in the south on the following day. This movement spread widely along the front of the French. By the 8th the Germans, their peril undiminished, were back to the Crozat Canal. North of this their line included Vermand, Epéhy, and Havrincourt. During the withdrawal rear-guards had been cut off and great execution done on the retiring columns by artillery and aeroplanes. The captures of guns and material were considerable, the total captures since August 21st amounting to 53,000 prisoners and 470 guns.

South of Havrincourt the enemy stayed his retreat on the edge of the old British trench systems west of the Hindenburg Line. The possession of these was indispensable to the assault of the Hindenburg system. Accordingly on September 12th four divisions of the Third Army drove the Germans from the old defences about Trescault and Havrincourt. To the south some days were spent in manoeuvring the enemy out of his most advanced positions. Skilfully fought local actions caused him to leave Holnon and Maissemy.

The 18th of September was a day of heavy rain. At seven in the morning 10 divisions of the Third and Fourth Armies attacked some 17 miles of the German front between Holnon and Gouzeaucourt, and almost everywhere the defenders were driven out of the old trench systems. The depth of the advance made exceeded 3 miles. The enemy resistance was strong, particularly south of Holnon and at Epéhy, and it was favoured by the maze of obstacles, trenches, shelters, and wire; but the courage and skill of the assaulting troops overcame all. Minor operations on this front during the next few days extended the gains. All was then ready for the attack on the Hindenburg Line.

A noteworthy feature of the action at Epéhy is the success attending the use of dummy tanks. The value of this stratagem had never previously been ascertained in a serious attack, and its results show clearly the turn given to warfare by the use of mechanised weapons. The hopelessness of facing tanks had taken a deep hold on the mind of the German soldier; he had faced them bravely many times of late, but bootlessly. It is possible that the illimitable foulness of the war of 1914–1918 would have never been if military theory could have been held closer to the great practical advances of invention during the preceding years. Weapons such as the aeroplane and the tank now hopelessly outmatch all that unassisted physical courage can do against them.

SUGGESTIONS FOR READING:

The World Crisis, 1916–18 by W. S. Churchill, pt. II, pp. 500–1 and 504–5.
   The Fifth Division in the Great War by Brig.-Gen. A. H. Hussey and Major D. S. Inman, p. 239.

Chapter XXIV: THE FINAL OFFENSIVES IN ITALY, THE BALKANS, PALESTINE, AND MESOPOTAMIA

(See maps on pp. 169, 79, 237, *and* 138)

On the Italian front the Allies turned at length from defence to attack. Late in September the 7th and 23rd Divisions were withdrawn from the Asiago Plateau and transferred to the Piave line. Reconnaissances were made in Italian uniforms and boat practice was carried out at Treviso. Artillery moved into position along the river, but did not register. The treacherous Piave delayed the preliminaries, for the weather had broken.

On the front of the British attack, the Austrians held the Grave di Papadopoli, an island about three miles long, as a detached post in advance of their main position on the left bank. On the night of October 23rd–24th troops of the 7th Division crossed by ferry-boat and secured a footing at the north-west point of the island. By skilful and gallant fighting they completed the capture of it on the 25th and threw a foot-bridge to its lower end. This served for the assembly of attacking troops of the 7th Division during the night of the 26th–27th. The 23rd Division, further up-stream, at first used the ferry-boats to put their troops on to the island. In the black darkness, under harassing fire and across a ten-mile current, these boats were skilfully worked by Italian Pontieri (Bridging Company troops), and each hour about a hundred men were thus passed over. During the night of the 26th–27th this means was supplemented by a light boat-bridge. By 3.30 a.m. on the 27th the assembly on the Grave di Papadopoli was complete. Since 10.30 p.m. the British guns had been cutting the Austrian wire, having only reached their positions for this work at dusk.

To gain the further shore of the Piave, the infantry were to cross, in places, as much as seven hundred yards of shoals and channels. Arrived there, they would deploy behind the artillery barrage, in readiness to advance under cover of it as it moved forward over the four hundred yards which separated the water's edge from the embankment along which lay the enemy's line. At 6.45 a.m. the guns would lift from the line to open the way for the infantry assault.

Drenched to the skin by heavy rain during the bitterly cold wait on the island, the troops got no wetter crossing the remaining channels. Led through these in the darkness on compass bearings, they struggled against the swirling waters with linked arms, immersed beyond their middles. Men were swept away and drowned, snatched by the greedy flood and weighed down by their equipment. Others fell under the fire of the enemy's guns and machine-guns and were lost. Notwithstanding, the deployment was made with precision in good time.

Both flanks, however, were exposed. The Italian troops on the right had been unable to effect a crossing in the face of the opposition they encountered, while on the left the situation was even more serious. Here the bridges of the Italian division which was to have crossed further up-stream had been swept away during the night, and its attack was therefore abandoned.

When the moment of the assault came, the main difficulty was on the left flank, where uncut wire was met, swept by machine-guns and guns beyond the flank barrages. The 11th Northumberland Fusiliers, left of the line, lost every officer over the rank of subaltern and were momentarily isolated; but there was no wavering. The 12th Durham Light Infantry on their right were checked at the wire. Captain Gibbon dashed out to cut it, four men at his heels, but the men were killed and the officer wounded. A wounded man, Private George Brown, crept in and assisted the officer, who was continuing the work; thus they succeeded shortly in making gaps, through which the Durhams stormed the trench. In the meantime the centre and right of the British line had carried their objective; the capture of the Austrian front line was complete by 7 a.m.

The British advance was then continued. On the right the strongly held village of Cimadolmo was carried by the 2nd Gordon Highlanders, led by Colonel Ross; he fell shortly afterwards, the fifth officer killed in command of this battalion during the war. By 8 a.m. the second objective, a heavily wired line, had been taken, and the Italian division on the right was then able to get forward. By noon the final objective for the day, the Tezze–Dalmadella road, had been reached.

Four days of fighting in close country followed. The rivers Monticano and Livenza were crossed in spite of firm Austrian rear-guards. Cimetta fell to the 7th Division on the 29th of October, Sacile to the 23rd Division on the 31st. Meanwhile the Allied airmen had been taking a terrible toll along the Pordenone road. The merciless ubiquity of the newest arm has doomed retreat in its old form. The road-sides became heaped with the ghastly débris of men, animals, weapons, and vehicles. Those who later viewed the grim tokens may well have wondered that men presumably too demoralised to fight on could yet work to keep clear that road of terror and wearily toil along it, expecting a similar end. Modern warfare has added that to its engines which gives a new turn to the savage Gaul's rejoinder, "Vae victis!"

In these operations the British Fourteenth Corps formed the left of the Italian Tenth Army commanded by Lord Cavan. Left of this, two other Armies, the Eighth and Twelfth, crossed the Piave towards Vittorio Veneto, a point of vital strategic importance to the Austrians. The two British divisions of the Corps achieved a brilliant success; their year of work in aid of the Italians found in it a fitting climax.

On the second day the advance outdistanced the support of the field artillery on the right bank. The guns could not be got across at once, nor would it have been possible to supply them with ammunition if all had been across. This had been foreseen, and 6-inch mortars and captured Austrian guns were accordingly used. Signal services adapted themselves at need with great devotion, supplies and ammunition never failed, and the care of casualties was as prompt as ever. No decisive victory was ever more decisively planned.

Meanwhile, on October 29th, the 48th Division had early discovered a withdrawal of the Austrians from the forward defences of Asiago. In the course of the next two days the enemy's positions in the mountains about the southern end of the Val d'Assa were assaulted and taken. Then the retreating enemy was followed up closely through this defile, 3000 prisoners and several hundred guns being captured. The advance of the division continued rapidly until the Armistice; during this time the progress of the rest of the Allied line in the mountains had been far out-stripped. The country passed through betokened in the litter of material in all stages of neglect and damage, the straggling groups of Austrians hungry to the point of truculence, the miles of road blocked with transport in confusion, the starving animals, the ill-slaughtered carcases, the chaos on the railways—even to the wreck of an ambulance train full of wounded in a lonely cutting—the pitiable disintegration of an army.

On the 3rd of November an armistice was signed with the Austrians, to begin at 3 p.m. on the following day. On the 27th the King of Italy reviewed troops of the Fourteenth Corps. As they marched past, a French division commander appealed excitedly to all in the royal enclosure—"have ever such troops been seen before!"

SALONICA

The year 1917 wore away without any further attempts being made to break the Bulgarian line. Meanwhile the Army of Salonica was gradually furnishing itself with the general reserve it needed for offensive action. In May the Greek Venizelist or Hellenic Army supporting the Allies numbered 60,000 men, and it continued growing. Yet more than a year was to elapse before it was deemed expedient to thrust at the Bulgars again. During this time the British divisions underwent reorganisation to provide drafts for the Western Front. The British strength in the Balkans was thus reduced by one-third.

The minor activity of the front grew remarkably; raiding and patrolling were more and more actively carried on, that the enemy might be given no rest, and perhaps also as an antidote to the weariness of the long-exiled British. As 1918 grew to summer and matured to autumn, the preliminaries of a great offensive stroke were completed by the Allies. Before it was due, the war had taken a decisive turn, and it was therefore of the greatest urgency and the first importance to get the upper hand in the Balkans. Thence the rickety Austrian flank might be turned and crushed, with fatal consequences to the Central European confederation.

To confuse the enemy, the British attacked west of the Vardar on the 1st of September. The enemy's reserves were thus attracted to the valley of the Vardar on account of the threat to Ghevgeli. Next, on September 8th, a Hellenic Corps made an advance on the Struma front.

On the 15th the Franco-Serbian Armies engaged the Bulgarian Second Army thirty miles west of the Vardar, and defeated it. The remnants were routed and the remainder of the line to the east was decisively turned. This main thrust was supplemented by a strong attack on the Doiran hill positions. On the 18th two British divisions, two Hellenic divisions, and a French regiment began the assault, which was renewed daily for three days with but little gain, such was the strength of the defences.

On the 21st the Bulgar Second Army to the west was broken and in flight, and Serbian cavalry was moving against the communications of the eastern Armies; so these withdrew from the positions they had held successfully and the enemy repassed the mountain-barrier into his own country. As on the final retreats of the Austrians and the Turks later, the Allied air squadrons swooped destroying. The Kresna defile, through which flows the Struma north of the Rupel Pass, became an air-made inferno through which the helpless retreating columns needs must pass. The carnage and overthrow they suffered in their passage remained long heaped in gruesome testimony.

The British and Allied troops steadily followed up the enemy's retreat, which was not marked by any considerable

action. The main lines of advance led up the valleys of the
Struma and the Vardar, but columns became involved in
mountain warfare on the flanks. Night-marches by narrow
mountain-tracks and fierce little fights at dawn—here in a
defile defended by machine-guns only overcome with
howitzer aid; there before a village, through a shrapnel
barrage, till aircraft arrived and bombed out the enemy's
guns—thus was the mountain barrier crossed into Bulgaria.
And whilst yet the issue between a Hellenic Corps and the
Bulgar rear-guards at Yenikoi was undecided, an armistice
was declared. Hostilities ceased at noon on September
30th, 1918.

PALESTINE

Not far ahead of the British line at the end of its advance
in 1917 lay the plain of Jezreel, one of the world's traditional
battle-grounds. On its nearer margin lay Megiddo. The
last surge of the struggle was to race irresistibly around the
place which wrought the conception in the mind of De-
borah "when the people willingly offered themselves". Over
ground oft-trodden in fight the decisive onslaught of a great
campaign fell to be delivered.

Although a portion of the troops had still not reached the
requisite stage of training, it was impossible to postpone the
offensive beyond the middle of September, since the rains,
which generally begin before the end of October, would
make the plains of Sharon and Esdraelon unfit for a rapid
advance. The plan of campaign was an ambitious one. Four
infantry divisions, concentrated on a sector of five miles next
the coast, were to break through and roll up the enemy line
eastwards. Three divisions of cavalry would pour through the
gap thus made and, swinging north-east, would capture the
nodal points in his communications (Afule and Beisan), thus
cutting off the two Turkish Armies west of Jordan from their
base. The Arab Army, by striking at Deraa, would at any
rate hamper the retirement of the Turkish Army beyond
Jordan. The enemy held two strongly fortified positions on
the coastal plain. It was vital that he should be driven from
these by the opening blow in order that the cavalry should

reach their first objectives (at distances of 45 to 60 miles) before the Turkish Armies could escape.

The Allies began the battle with a great numerical superiority over the enemy, amounting to as much as three to one in mounted troops and almost two to one in infantry. The preparations for the attack, involving as they did the concentration of a vast number of troops in a small area and demanding complete secrecy, were carried out with the greatest skill and care. All movements were made by night, troops being concealed by day in the numerous olive groves that surrounded Ramleh, Ludd, and Jaffa. Camps vacated were left standing to deceive the enemy. The success of these preparations was due to brilliant and untiring staff work and to the supremacy in the air that had gradually been attained during the past two months.

A preliminary attack was made on the right flank, north of Jerusalem, on the night of September 18th, to place the 53rd Division in a more favourable position to advance. In the small hours of the 19th, Turkish Army Headquarters at Tul Keram and Nablus were heavily bombed from the air. At 4.30 a.m. a hurricane bombardment of 15 minutes duration was opened by the massed artillery on the coastal plain, and at 4.45 the infantry went over the top.

Perhaps the heaviest fighting fell to the 54th Division and the French and Armenian contingents in the foot-hills, and to the 75th Division on their left, whose task it was to capture the strong El Tireh position. The 60th Division on the coast captured their objectives with such rapidity that the cavalry were through by 7.30, and had by midday reached a point 18 miles beyond the old Turkish front line.

Disorganised bodies of the enemy were now streaming across the plain towards Tul Keram, pursued by the 60th Division and the 5th Australian Light Horse Brigade. Great confusion reigned at Tul Keram. Bodies of troops, guns, motor lorries, and transport of every description were endeavouring to escape along the road leading to Messudie and Nablus. This road, which follows the railway up a narrow valley, was already crowded with troops and transport. The confusion was added to by the persistent attacks of the R.A.F. and Australian Flying Corps, from which there was no escape. Great havoc was caused and, in several places, the road was blocked by overturned vehicles. Later in the evening an Australian regiment, having made a detour, reached a hill four miles east of Tul Keram, overlooking the road. As a result, a large amount of transport and many guns fell into our hands.[1]

As the divisions in the coastal sector advanced, they wheeled to the right, till they had taken up a position facing due east. The 60th Division, after a fighting march of 18 miles, entered Tul Keram in the evening; while the 3rd (Lahore) and 7th (Meerut) Divisions had crossed the railway and stormed the strong positions in the foot-hills.

On the next day the 60th Division advanced eastwards from Tul Keram along the Nablus road without any heavy fighting. The Meerut Division pressed on through extremely difficult country, though suffering great hardships from water shortage, and after overcoming a strongly posted enemy rear-guard found themselves across the road and railway north of Messudie by the small hours of the 21st. The 3rd Division made good progress in face of strong enemy rear-guards. The advance was continued by the 10th and 53rd Divisions on the right of our line, where the enemy defence was still strongly organised in country most unfavourable to attacking troops.

Meanwhile the 4th and 5th Cavalry Divisions had pressed on all night and dawn found them in the plain of Esdraelon. Afule and Beisan were taken during the day by the 4th Division, and the 5th Division occupied Nazareth early in the morning. A German aeroplane landed in Afule, unconscious that it was in our hands. At Nazareth Marshal Liman von Sanders, the German Commander-in-Chief, escaped capture by a hair's-breadth (in his pyjamas, so it is said). His papers and some of his Staff were taken. Thus "...while the infantry were breaking the last organised resistance of the enemy, the action of the cavalry had ensured, the destruction or capture of the whole Turkish force west of Jordan".[2]

---

[1] Allenby's Despatch, Oct. 31st, 1918.
[2] *A Brief Record of the Advance of the E.E.F.*, *June* 1917 *to October* 1918.

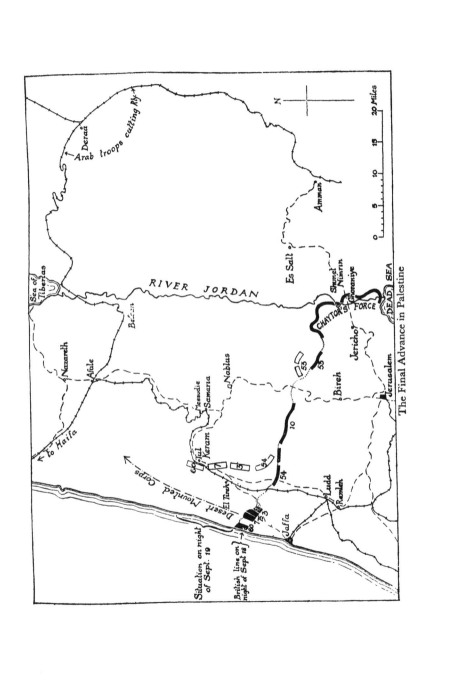

The Final Advance in Palestine

We must return for a moment to the Turkish Fourth Army east of Jordan. To hold this in check while the main attack was being made, "Chaytor's Force" (the Anzac Mounted Division with a contingent of infantry equivalent to two brigades) had been created and was posted on the line of the Jordan facing east. By the 23rd this force had cleared the country west of Jordan and crossed the river, and was pursuing the enemy, in face of stout opposition from his rearguards, towards Es Salt and Amman. Amman was captured on the 25th and 5000 prisoners with 28 guns fell into the hands of the Anzac Mounted Division. Meanwhile the Arab Army had been relentlessly harassing the Turks from east and north, and on September 28th the Turkish Second Corps, 5000 strong, surrendered to Chaytor's Force. By the 27th the Arabs had captured Deraa and entrenched themselves across the enemy's northward line of retreat, thus ensuring the capture of the remnant of the Fourth Army.

The rest of this amazing story must be told in few words. On the 23rd Haifa, a valuable gain as a landing place, and Acre were occupied. Acre fell without resistance, but Haifa was strongly defended, and but for two gallant charges—by the Jodhpur Lancers from the south and the Mysore Lancers from the east—might well have held out for some time.

On the afternoon of the 26th the 4th Cavalry Division started its 120-mile march on Damascus. The 5th and Australian Divisions, converging on the same objective but from a lesser distance, set off on the following day. Both columns met with considerable resistance, but the distance was covered in good time and Damascus was entered by the Desert Mounted Corps and Arab Army on October 1st.

The Meerut Division, which began moving from Haifa along the coast on October 3rd, was warmly welcomed by the inhabitants of Tyre and Sidon and entered Beirut, most valuable to us as a port, on October 8th. Ships of the French Navy had already entered the harbour. Tripoli was occupied on the 11th and Homs on the 15th, and the 5th Cavalry Division, accompanied by armoured cars, was ordered to march on Aleppo. Their advance-guard reached the town on the morning of the 25th, and the Jodhpur Lancers gallantly charged a strong enemy rear-guard, but were forced by lack of numbers to withdraw and await the main body. Detachments of the Arab Army were, however, attacking the town from the east, and by evening the Turks had withdrawn.

In five and a half weeks the Allies had advanced 300 miles, taking 75,000 prisoners (including 3700 Germans and Austrians) and 360 guns, with a countless store of transport, equipment, and baggage. An armistice was concluded with Turkey and came into force at noon on October 31st.

MESOPOTAMIA

On the death of Sir Stanley Maude the command devolved upon his senior Corps Commander, Lieutenant-General Sir W. R. Marshall. The watch upon the Turks during the year that followed was not suffered to relax. At favourable opportunities forces moved out against them and administered severe punishment, with only slight losses.

In order to establish free commerce with northern Persia and to co-operate with the Russians there, it was desirable to dislodge the Turks from the Jebel Hamrun range, to the west of the trade route. Accordingly, on December 3rd, 1917, strong columns cleared the right bank of the upper Diala and secured the crossings. During the next two days the troops struggled against the natural difficulties of the ground and the inclement weather. Thereafter they got to grips with the enemy, drove him from the western passes, and pursued him in retreat through Kifri, where there are coal-mines. On the 9th Khanikin, on the Persian border, was occupied. A bridge-head at Kizil Robat was maintained subsequently.

During December and January the Turks massed about ancient Hit and felt their way gingerly down the Euphrates. Soon after the middle of February the enemy's advanced detachments were driven back. Strong forces then marched for Hit and drove the Turks from the place. They began a hasty retirement, but extra mounted troops and light armoured cars moved to Hit, and on March 26th the cavalry gained the Aleppo road on the enemy's line of retreat. The Turks flung themselves desperately on the sudden check, near midnight, but they failed to break through and lost a thousand prisoners. With the dawn the British infantry fell on them and completely defeated them. The pursuit was pressed as far as Ana during the two following days, and before they withdrew on the 30th of March the British destroyed the Turkish dumps at Haditha and Ana.

In a further operation to protect the communications into Persia, undertaken in May, the Turks received like punishment. A body of retreating infantry on the way to Kifri was charged by the 6th Cavalry Brigade. Two hundred of them were killed, including two battalion commanders; 565 prisoners and a mountain gun were taken. Passing through Kifri, the advance broke down the enemy's opposition before Kirkuk, the chief town of Kurdistan, which was entered on the 7th of May.

The plunging of Russia into Bolshevism brought about the withdrawal of Russian troops from north Persia, where anarchy and starvation reigned. So a British military mission penetrated the region by way of Kasvin, Kermanshah, and Hamadan to the shores of the Caspian at Enzeli. So evil was the state of the country, torn with internal dissension and harried by Russian and Turk, that cannibalism was not unknown. In spite of the hostile attitude of the miserable people, the mission found it possible to do much to alleviate their sufferings.

But the political unrest about the Caspian, aggravated by the intrigues of Turk and German, drew the mission further afield. In June the Bolshevik committee at Baku was overthrown, and on the invitation of its successors, the Trans-Caspian Directorate, Major-General Dunsterville (Rudyard Kipling's "Stalky") went there with a platoon of British infantry and was rapturously received. The Turks attacked Baku late in August. By then a weak brigade of the 13th Division and some light armoured cars had reached there. Isolated across the Caspian in the midst of anarchy and treachery, hundreds of miles from their parent army, they put up a glorious fight, holding out against great odds till the middle of September. Then, having paid the last honours to the dead which they must leave in this inhospitable place, they re-embarked for Enzeli, prepared to fight their way out of a harbour commanded by the Turkish guns at 3000 yards.

Acting in conjunction with Allenby's great drive in Palestine, the two British Corps in Mesopotamia began to advance on Mosul at the end of October. One column marched up the Tigris; it outflanked and enveloped the enemy's main force there and 7000 surrendered. The other column took the road through Kifri and Kirkuk. On the 3rd of November, 1918, after the conclusion of the armistice with Turkey, the British entered Mosul.

SUGGESTIONS FOR READING:

The 23rd Division, 1914–19 by Lt.-Col. H. R. Sandilands, pp. 315–16. *With the 48th Division in Italy* by Lt.-Col. G. H. Barnett, pp. 138, 148–9. *Revolt in the Desert* by T. E. Lawrence, pp. 392–3, 412–13.

Chapter XXV: THE ALLIED COUNTER-OFFENSIVE PREVAILS

(*See map on pp.* 216–7)

THE line St Quentin–Cambrai, the objective of the British Army, now lay directly before it. In two months of successful fighting the enemy had been deprived of his spring and summer conquests; moreover his offensive base had been breached east of Arras, about Quéant. Six weeks of good campaigning were yet possible. The Armies, despite their labours, were in good heart; their victories had been won without too great a sacrifice of men, and though the British reserves were running low, an unexpectedly large margin remained. Under the exceptionally favourable conditions brought about by the recent actions, these might suffice to achieve an end earlier than had been hoped, notwithstanding that further operations would immediately involve the attack of a fortified position of very great strength.

Elsewhere along the Western Front the Allies were dealing

the enemy severe blows. On September 12th the First American Army and some French troops assaulted the St Mihiel salient and during the following days completely reduced it, 16,000 prisoners and 450 guns being captured. On the 14th a French Army under General Mangin took the Laffaux salient, north of the Aisne, the southern bastion of the Hindenburg Line.

THE BATTLE OF CAMBRAI AND THE HINDENBURG LINE

All was now ready for a combined offensive. It was planned that the American Armies should advance on Mezières, east of the Argonne Forest. The French west of the Argonne would make for the same objective. To the British was assigned the task of forcing back the great enemy concentration about Cambrai. The object of this concentration was to protect the only route of supply to the German Armies south of the Ardennes, which lay through the railway junction of Aulnoye, near Maubeuge. A subsidiary operation to clear the Belgian coast was to be begun by the Second Army and the Belgian Army when circumstances were favourable.

On September 26th the attack in the Argonne opened and was immediately successful. Progress was made thereafter at the rate of about a mile a day for several days.

The British advance began on the 27th. The work before the British Army was formidable enough. North of St Quentin the Germans occupied the Hindenburg Line to near Havrincourt. Thence northwards they defended the line of the Canal du Nord, and their right flank rested on the marshes of the Sensée. The British line ran east of Sélency, Gricourt, Pontruet, Villeret, and west of Villers Ghislain and Gouzeaucourt.

The axis of the Hindenburg system north of St Quentin was the Scheldt Canal, and the main line of defence, a double trench system full of concrete works, lay mostly to the east of the Canal. Between Bellicourt and Vendhuille the Canal is tunnelled for over three miles; elsewhere it is mostly deep in sixty-foot cuttings, but south of Bellicourt the cutting shallows towards Bellenglise. Further south, at Tronquoy, is another tunnel, a short one. The tunnels and numerous deep shelters in the cuttings housed the garrisons. To the west of the Canal complicated forward defences had been developed wherever necessary to ensure fire supremacy. Two and a quarter miles east of the Hindenburg Line lay the Hindenburg Reserve Line or Beaurevoir–Fonsomme Line. Like the former, it was a double trench with shelters and emplacements of concrete. Belts of wire entanglement were spread in protection of the whole system, along and within it. The whole depth of the defences was from 4 to over $5\frac{1}{2}$ miles and incorporated many fortified villages. Even troops borne forward on a great wave of victory might pause in their career towards such a carefully elaborated fortress. The British only paused to make final arrangements.

During the night of September 26th–27th the guns of the Fourth, Third, and First Armies began a preliminary bombardment on the whole front from Sélency to the Sensée. At dawn in rain and mist the infantry of the Third and First Armies attacked the line of the Canal du Nord, whilst the Fourth Army's guns continued their work of preparation south of Gouzeaucourt.

The forward slopes to the Canal du Nord from the west were deadly exposed. Moreover the northern stretch of the Canal was not deemed practicable for assault; it had to be turned by way of Moeuvres. South of this the crossings were most gallantly won and as gallantly bridged forthwith. The greatest strength of the attack was deployed from about Moeuvres. Here crossings were made on a narrow front; thence diverging advances pushed on and outwards across the Bapaume–Cambrai and Arras–Cambrai roads.

The Cambrai battlefield of the year before was overrun with precision and thoroughness. The enemy resisted strongly, and counter-attacked the southern flank of the advance, about Beaucamp, persistently. But this availed nothing. The dominating heights about Bourlon and the length of the Flesquières ridge were taken and held. It soon became possible to pass troops across the northern stretch of the Canal, now undefended, and these drove the enemy from the angle between the Canal and the inundations of the Sensée.

Thus at one stroke the northern end of the remaining Hindenburg Line had been turned and the crossings of the Sensée reached. The results were that Cambrai lay helplessly exposed; that the rear of the enemy north of the Sensée was seriously threatened; and that the offensive power of the artillery on the left of the Fourth Army was terrifically increased. Withal over 10,000 prisoners and 200 guns had been taken. Considering that the immediate results differed little from those of the battle in November, 1917, the incomparable possibilities of the later action are the more remarkable.

Next day the British crossed the Scheldt Canal at Marcoing, and they took Aubencheul on the Sensée Canal. Meanwhile the Fourth Army guns had worked up to a destructive fury which kept the defenders of the Hindenburg Line underground and prevented supplies and ammunition reaching them for two days. The general bombardment changed to barrage fire at 5.50 a.m. on the 29th. Simultaneously the Fourth Army infantry, including that of two American divisions, began the assault. Tanks were used in strength. Support on the right was provided by the attacking First French Army moving on St Quentin; on the left two Corps of the British Third Army pushed forward north of Vendhuille.

A great deed of arms dominates this day's fighting—the storming of Bellenglise by the 46th (North Midland) Division. Bellenglise lies in a loop of the Scheldt Canal, on its east bank. The infantry wore lifebelts and dragged with them mats and rafts as they went forward to the cutting. Some were fortunate in finding foot-bridges which the enemy had had no time to destroy, the rest seemed to make light of their amphibious task—they scrambled down the steep banks, dropped into the low water, splashed across, and scaled the farther bank in little knots and groups and strings, pushing and pulling one another to the top. Arrived there, they reformed, broke into the village from the west and north-west, cleared it, and rolled up the German defences along the canal south of it. Then they pressed on to the taking of Lehaucourt. During the day they took over 4000 prisoners and 70 guns.

The 46th Division was the first Territorial Division to land in France. Since then, late in February, 1915, they had toiled and learned and died. In the last great critical stroke of the war they gained the fame they had for so many years been earning. Doubtless their thoughts turned to the 13th of October, 1915, and the silent alignment of the ranks of their dead before the Hohenzollern Redoubt; and it was not too late for the dread cycle of experience to turn afresh. Five miles to the north, before Bony in the tunnel sector, the dead of the 27th American Division lay just as those of the 46th had lain in the Hohenzollern Redoubt years before. A mistake had been made in plotting a preliminary advance— inexperience in the treacherous work of identifying the few landmarks left on contested ground was the cause. Accordingly, at the opening of the main action the American infantry was nearly a thousand yards from the barrage line. Trying with commendable but fatal zeal to catch up the moving barrage, they were mown down by machine-gun fire from the strong-points which they had imagined already in their possession. Their fine physique and their spirited conduct in carrying on the attack only magnified this disaster lamentably. The efforts of two Australian divisions which were to have carried on the attack begun by the Americans were directed to retrieving this early set-back, and it required the exercise of all their famous skill and fighting powers.

Further north the fighting was fierce. The Third Army gained the crossings of the Scheldt from Masnières to Cambrai, and the First Army was closing round the north of the city.

During the next few days there was continued severe fighting. To the limit of his failing power the enemy strove to retain the remains of his last stronghold, and even to recover what he had lost of it. But the inexorable pressure never relaxed. It was indeed increased, for the French First Army threw its whole weight into the battle and took St Quentin on the 1st of October. All along the Scheldt the Germans were gradually dislodged. The Beaurevoir–Fonsomme defences were first broken through at Le Catelet on

October 3rd; Montbrehain and Beaurevoir villages themselves were taken on the 5th; finally the enemy abandoned
the high ground in the Masnières loop of the Scheldt and
left the last hold he had kept on the Hindenburg Line.

The captures made during the whole series of operations
had increased to more than 36,000 prisoners and 380 guns.
The frontage attacked, the depth of the defences, and the
number of prisoners taken provoke comparison with the
details of the battle of the Somme in 1916. But the number
of guns taken in four and a half months of the Somme battle
was only 125; the later achievement occupied only nine days
in the doing.

In the ridge of the roof of the old citadel of Cambrai the
Germans had rigged an observation station which commanded a wide view of the surrounding country. A long and
ricketty ladder led from it down to the garret floor. The
tottering rungs may well have stressed the feelings of the last
German observer, descending from this eyrie on the
abandonment of the defences he had seen overwhelmed in
the storm of battle.

THE LAST BATTLE OF YPRES

Constrained by the peril threatening his vital railway
communications from the Allied advance towards the
Sambre, the enemy had reduced his strength in the north to
little more than a screen—some 5 divisions.

As soon as the battle was well joined before Cambrai,
General Plumer's Second Army and the Belgian Army, both
under the command of the King of the Belgians, struck at
the weakened enemy. On September 28th at dawn, without
preliminary bombardment, the whole line from Voormezeele
to the Yser inundations moved to the assault, and the Germans were simply swept from the old battlefield north of the
Comines Canal in one day. The arena of the grimmest
struggle in history passed out of the war. Within its confines
youth and the ideals of youth had quenched themselves until
it had become abominable. On this last day of the long
struggle to and fro over its slopes the attacking British
division of the right flank was the reconstituted 14th, once

the "Light Division". All the *esprit de corps* of young manhood had risen to the famous title in 1914. Such honour as that which invests the century-old memories of Craufurd's Light Division had been their ideal; the classic labours of Sir John Moore had prepared the tradition they would follow. At Ypres, the Somme, and Arras the Division had been tried in the fire, and finally at St Quentin and Villers-Bretonneux it had been reduced to a handful of survivors. Thereafter it had been reformed; men too old and otherwise unfit for general service in the field mainly composed it now. Its G.O.C. found it a source of pride that his "rheumaticky old gentlemen" made such a fine advance to the Lys on this and the succeeding days.

By the evening of the 1st of October the German hold on the left bank of the Lys above Comines had been ended. The Second Army took 5000 prisoners and 100 guns in effecting this, without suffering much loss. Another German withdrawal followed, closely pressed by the Fifth and First Armies between Lens and Lille and south of the ruins of Lens. On October 4th the enemy paused on the fortified high ground west of Douai, but on the fall of the Hindenburg defences south of Cambrai he resumed his withdrawal. The encirclement of Lens and Lille then proceeded.

Work was rapidly done on the shattered communications across the battlefield of Ypres. By dint of great exertions this was sufficiently forward to permit of the Second Army resuming its advance before dawn on the 14th of October, just four years since the Germans had appeared in strength north of the Lys. By the 20th, the date on which the First Battle of Ypres had begun, the northern flank of the Allies rested on the Dutch frontier. The Germans had at last been driven from the Belgian coast and were in hasty retreat to the Scheldt.

The First and Fifth Armies were pushing forward also, the latter now commanded by General Sir W. R. Birdwood. On October 17th the First Army occupied Douai and the Fifth Army Lille, Roubaix, and Tourcoing. But the impetus to these events had come not only from the north, nor mainly so. A week earlier a great drive against the few remaining defences east of the Hindenburg Line had begun in the south. Between the two the enemy clung desperately to a pivotal position on the Sensée inundations.

The line of the Sensée is one of the cardinal natural lines of defence of Flanders; it played an important part in the campaigns of Marlborough. The use made of it by the Germans during their evacuation of Flanders in October 1918 was invaluable to them. Notwithstanding the difficulties presented by a line of such strength, there were both the men and the leading ready to attempt its assault. The fame of two of the men has come down to us. They were both sappers, who for the greater part of two rainy October nights and a day had been maintaining a floating bridge across the Sensée Canal during an assault on Aubigny-au-Bac by two companies of the 2nd London Regiment. The assault at 5.15 a.m. on October 13th had had an immediate success, but it had been heavily countered by overwhelming numbers of the enemy; yet a resolute attempt was made to re-establish a footing on the northern bank. On the 14th in the darkness of the last hour of a stormy night a patrol began to cross the seventy feet of flimsy floating bridge, to establish a post on the other side. The enemy lay within bombing distance. The bridge broke. Sapper-Corporal McPhie and Sapper Cox dropped into the water and held the cork floats together, in spite of having their fingers trodden on. Daylight was at hand when the Corporal, after a hasty search for material to repair the damage, returned to the bridge. "We've got to make a way for the patrol", he said; "it's a death-or-glory job". It was both. Working under the fire of snipers McPhie was at last hit in the head and fell into the water. When Cox laid hold of him he was told by McPhie to let go—"I'm done", he said. Cox held on whilst his Corporal was hit again and again and killed; he himself was hit six times before he let go of his comrade's body. Sapper Hawkins then got a rope to Cox and drew him ashore, but he died in hospital two days later. The Victoria Cross was conferred upon Corporal McPhie. The whole operation cost in casualties 3 officers and 140 other ranks out of 6 officers and 165 other ranks who took part in it. But they consolidated the bridge-head and patrolled the northern bank, and they took prisoners 4 officers and 203 other ranks of the enemy.

THE SECOND BATTLE OF LE CATEAU

The great drive in the south culminated for the British in a battle about Le Cateau, which began on the 8th of October on a front and with forces greater than at any period of the war. The Americans resumed their offensive east of the Meuse. The French on their immediate left acted with them, extending their attack across the whole of Champagne. From Cambrai southwards to St Quentin the Third and Fourth Armies and the French First Army began a new advance. The remaining sectors were anything but inactive; it was the Third and Fourth Armies which were fighting for the decisive advantage, however, and they had to fight hard and work hard.

Assisted by tanks, the first onslaught overcame the resistance of the enemy and threw his troops into confusion. On the whole front of 17 miles the British line was advanced four miles. Cambrai, blazing fiercely, its streets blocked with the débris of wilful destruction, was in the hands of British patrols.

On the morning of the 9th, the attack having reformed and the guns advanced, the enemy was pressed yet further eastwards. Cavalry began to be used and were able in important instances to stop the work of the enemy's demolition parties. By the evening of October 10th the left bank of the river Selle was held to within a mile of Solesmes; the French First Army held Bernot on the Oise–Sambre Canal; the left of the advance rested on the Scheldt near Iwuy.

The ceaseless activity of the British Army during these days exceeded anything in its previous experience. The comparatively rapid advance of so vast an organisation is a great undertaking. In the face of the obstacles due to demolitions carried out as thoroughly as the Germans knew how, the work to be done was enormous before a further stage of progress was possible. After an action the traffic filled the roads for miles in an unending column, and even so, much light horse transport moved across country, off the roads. Progress at such times was slow, two miles an hour being a normal rate. Railheads began to be pushed up; wagon-lines and lorry parks moved ground frequently; the whole Army lived largely on the roads again.

The civilian population, too, were again in a lamentable state of flux. After each action, each day of fighting even, a straggling crowd of the inhabitants of villages now redeemed would find their precarious way across the battle-zone, bringing with them little hand-carts, which they had made by order of the Germans to hold their valuables and necessaries. Driven eastwards with their few movables by the tide of battle, they early braved all weathers and all physical dangers to return, hoping and fearing for the homes and lands over which the storm of war had passed. The poor wretches on arrival were fed and loaded with their few possessions into motor-lorries held ready for this service after bringing up supplies and ammunition. Thus they were carried off to their homes or to temporary refuges where they were cared for as well as possible, though many died through exposure and privation.

The destruction wrought by the Germans in their retreat was amazing. They justified what they did by the plea of military necessity; but the lengths they went to have been regarded as barbarous. The limits of military necessity, however, are not easily defined, and the conditions of war existing between 1914 and 1918 were quite unprecedented. The wrecking of roads, railways, and bridges was actually the only means by which their exhausted armies could put off the day of decisive defeat.

British engineers had to work day and night to put the communications into a condition to bear the traffic on which the next "push" depended. The extent and urgency of this work can only be guessed at by those who did not see the actual destruction. Arterial roads were blocked in the towns by buildings carefully collapsed on to them; in the country the great trees which had shaded them were felled across them. At road-junctions fifty-foot craters were blown. Railway lines were wrecked regularly and completely. Culverts were destroyed and the channels blocked, so that large areas were flooded. The numerous bridges of a country-side richly laced with roads, railways, rivers, and canals were blown up almost without exception. Often delay-action mines concealed in the neighbouring embankment or cutting destroyed the new construction. The only bridge of the many in the neighbourhood of Cambrai which escaped being broken was an ancient structure spanning the Scheldt from Ramillies to Escaudoeuvres. The Victoria Cross was awarded the Canadian Engineer officer who miraculously saved it. His party killed the German machine-gunners whose guns protected the approaches, and during the fight he cut the firing circuit and drew the detonator from the charge under the middle of the arch.

All this was justifiable, by common consent, even in its remarkable thoroughness. But the orgy of demolition had not stopped at this. All means of useful supply had been dealt with also—coal-mines particularly. Numbers of in-dustrial plants had been wholly wrecked, some after they had been carefully rifled. Even the co-operative dairy-produce factories in small villages were not spared. The residential quarter of Cambrai was damaged and set on fire by trench-mortar detachments—their guns were found abandoned in various gardens—and the main shopping thoroughfare of Douai was razed.

The pictures of war at this time lacked nothing of its classic mood. The night sky was lurid in a dozen different directions with conflagration. Gun-flashes showed pale and electric. Along the rain-soaked roads interminable bus and lorry convoys with troops relieving and relieved glinted wetly. A red gleam of a tail-light cast now and then a crimson streak. Faint half-shrouded flickers came from cottage casements. The open doors of churches showed moving lanterns within, and bandaged heads and limbs were raised from among the straw spread on the pavement of the nave. Near-by, the dull glow of a cooker fire struck the ground and outlined the putteed legs of busy cooks.

By day the country was a waste hardly broken by tillage. The village chimneys were smokeless and dead. Black window-gaps and shell-scars defaced warm red walls.

Furniture stood in the streets. An unimaginable litter of clothing, equipment, arms, ammunition, artillery weapons, and tanks lay strewn over the land and hidden in every corner of villages and houses. Troops wandered idly about newly taken towns. They sat before the lifeless cafés, the music of a mouth-organ or an accordion making the little groups gay against their macabre surroundings. The potted bay-trees stood dismally out in the wet before them. What were bays to them, or the joys they caricatured to the bays!

With hardly a glance the steel-hatted columns went by.

THE BATTLE OF THE SELLE

Between September 27th and October 10th the British took 48,500 prisoners and 620 guns. In the Argonne the French had taken 21,500 and the Americans 17,000 prisoners by October 12th. The Germans had been feeling their losses in guns for some time. Now they began to lack men to close the gaps in their line—this in spite of the fact that their front had been shortened by the withdrawal north of the Sensée and that from the Lys. For this and for other reasons of tactical moment another withdrawal was made in the south. The great salient which had developed about Laon was abandoned and the French entered the town on October 13th.

It almost seemed that the German Supreme Command had lost its grip of the situation. For this withdrawal was set going too late to ensure the line of the Meuse being reached as part of a combined movement of the German Armies. It was certain that only on the line of the Meuse could they hope to recover their cohesion and prolong their resistance into the coming year. The Allies now had a growing advantage, for one more onslaught by the British would almost certainly bring the vital railway junction at Aulnoye within effective range of their artillery. Then all hope for the Germans of making a retirement to the Meuse would be gone.

For nearly three months the British Army had been pressing attack after attack with constant and even growing vigour. Victory and the hope of victory inspired it. But its strength was daily diminishing and had now fallen to 470,000 rifles, less than that of the force handed over to Sir Douglas Haig by Sir John French three years before. There was no time to lose if the endurance so far shown by divisions engaged in battle repeatedly was to be maintained to the end. With all speed, therefore, preparations were made, and on the 17th of October the Fourth Army and the French attacked west of the Oise–Sambre Canal. During the next three days they drove the Germans out of a three-mile belt of wooded country south of Le Cateau. For two days the enemy fought stubbornly; then his resistance broke down.

On the 20th the Third Army and the right divisions of the First Army attacked the line of the Selle north of Le Cateau. Starting at 2 a.m. they gained the crossings against strong opposition. Particularly fine was the spirit shown by the Royal Engineers in bridging the stream; a Field Company of the 38th Division lost half its strength whilst working at its bridge, but finished it. Tanks were got across the river and materially assisted in the fight for the high ground to the east, towards the river Harpies.

Meanwhile, allowing the beaten enemy no respite, the Fifth and Second Armies and the Belgians were following up his retreat. On the 23rd the Fifth Army reached the line of the Scheldt north of Valenciennes; whereupon the Fourth and Third Armies and the right of the First Army thrust forward again. The attack opened at 1.20 a.m. on the 23rd with such a barrage as could hardly be credited in mobile warfare, and the infantry advanced steadily on a 17-mile front south of Valenciennes. Next day the First Army prolonged the attack seven miles to the north of the city. In wretched weather the troops went forward steadily and by the evening of the 24th had made 6 miles. Their line lay along the western edge of the Forest of Mormal and the Scheldt north of Valenciennes.

In this series of actions, entitled the Battle of the Selle, 24 British and 2 American divisions defeated 31 German divisions, taking 20,000 prisoners and 475 guns. Towards the end of it the fighting of the German troops was of very varying merit. In places they still resisted stoutly, but instances multiplied of retirements in front of the British barrage, and in one case a weak battalion, complete with a major in command, crossed No Man's Land and surrendered just before the barrage opened. Their apathy as they marched off to captivity was notable; their bearing generally was that of civilians somehow uniformed; the military cult of the Germany which went precipitately to war had no part in them. The German defence, in fact, seemed to be held together by the skill and tenacity of their machine-gunners.

If the German spirit was breaking, the victors could with difficulty sustain the labours of victory, unbroken as was its sequence. Their flagging energies had to be carefully encouraged. A great effort was made to give them food for thought, not apart from the war, but apart at least from the deadening spiritual influence of the making of war. "Education officers" had been appointed late in the summer. As the prospect of a winter campaign mercifully dwindled, these had been set to the work of improving the knowledge of all troops on the international issues of the future. They gave an account of what the Germans had intended, had they won the war, and what the Allies hoped now to achieve. It was in this vital culture that autumn evenings were passed in half-lit, out-of-business estaminets by crowded gatherings. Officers and men joined in getting a clear view of the causes and the solution of the state of war which they had so long accepted dutifully.

THE BATTLE OF THE SAMBRE

The last great stroke of the war on the Western Front impended. A preliminary operation for the clearing of Valenciennes, however, was required, and on the 1st of November it was begun. The northern Corps of the Third Army and the two on the right of the First Army attacked on a 6-mile front south of Valenciennes. In two days of fighting the Germans were driven from the Rhonelle river and for two miles beyond it. Valenciennes was entered once again by British soldiers and Famars also was taken.

The main action was begun on November 4th. Thirty miles of front from Oisy on the Sambre to Valenciennes erupted in the flame and thunder of countless guns. At dawn the infantry went forward behind a heavy barrage, and by nightfall an advance of 5 miles had been made. The crossings of the Sambre had been forced by the Fourth Army at and south of Landrecies; at Catillon the Royal Engineers of the 1st Division did gallant work bridging. The western half of the Forest of Mormal fell into British hands on this day. Le Quesnoy was first surrounded and its ramparts then stormed. Though at first the enemy stood firm against the centre of the Third Army, they gave way completely to the impulse of its purpose and retreated with all speed. Further north the advance of the First Army was hardly opposed at all. Nineteen thousand prisoners and 450 guns were taken in this operation, whilst the French First Army on the right of the British took 5000.

That night the enemy retreated hurriedly eastwards. Not only his spirit but his military power was now broken. Flanders had betaken itself to its autumn mood under a streaming rain, and heavy cloud lay low over the sodden landscape. But the pursuit was pressed and even the aeroplanes braved the conditions to harass the fleeing enemy. By the 8th the enemy was moving away steadily along the whole line as far north as Tournai. His anxieties were limitless; his lines of communication were choked and almost paralysed. Behind him thronged a relentless enemy. The most desperate efforts to cope with the situation could evoke no response from troops whose one thought was how soonest to get home from the war. Some few still resisted, forced to do so by their unhappy propinquity to the converging divisions of a victorious host; these fought stubbornly to the last, without fear and without hope.

In face of the opposition of such hapless groups, on November 9th the Guards and 62nd Divisions entered Maubeuge, the Canadians approached Mons, the Fifth Army reached Tournai, and the Second Army crossed the Scheldt to Renaix. Fighting in the neighbourhood of Mons during the 10th ended on the 11th with the destruction or capture of the defenders. The whole of the British line had passed from France into Belgium, as it was in the beginning.

THE ARMISTICE

Faced with the insoluble problem of evacuating what remained to them of northern France and Belgium, the German Supreme Command on the 8th made overtures to Marshal Foch that he should receive a delegation empowered to conclude an armistice. Germany was in the throes of political revolution and its royal representatives were abdicating. The German Army was no longer controllable as a military organisation; its retreat threatened to become a chaotic struggle to move. The pressure of the Allied Armies would soon confine still further the already seething area in which the masses of defeated troops were hastening eastwards. What the consequences might be was terribly plain.

After dark on the 7th the cars containing the German plenipotentiaries were admitted through the lines of the Allied Armies and negotiations were opened at Rethondes in the Forest of Compiègne, where stood the advanced headquarters train from which Marshal Foch and his Staff conducted the campaign. In the dining-car of this train an armistice was signed at 5.15 a.m. on the 11th of November, to take effect at eleven o'clock the same day.

The orders for the cessation of hostilities reached the British troops during the night. Till the moment at which they took effect the fight was maintained and the advance was pressed. The last stage on which it entered that night was, to all intents, as purposeful as the first stage on which it had entered roughly a hundred days previously. In this period the British Army had driven its enemy before it uninterruptedly more than 60 miles in the north and 80 in the south, and in doing so had taken 187,000 prisoners, 2850 guns, 29,000 machine-guns, and 3000 trench-mortars. Latterly it had re-ordered and helped to resettle the devastated country through which it passed; the history of the 56th Division records that "on the 6th November 16,000 civilians were receiving rations under arrangements made by the Division".

Of the last moments of fighting Major Dudley Ward writes:[1]

Just before 11 a.m. all batteries opened fire. Each gunner was determined to be the last man to fire a shot at the Germans. And then in the midst of the rolling thunder of rapid fire, teams straining every nerve to throw the last shell into the breech of their gun before the "Cease Fire" sounded, eleven o'clock struck, the first blast of the bugles pierced the air and with the last note silence reigned.

For what followed he quotes the diary of Brigadier-General Elkington, who set down: "There was no cheering or excitement amongst the men. They seemed too tired, and no one seemed able to realise that it was all over." On the German side the gunners were seen to get up and walk away —homewards.

By evening a pall of fog lay over the battlefields of Flanders. Heroically a few regimental bands played rag-time tunes in village squares. Determined to rejoice, some ardent spirits hit on the expedient of discharging S.O.S. lights. But the music was muffled and the now unfamiliar-looking red-green-red call for artillery support was dull. The silence of the night that followed, unbroken by any gun, was deadly strange. Sounds of peace had long been stilled. Neither lowing of cattle, bark of dog, nor crow of cock broke the nocturnal quiet of the paralysed country-side. The means of man's work was in ruins and dead. Stagnant and dumb, the land seemed to exhale the phantoms of former wars. Charles V, Alva, Don John, Condé, Turenne, Marlborough, the Prince of Orange, the Prince Eugene—the little warren-like moated châteaux, the convents even, had quartered them, and their wars still speak from many a storied page. Ours—our great combat—our prodigious, world-shaking strife had now faded into a silence from which the soul of it might never be reclaimed.

The grey silence of the 11th of November in Flanders contrasted with the gay tumult in London, where the nearness of the end had been less clearly realised. Soon after ten o'clock all London was thronging the streets in noisy exultation. Shouting, singing, laughing and crying, beating

[1] *The 56th Division*, by Major C. H. Dudley Ward, D.S.O., M.C.

or blowing some sound-producing improvisation, the crowds invaded every vehicle and gave way to an impulse of rejoicing which they hardly understood. Just before the appointed hour a great quiet concourse had collected before Buckingham Palace. Some minutes after the signals had been made which betided the beginning of the Armistice, their Majesties appeared on the balcony of the first-floor window and were rapturously acclaimed.

The wild doings of the day were carried on through much of the night, and indeed continued spasmodically on the following day; but behind them the nation's heart was heavy with the emotion which is now uppermost on Armistice Day —the sense of grievous loss.

The retreat of the German Armies continued steadily and now indeed happily. The roads and railways to Germany bore a tremendous traffic. At the bridges of the Rhine the returning troops arrived garlanded like victors and gaily singing; the country to which they returned had become a republic and its ruler had fled ignominiously to Holland. During and immediately after their withdrawal the Germans delivered to the Allies the items of armament, war stores, transport—road and rail—which they had agreed to surrender at the time of the Armistice.

Then the Allies prepared to advance into Germany. The line of the Rhine was to be occupied. Beyond it Allied troops would hold bridge-head areas, the French at Mainz, the Americans at Coblenz, the British at Cologne, and the Belgians at Aix-la-Chapelle. These were the military measures considered necessary to guarantee Germany's neighbours against aggression such as the precedent of 1914 had given grounds to fear. The advance began on November 17th and the British reached their bridge-head, after much hardship owing to bad weather and difficulties of transport and supply, on the 12th of December. On the preceding day the British Military Governor had hoisted the Union Jack on his headquarters in Cologne, and the British divisions of the Army of Occupation, crossing the river on the following day, passed their Army Commanders in review as they reached the further bank.

On the 21st of November the German Fleet crossed the North Sea for the last time. It was met by squadrons of the Grand Fleet under the command of Admiral Beatty at an appointed rendezvous, whence it was conducted to the Forth and came to anchor there. At sunset the German Imperial Naval Ensign was struck for the last time by order of the British Commander-in-Chief. Later, the Germans sank their ships at Scapa Flow; and there most of them still remain submerged.

SUGGESTIONS FOR READING:

The Last Six Weeks by Major-Gen. Sir F. B. Maurice. *The 56th (1st London) Division* by Major C. H. Dudley Ward, p. 310.

Chapter XXVI: CONCLUSION

IF the Armistice was the end of a long nightmare, it was also the beginning of a new and vital set of problems. The demobilisation of hundreds of thousands of temporary soldiers fretting to return to civil life was in itself a difficult problem which each nation had to settle for itself. But the matters which affected the conflicting interests of many nations were infinitely more difficult and momentous. The terms of the Peace of Versailles and the birth of the League of Nations belong, however, to the main stream of history and are dealt with in the ordinary text-books.

The theme of this book closes with the Armistice. Whatever troubles might lie ahead, at least the sun showed through the clouds once more. The war, indeed, had been like a dense fog, closing down on street and country-side. The novelty of groping through the fog, the sound of invisible traffic, the adventure of crossing the road, the sudden encounters—all these experiences have their momentary thrill. But if day follows day with no lift in the fog, the oppression becomes intolerable. The declaration of war brings a nation in a moment to the climax of its exaltation. The sudden break in the daily routine, the sight of troops on the march or warships off the coast, the flying rumours, the thirst for news of strange happenings, the call to service—all quicken the pulse and bring a thrill into the life of every citizen. But when the novelty has passed and month follows month with increasing anxiety, sacrifice, and privation, the sunshine goes out of life and the strain becomes almost insupportable.

For the fighting man himself the experience is much the same. It is untrue to say that there is no glamour in war. There is glamour for the civilian in the mere change into uniform, as there is in the new comradeship with men of all classes and trades, the finding of billets in an English country-side, and the hard and healthy days of training. The first furtive crossing of the Channel with a destroyer-escort, the endless march of a division through a foreign village street lined with British lorries, the glitter of an aeroplane wheeling amid white shell-puffs in a blue sky, the savage black spurts of a distant bombardment, Vérey lights, infinitely mournful, fringing the horizon on a dark night—these were experiences which no man wants to forget. Even the ducking at the first smack of rifle-bullets or the dodging of the first stray shell brought, to some at all events, only the excitement of novelty. But with the first sickening cry of "Stretcher-bearers!" glamour died. For those who got down to the real business of war exhilaration soon gave place to boredom, boredom to anxiety, and anxiety to fear and the dread of showing fear.

Modern warfare has few moments of excitement and is utterly unlike the cheerful word-picture of "Our Military Correspondent". The average soldier might, and did, spend months without a glimpse of an enemy, though in imminent peril of death or mutilation at almost any moment. Death, too, often found him employed in cold blood on tasks that had little to do with fighting, for the troops staggering to and from the line at night under a load of rations and trench-stores or doing a labourer's job on a reserve-line of trenches paid a steady toll. Mud, monotony, and deadly fatigue be-came the daily portion, varied only by occasional periods of intense fear and less frequent interludes of comparative safety and comfort. No wonder that the infantryman felt that his was the grimmest share in the war. But as science came to play a larger part and weapons of destruction developed, he began to realise that other branches of the fighting services had their peculiar terrors, and was less disposed to envy the gunners living in areas reeking with gasshell and battered by high-explosive, the signallers mending their lines under a barrage, and even the lorry-drivers plying their perilous loads of ammunition along shellswept tracks, axle-deep in mud, on dark nights. The dangers of the war at sea and in the air he could only vaguely imagine.

A rapid survey of the course of the Great War cannot stress these grim details, and they are thus apt to be forgotten. The dramatic quality of the story in outline—the first wave of German invasion sweeping all before it, the turn of the tide at the Marne, the "race to the sea" followed by deadlock on the Western Front, the spread of the war to fresh peoples and lands, the imminence of final defeat converted with amazing suddenness into victory—gives an appearance of rapidly-moving events to a scene to which the individual's contribution was months of stagnation and sordid horror.

It is a merciful provision of human nature that memory lets slip the unpleasant and leaves the pleasant uppermost; that for most of the war's survivors the gruesome episodes are overlaid by the recollection of a comfortable billet, a cheerful mess, the smoke-laden atmosphere of an *estaminet*, the unexpected encounter of a friend, or the bliss of getting into the "leave-train". It would, indeed, be foolish to pretend that the war had no redeeming features. Though the highest flights of heroism might be only for the few, the call to serve, whether in the forces, in hospital, canteen, factory, or office, was general and was generally answered with sacrifice. Class barriers were largely broken down and comradeship became a real and unforgettable thing. That the ideals which found their focus in a certain rest-house for troops in Poperinghe have become the basis of a world-wide Christian brotherhood is a hopeful portent; and if "Toc H", or any other movement, succeeds in transplanting in peace-time soil the noblest of the spiritual products of the war, it will not have been fought in vain.

Yet not one of those who felt the scorch of the war would willingly live through all his or her experiences again. If war can ever be ruled out as a means of settling disputes, the foundations of the new order must be well and truly laid in the life-time of those who have experienced its horrors. A younger generation will lack the means to envisage what hideous forms these will take and may be liable to forget one supreme lesson taught by the years 1914–1918—that in the next war there will be no non-combatants.

SUGGESTIONS FOR READING:

Foundations of the Science of War by Col. J. F. C. Fuller, p. 29. *The Memoirs of W. H. Page,* vol. I, pp. 272–83, 355. *Legends of Smokeover* by L. P. Jacks, p. 111. *Undertones of War* by Edmund Blunden. *Disenchantment* by C. E. Montague. *The Secret Battle* by A. P. Herbert. *Tales of Talbot House* by P. B. Clayton.

INDEX

www.ingramcontent.com/pod-product-compliance
Ingram Content Group UK Ltd.
Pitfield, Milton Keynes, MK11 3LW, UK
UKHW042154280225
455719UK00001B/331